Messengers in Denim

Read complete endorsements at
http://www.MapletreePublishing.com/MessengersInDenim

I know that when my children reach their adolescent years, my wife and I will ... be pulling [Dr. Donahue's] book off our shelf for a few lessons from a wise man who spent his entire life studying, mending, and truly listening to these young men and women.

Matthew D. Eberly, M.D.
Major, USAF Medical Corp

Of the many talents that Dr. Donahue displays in writing this most engaging and useful book, the two most important are story-telling and listening. ... It is a book about sound medical advice — but even more so, in the biggest of pictures, it's about how to live a healthy life. The good doctor proves time and again that the deepest wisdom and the most practical common sense often go hand-in-hand.

Dennis M. Doyle, Ph.D.
Professor of Religious Studies
University of Dayton

Messengers in Denim should be required reading for every professional who works with teens or their parents. ...[T]he unique needs of the teen patient are sadly absent in theory as well as practice. Dr. Donahue's book has at long last provided a very comforting and heartwarming glimpse into our future by highlighting the remarkable young people currently preparing for adulthood.

Chris Eickman, M.A.
Marriage, Family & Child Counselor
California

Readers may not agree with all of [Dr. Donahue's] recommendations, but they will find them thoughtfully and compassionately presented. It is the only book of its kind that I know of, and am happy to recommend it not only to parents, but to teens as well.

Fr. James L. Heft, S.M.
Alton Brooks Professor of Religion
President of the Institute for Advanced Catholic Studies
University of Southern California

Dr. Donahue's forty years of clinical experience coupled with his old school wisdom and careful research will make this a well-worn addition to your parenting library!

Mark H. Deis, M.D.
General Pediatrician
Pediatric Associates, PSC
Crestview Hills, KY

As a father, grandfather and great grandfather it is heart warming to know the old-fashioned ways my wife and I believed in and used to raise our children are still being promoted today. I recommend this book very highly to all parents.

Don Lage
New Ulm, MN

Dr. Donahue's techniques and attitude can be learned by adults who read this book as he applies them to most of the problems that teenagers face as they become adults, including too much television, how to handle finances, substance abuse and teen age sexual problems. Underlying it all is Dr. Donahue's strong personal morality and his religious faith.

Wend Schaefer, M.D.
2009 Humanitarian Award
Marquette Medical College, WI

Messengers in Denim covers years of his Pediatric experience and is a necessary book for every parent. For many reasons, today's Pediatricians and Primary Care Providers rarely have the time to develop close, personal relationships with their patients. But, as children grow, it is essential that doctors hear what they have to say. Without the benefit of Dr. Donahue's book, physicians may only hear the parent's concerns while the child's message may be different and unheard. There are many methods of parenting, but some things remain the same, and what our children need most is our time, love, support, and trust. Parents and doctors can rely on *Messengers in Denim* for the insight they need.

Thomas Kowalski M.D.
Medical College of Wisconsin Class of 1963
Clinical Professor of Pediatrics (retired)
Pediatrician an dNeonatologist (retired)
Former President, Medical Society of Milwaukee County

This book is a must-read for anyone looking for a deeper understanding of the psychology of teens and the importance of family in their lives. These precious (and sometimes turbulent) years are in fact so formative, and actually launch the adult years where they really begin to act like us, their parents! I will always keep a copy of *Messengers in Denim* in my medical library and personally recommend it to anyone who has children in their lives.

Daniel Salinas, M.D.
Senior Vice President
Chief Medical Officer
Children's Healthcare of Atlanta

I am not at all surprised to see how wonderful this book is, and I'm thankful to be learning even more lessons from Dr. Donahue. As a physician and a first-time new parent, I realize raising a child in these complex times is scary and difficult. I'm both anxious and excited to see my young son grow and mature, and Dr. Donahue's book will serve as a valuable resource in the challenging and rewarding task of parenting.

Fred Reifsteck M.D.
Head Team Physician
University of Georgia

Messengers in Denim is much more than a guide to listening and connecting effectively with teenagers. It models a way of living in integrity and provides a framework for positive interaction in all our relationships. This is a serious book full of important information written by a very wise physician with exceptional insight and a healthy sense of humor.

Edward S. Gallagher, M.D.
Medical Consultant/Pediatrician
Oakland, CA

Dr. Donahue draws on forty years experience to equip parents, coaches, and pastors to work with the unique challenges of to-day's teens. From faith and family to sexuality and self-image, *Messengers in Denim* allows teenagers to speak for themselves and shows us grown ups how these kids want—and need—to be led.

Dave Ramsey
New York Times best-selling author
host of The Dave Ramsey Show

Today's parents desperately need to understand what being a teenager in these tumultuous times is all about, and Dr. Donahue offers them that understanding straight from the proverbial horse's mouth. Chock-full of illuminating, helpful insights.

John Rosemond
Gastonia, NC

Dr. Donahue writes with the poise and grace of a seasoned

physician and the insight and sensitivity of a brilliant but humble man. Every parent should read *Messengers in Denim* to gain a peek into the world our kids know.

Meg Meeker, M.D.
author of Strong Fathers, Strong Daughters:
Ten Secrets Every Father Should Know

As a Pediatrician who is also a parent I enjoyed reading *Messengers in Denim* by Dr Parnell Donahue. This book contains a message of hope for parents of teenagers while gently reminding us that "the apple doesn't fall too far from the tree."

Elizabeth Lynn Wells, M.D.
Pediatrician

I enjoyed reading *Messengers in Demin* by Dr. Donahue. His insight into teen behavior and use of their stories to highlight important lessons parents should know when raising their children are a welcome addition to my parenting library. I highly recommend this book to parents with children of any age.

Tommy Thompson
Former Secretary
U.S. Health and Human Services

All new parents should read this book to learn how children should be loved and respected, and to learn how a parent's behavior plays a major role in a teen's life and the adult they will become. ... Likewise, it is a book to be read by teens. I will remember the example of Eric, who explained his positive and optimistic attitude by saying, "You will become the man you pretend to be."

Jacqueline A. Noonan, M.D.
Professor Emeriti of Pediatrics
University of Kentucky

Welcome Dr. Donahue and thank you for *Messengers in Denim*

— *The Amazing Things Parents Can Learn From Teens,* in which he elucidates why some children become competent and empathetic teenagers and others do not. From the crucible of his experience exemplified in insightful vignettes and enhanced by summations of medical studies and surveys, Dr. Donahue deduces into "parenting tips" the key components of how to be a parent. Implement these and how to parent will follow.

Bill Dukart, M.D., F.A.A.P.
Lewisburg, West Virginia

Other Books by Parnell Donahue, M.D.

Germs Make Me Sick
ISBN 978-0-394829-09-8
Knopf Books for Young Readers, 1975

Sports Doc
ISBN 978-0-394939-58-2
Knopf, 1979

MESSENGERS IN DENIM

The Amazing Things
Parents Can Learn
from Teens

Parnell Donahue M.D.

MESSENGERS IN DENIM

The Amazing Things Parents Can Learn from Teens

Parnell Donahue M.D.

Mapletree Publishing Company • Silverton, Idaho

Mapletree Publishing Company
an imprint of WindRiver Publishing, Inc.
72 N WindRiver Rd
Silverton, ID 83867-0446

http://www.MapletreePublishing.com

**Messengers in Denim: The Amazing
Things Parents Can Learn from Teens**
Copyright © 2010 by Parnell Donahue

ISBN 978-1-60065-106-9

Library of Congress Control Number: 2009943269

10 9 8 7 6 5 4 3 2 1

Printed in the United States of America

*T*HIS BOOK IS dedicated to my parents, Gertrude and Melvin Donahue. Melvin, my father, died in January of 2007 at the age of 94. My mother, Gertrude, is in her mid-nineties and lives in Sleepy Eye, Minnesota. It is also dedicated to the memory of Emma and James Betthauser, and to Mary, whom they parented. She is the most amazing woman I have ever known. We met during my first year in medical school and she became my wife on August 26, 1961. She has been my inspiration, my driving force, my constant companion, and my best supporter. I will love her forever. We have parented four children: Sean, Brian, Rafe, and Maura. All are very successful, brilliant professionals from whom I have learned much. You will meet all of them in this book and will see why I admire them as I do. I also dedicate this book to them and their children. God bless them all.

ACKNOWLEDGMENTS

I WISH TO THANK my son Rafe who was my library research worker and helped with my word processor and computer. I owe him a big thank you. Also a warm thank you to Doreatha Page, my sister-in-law, for coming up with the title. I love it; thanks, Doreatha! My grandsons, Marc and Patrick, who as high school sophomores read and proofread the text and offered constructive evaluation and comments, I thank them. Tim Chavez, a columnist with *The Tennessean*, supplied socially relevant content. I see few movies and only rarely watch television—some say I am not in the real world—so his additions make the stories germane to today's world and today's parents. Regrettably, he became ill early in the writing process and was unable to complete the task, but his style stayed with me, allowing me to find similar current analogies to finish the manuscript. Tim lost his battle with leukemia on June 18, 2009, but his good works live on; he requested memorials be made to Smithson Craighead School. This inner city, charter school has long been one of his favorite charities and will receive part of his share of the royalties from this book. I thank Tim for his hands-on help and his writing lessons. Also, thanks to my agent, Jeff Olson, and my editors, Rachel Terry, Laurisa White Reyes, and Gail Howick who gave much-needed support and helpful suggestions as well as excellent critique. Laurisa nearly worked me to death. Editor-in-Chief Gail Howick was ever a stickler for detail, which made everything clearer and, in fact, better. Thank you, Rachel, Laurisa, and Gail!

And thanks to my wife Mary. Without her support and the wisdom of our own teens, this book could never have been written. Together, we have raised three sons and a daughter. They all have their Ph.D.s. Our two oldest sons, Sean and Brian, are also medical doctors. Sean is director of pediatric ophthalmology at Vanderbilt University School of Medicine and is known worldwide as the authority in visual screening of preschool children. Brian is director of pediatric cardiac anesthesiology also at Vanderbilt University and does research in perioperative genomics. He told me that when I think of perioperative genomics[1] I should think of him. I think of him many times each day, but until he became one, I didn't even know what a perioperative genomist was. Our third son, Rafe, has his Ph.D. in statistics and is an adjunct professor and research consultant at Vanderbilt's School of Medicine. He works full time as senior statistician for BMTI, a medical research facility in Franklin, Tennessee. He's a highly insightful young man and has contributed a lot to this book. Daughter Maura has her Ph.D. in finance. She directs the Program for Christian Leadership at the University of Dayton in

Dayton, Ohio, where she also teaches corporate and international finance. She is currently pursuing a master's degree in Theological Studies and is as beautiful as she is smart. Her seemingly unlimited abilities continue to amaze me.

I also want to thank the thousands of kids whom I have known over the years, especially those who shared the stories mentioned in this book. They taught me about children, teenagers, parenting, and life in general. And a final word of gratitude to all those parents who trusted me to serve the medical needs of their children; you have been a blessing.

FOREWORD

WHEN DR. DONAHUE approached me to write a Foreword to his book, I felt deeply honored to receive such a request by a man who has greatly impacted my life. I first met the good doctor 15 years ago as a teenage patient in need of a yearly physical prior to starting my sophomore year in high school. My mother's announcement of my upcoming appointment with a Dr. Parnell Donahue was met with anxiety, resentment, and frustration knowing full well that a perfect summer day would be ruined. Curious to see just exactly what a "Parnell" looked like, I looked for and found his picture in the Kaiser booklet. He had white hair, glasses, and a big smile spread across a reddened face. I realize now that I was looking at an Irishman who spent a good amount of time outside in his garden.

I remember first meeting Dr. Donahue in the exam room. He greeted me with a firm handshake and loudly said with his Wisconsin accent, "So Matthew, how are you, my son?" It was like he had known me for years.

As we concluded the health history, my mother was asked to step out of the room for the exam and the health habits questioning. It had only been a total of 10 or 15 minutes of face-to-face time, but somehow Dr. Donahue was able to gain my complete trust. Just as you'll see in his book, we discussed in "shoulder-to-shoulder" fashion some of the typical teenage woes. I felt surprisingly comfortable opening up to him about my family, friends, school life, interests, likes, and dislikes. Dr. Donahue was unlike any other doctor I had encountered—he was an outstanding listener and was genuinely interested in my well-being. How was he able to spend so much time with me? Was I his only patient for the afternoon? It certainly felt that he was in no rush. In past experiences, the physician's hand was already on the doorknob by the time I wanted to ask follow-up questions.

As the conversation concluded with a joke and some laughter, we walked outside the room to find my mother. He said his good-byes and told her that he would be proud to have a son like me. I felt very appreciated and respected as I left the building. The following summers when I had my school physicals, I looked forward to conversing with Dr. Donahue, but I soon discovered that Dr. Donahue's influence did not end there.

Midway through my senior year, I found myself struggling to decide what to do for Career Week, our school-sponsored program that gave students the opportunity to shadow a professional. I had planned to study engineering in college, but I was short on possible contacts. Ultimately, I searched through a large binder in the guidance office that included names of adults who had had students work with them in the past. Suddenly I spotted "Parnell Donahue, MD, General Pediatrician." Wow! I called him up and asked if I could tag along for a few days. He welcomed the idea wholeheartedly. So starting one Monday morning two months prior to graduation, Dr. Donahue introduced me to the world of pediatrics.

I was impressed by how much he loved his work; his passion was contagious. The highlight of each day was discussing over lunch the cases we had seen in the morning: from mono to ear infections, asthma to obesity, back pain to diabetes. Dr. Donahue was pretty old school, which I didn't mind—it's just what the MTV generation needed. His teenage patients admired his ideologies, though, making them want to come back. In a nutshell, he taught us to turn off the television and go outdoors for a jog, work hard for what we want, don't expect handouts from our parents, fight for what we believe in, speak the truth and trust others, watch our mouths, make no excuses, accept blame when it's due, respect and love one another, tell a joke, fear God, and save sex for marriage. I must admit that Dr. Donahue provided me only one free handout during my week there—he paid for my blueberry pancakes at Cracker Barrel (I never received free ice cream like Nicole and Maria [see Chapter 7]).

I should not forget one last adage from Dr. Donahue: manual labor is humbling and therefore good for you. Maybe that's why he asked me and my brother to work in his "garden" for the following few summers. Planting flowers didn't seem so tough, especially if it came with some monetary compensation and a free meal courtesy of his wife, Mary. Little did I know when I "signed up" for the task that this "garden" was actually a five-year backyard project involving the planting of many large crepe myrtles, spike-aerating his lawn, painting a fence, and moving 100-pound stones and bricks in a wheelbarrow from a nearby abandoned construction site! (Later, Dr. Donahue would give us a caricature print made of himself that soon after being posted on our refrigerator door, mysteriously acquired the caption: "Boys, money doesn't grow in *my* garden." It remained there for nearly ten years.) I stuck with it, though, because I enjoyed working for someone I really respected. And our afternoon quitting time lunches at the Donahue's gave us more opportunities to discuss pediatrics, adolescent complexities, and ... well ... the meaning of life. He was right. The manual labor and early sunrises were good for me, after all.

The time I spent with Dr. Donahue in the clinic and working for him in his Versailles garden ultimately had quite an impact on me. In the first two weeks of college, I switched my major from engineering to the pre-med science program. He inspired me to learn more about the field of medicine and broaden my experiences by volunteering at hospitals and shadowing other doctors. Sometimes I wonder where I would be today had it not been for Dr. Donahue's influence. My life would be very different. I would not be married to my lovely wife, Rachel, whom I met in medical school; have two wonderful children; or be practicing pediatrics. Now as I am just starting my career in pediatrics at a time when Dr. Donahue is concluding his,

I could not be happier or more honored to recommend his book for parents and teenagers alike. I know that when my children reach their adolescent years, my wife and I will once again be pulling his book off our shelf for a few lessons from a wise man who spent his entire life studying, mending, and truly listening to these young men and women. Thanks, Doc.

Matthew D. Eberly, MD
Major, USAF Medical Corp

TABLE OF CONTENTS

Substance Abuse ·······································

Teen Sexuality ·······································

Adolescent Medical Issues ·····················

Living Well ·······································

INTRODUCTION

S OME YEARS AGO, I was telling a friend of mine that as a youth I wanted to become an architect. He looked at me and said, "You are an architect. You help people design their lives and build the lives of their children."

At first I thought he was patronizing me, but then I took it as a compliment and was about to thank him when I realized the enormous responsibility his comment implied. My face paled and I responded, "That's pretty scary."

"Maybe," he said, and then added, "But you're good at it!"

I thought about Doug's remark a lot over the months and years that followed. I became aware of the burden I had placed on myself when I began to study pediatrics. Fortunately, it is a burden shared with teachers, coaches, priests, rabbis, ministers, and all who interact with or are in any way visible to children. It indeed takes a village to raise a child, but the *final* responsibility for "building" children rests in the hands of their parents.

Messengers in Denim approaches parenting differently

than other parenting books. It is not a *how* to parent book, but a *how to be a parent* book. I have avoided using the situational approach which many parenting experts use in their books. These situational parenting books state problems or situations which a parent might face and discuss ways to handle them. No book can contain all or even most of these situations. Instead, I offer a basic, principled approach to parenting. These principles are based on the lessons I have learned from teenagers through the years. These ordinary teenagers neither think nor act like adults, but have a collective wisdom that we adults have too long ignored in favor of always wanting to impart our own "superior, more mature" knowledge.

Each chapter of the book is illustrated with stories told by these ordinary teenagers. They shared with me their beliefs, their personal philosophies, and the lessons they've learned from life. They discussed religion, sexuality, substance abuse, medical issues, suicide, anger, money, and much, much more. At first I was awed (and at times flabbergasted) by what they had to say; but as I listened, I realized they were teaching me—and all of us adults—how to parent. In essence, this is a book about ordinary teenagers teaching extraordinary lessons. All of them were either my patients, my neighbors, or the children of my friends. The stories are all true, though I have changed many of the circumstances and used fictitious names to protect patient confidentiality. To help the reader focus in on the attributes the teenagers illustrate, I have included "Parenting Tips" at the end of each section that summarize the parenting concepts discussed in the section chapters.

As much as it might scare you, your children mirror you. They reflect your opinions and values. They are becoming you! And that's how it should be. Obviously, there is no secret formula for raising healthy kids and ushering them safely through the teenage years. If there were such a formula, there would be no need for the more than 16,000 Web sites on parenting teens, nor the dozens of books written on the subject each year. For the most part, however, the teenagers referenced in this book listened to their parents and learned to respect them, their judgment, their values, and their way of life. And through them we learn the qualities their parents possessed that made it possible for them to raise emotionally, mentally, and physically healthy children. We even learn things that we as parents should attempt to correct or avoid from the few negative stories they recount.

As you turn these pages, be prepared to meet some kids who will entertain, excite, amaze, and enlighten you, just as they did me. And if you listen—really listen—to the teens you know, you, too, will hear many words of wisdom that will help you design a parenting style capable of producing a much needed commodity in today's world: honest, well-balanced, hard-working young men and women. Learn from them, and take pride in knowing that by applying the principles taught by the teenagers in this book, your kids can be just as capable and wonderful as those who related these stories to me.

Home And Family

In this section you will meet some ordinary teenagers who realize that the values needed to become outstanding, successful individuals are taught by parents. And you'll recognize that parenting is not a technique; it is a way of life. It is digging into the depths of your soul to find the character to transmit integrity, moral strength, and leadership to your children. This is easy if we as parents emulate these qualities ourselves, but without them, good parenting is impossible. Young people—teens especially—have acute noses for hypocrisy and abhor the insincere. On the other hand, they are drawn to leaders who practice what they preach ... and good parents are "leaders" in the truest sense of the word.

CHAPTER I

KIDS DO LISTEN

A wise son heareth his father's instructions, but a scorner heareth not rebuke.

Proverbs 13:1

ONE WARM SUMMER day not so long ago, my son Brian and I had been out riding bikes with his children. We took a break and were sitting on some rocks watching the kids play in the creek beside the bike path.

"You know, Dad," Brian said, "every time I go biking I think of what you told me in that Milwaukee parking lot 30 years ago when you were trying to teach me how to ride my bike. I told my kids that same thing when I was helping them learn to ride." Then he fell silent as he contemplated this memory.

What was this great pearl I dropped in my youth? I wondered, almost out loud. I was about to know how it feels to be a quoted authority, to be revered (or at least respected) by one of my progeny. My heart pounded as I waited patiently for him to say more.

"I remember I did okay going straight," he continued, "but every time I tried to turn, I tipped over. One time you picked me up again, put me back on the bike, and said, 'Brian, don't turn the handle bars. If you want to turn, just lean a little in the direction you want to go and the bike will turn itself.' And it did."

That's it? I thought. *A lesson on how to turn your bike. I'll be remembered for that?* I felt disappointed in a way, but Brian was sincere. It was his way of acknowledging advice that had worked for him. The more I thought about it the prouder I felt; my son had actually listened to me and followed my advice. And then it dawned on me. I had always told parents that their kids listen to them— and after 30 years, I realized that mine did, too!

Father Knows Best

Talking with kids is always the most exciting part of any health evaluation and also the most educational—if not for the patient, at least for me. I learn so much by talking and listening to kids of any age, but especially teenagers. The American Medical Association believes that talking with teens is the most important part of a teenager's health evaluation. To help physicians with that task, the AMA released Guidelines for Adolescent Preventive Services (GAPS) in 1992. (A synopsis of GAPS is contained in Appendix A.) These guidelines should be reviewed with every teen as part of their annual physical. Appendix B lists the questions I ask each teen to assure I am heeding the AMA's guidelines.

Harry is a case in point. He was in for an annual health evaluation (which he described as number 75, although he was only 16). He jokingly complained that his mother was always "dragging him in for another physical." I had never met his construction worker dad, but I was soon to learn something about his character.

"Do you smoke cigarettes?" I asked, already knowing what Harry's answer would be.

"Never, not a chance," Harry responded. But then anticipating many of the next questions he said, "My dad would kill me if I ever smoked or had sex!"

"Your dad would kill you?"

"Oh, no, no," Harry clarified. "He would never ever *kill* me; but I think it would probably kill him! He's been around a long time and has seen a lot of

DAD KNOWS BEST, SO LISTEN TO HIM

bad stuff happen, so he knows what's best. And he lets me know what's right and what's not. I can't imagine facing my dad with tobacco or alcohol on my breath, or worse yet, having to tell him I got some girl pregnant or had an STD. If I let him down, I don't know if we could get through it. I guess it's sort of like dad knows best, so listen to him."

"Harry," I responded, "that was a whole lesson in parenting. Know where you stand and let your kids know, then love them enough that they would not want to disappoint you by doing the wrong thing. Thanks for making it so simple. I'll have to have you talk to some of my parent groups," I kidded.

"Thanks," he blushed. "But it's true."

"Do you think you're unique in what you just said, or do other kids think like that, too?"

"Do you mean, 'Do other kids smoke, drink, do drugs, or have sex?' or 'Do other kids listen to their parents?'"

"I know the answer to the first question," I replied, "but what about the second one?"

"Pretty much kids do what their parents do or what their parents *expect* them to do. I know some kids whose dads gave them condoms. To me that says, 'Go ahead, have sex.' But that's not what my dad says. I have a girlfriend and sure, we'd like to have sex. But no way am I going to go against what Dad says, not in this life!"

"I sure would like to meet your dad," I said. "He must be some kind of a guy."

"He sure is. He played football for the University of Kentucky. I'd like to play there, too. Dad always works during the day so he can't come in here, but if you come to any of our home games, I'll make sure you get a chance to meet him."

"I'll do that," I promised. And I did. Harry's dad was as impressive as Harry. I also had a chance to meet Harry's brothers in the following years, and they had the same attitude as Harry. Apples don't fall far from the tree.

Too many parents today think they have no influence on their kids' beliefs and behavior, yet every study I've read (and there are many of them) shows that kids respect and listen to their parents.

In the 2005 Horatio Alger survey on The State of Our Nation's Youth,[2] 68 percent of the girls ages 14 to 19 and 70 percent of boys that age named a parent, sibling, or other family member as their role model. Only 15 percent named a friend, and even fewer mentioned an entertainment celebrity or an athlete. To test these national statistics, I asked the 103 teens I evaluated one summer who most influenced their values of right and wrong. Of these, 83 said mom, dad, or parents; three said brothers or sisters; three credited themselves as their main influence; three said others (teachers, coaches, ministers); while three had no one to credit. Only eight said friends. (One 15-year-old boy actually said Rush Limbaugh.) Like it or not, parents everywhere are the main role models for their children.

Not only do parents have a major role in influencing values, their expectations also greatly influence future performance. A study conducted by the University of Minnesota[3] on 12,000 kids in grades seven through twelve concluded: "If parents expect adolescents to get good grades and refrain from sex, those expectations influence the adolescents' behavior powerfully through twelfth grade, regardless of family income, race, or single- or dual-parent status." The lead researcher, Dr. Michael Resnick, said, "Adolescents are often very effective at convincing us that what we say is irrelevant to their lives, and the mistake we make as adults is that we believe it."

The study further indicated that "the more teenagers felt loved by their parents the less likely they were to abuse drugs or alcohol, smoke, have sex, or commit violence or suicide."

It's clear that kids adopt their parents' values. To clarify these values for their children, parents must let their kids know where they stand and why. This doesn't call for a lecture, which would most likely force the kids to hold their hands over their ears, physically as well as metaphorically; instead, parents should do as Harry's dad did and tell of the times he saw "bad stuff happen," why it happened, its consequences, and how it might have been avoided.

These teaching moments happen all the time: when we see someone drinking too much at a ball game; when we see inappropriate displays of affection in public; when we see scantily dressed adults; when we read about an outburst of anger leading to a shooting; and when news stories tell us about drug busts, lung cancer, teen pregnancy, AIDS, and other STDs. Unfortunately, the opportunities are countless.

Our instinct is to shield our kids from these stories. Yet these everyday experiences can become the basis for teaching values, and the way we adults handle them determines what values our children will adopt as their own. To fail to discuss someone's public drunkenness, for example, teaches that we place no value on sobriety. Laughing at such a calamity teaches that we enjoy others' misfortune. The involvement of the parents and the way they discuss these incidents is the key. These are the discussions upon which character is built; they create impressions that kids will take with them into the future and throughout their lives. There is no better way—perhaps no other way—to teach values.

I still remember a high school basketball game I

attended as a freshman with one of my friends and his parents. During the game, there was some booing of the referees from the student section. On the way home, my friend's father, Mr. Bondhus, assumed we had participated and told us in no uncertain terms that referees, like other officials, should be respected. Such behavior was wrong and was not to be repeated. For the rest of our high school days if refs were booed, Wayne and I were not a part of it. Mr. Bondhus had made his point.

In a similar vein, in the April 2001 edition of *Focus on the Family,* Dr. James Dobson said, "There is no sex education program, no curriculum, no school or institution in the world that can match the power and influence of ... parental involvement. ... [These] are the parents who are present and involved, who communicate and exemplify their own values and attitudes, who ask questions, who carefully supervise their kids' choice of escorts and points of destination, and who insist on a reasonable curfew."[4] Red-headed Harry's father knew this, and Harry learned and profited from it.

Parental Unity

Harry's dad also had the support of a loving wife who believed as he did. It is so important that as parents, we agree on the values we wish to pass on to our children. Certainly, no two people can agree about everything. Seeing one's parents disagree, have a rational debate or argument, and come to an agreement with which both can live is an important lesson. But when it comes to imparting values, parents must be united. Children without guidelines become adults without guidelines, and both can become confused and fearful, feel alone and unloved, and make poor choices.

It is especially important that divorced parents agree on the values they want their children to learn. Disagreement not only confuses kids, but teaches them that values are unimportant. Whatever conflicts you may have with your divorced spouse, take time to have a rational discussion with him or her and decide what values are important to teach your kids. Such discussions may be difficult, but watching your children face the consequences of their poor decisions is much worse.

Establishing Rules

Lynn Minton in her *Parade*[5] column reported on a youth from New Jersey who came from a house with no rules. This teen got into trouble with drugs at age 14. His dad said it was good to get that out of his system at a young age. Later, Dad was "understanding" when he began to have sex. At last the boy said, "… I turned myself around without any help from my 'understanding' father. You may think it would be great to have no rules and be able to do whatever you want. But trust me. I've been there. It's a lonely road when nobody really cares what you do."

Too often we think of values as something ethereal or hypothetical; something imposed on us to curb our fun or lifestyle. But the values we're talking about are simply codes of conduct—rules, if you will—that have developed over time to protect us and society and to put order into our lives. These values include honesty; thrift; morality; respect for the rights, possessions, and lives of others; education; honoring parents; respecting the law; honoring our faith; respecting our leaders; etc. Parents who teach these values to young children make life easier for them. These kids know their parents love them and care about how they live their lives, and they tend to be looked on more favorably by society than the kids who don't receive this training.

Like people of all ages, teenagers need, want, and are searching for rules. Although these rules may vary from culture to culture, good parents provide boundaries and show their children how to follow them.

The most illustrative story I ever heard about kids listening to their parents comes from Father Richard Lopez,[6] a religion teacher at St. Pius High School in

KIDS LISTEN TO THEIR PARENTS AND DO WHAT THEIR PARENTS DO

Atlanta, Georgia, and one of the best homilists I ever heard. He once asked his students to draw a picture of their conscience. "One drew a big circle," he recalled, "and in it the words 'my parents.'"

It is a parent's responsibility to help kids form strong consciences. Perhaps this is no more difficult than living the life you want your kids to live because, as Harry reminded us, kids listen to their parents and do what their parents do.

CHAPTER 2

TRUST YOUR CHILDREN

*Honesty is the first chapter of
the book of wisdom.*

Thomas Jefferson

MATTHEW'S CREW CUT, square jaw, and muscled body served him well as a high school varsity wrestler. His jovial flare and practically permanent smile said something more important—Matthew was a good kid. He was an honor student and a hard-working farm boy who was fun to be around.

One Sunday afternoon, however, Matthew stood at the front door of my home in tears; an unusual public display for a teenage male, let alone one usually as happy and tough as he was. But as you will see, his emotional state was the result of a series of strange events that had occurred recently.

Several days earlier, my six-year-old daughter Maura wanted to camp out in her brothers' tent. "We don't have to go to a park or anything," she begged. "We can set it up in the backyard and sleep right by the patio." She knew it would be fun because her older brothers were excited about their recent camping trip with the Boy Scouts. "Please," she pleaded. "I'll even help set up the tent." I reluctantly agreed, but her mother would have no part of sleeping on the ground just 50 feet away from her "Sealy comfort."

We set up the tent and prepared for a quiet night in the great outdoors. Along about midnight, neither of us was asleep because coyotes were baying in the distance. Then Maura thought she heard bears coming out of the nearby woods. We picked up our sleeping bags and crept quietly into the house, trying not to waken her brothers lest they taunt their "chicken" father and sister.

Just as we approached the stairs, we were startled by a car screeching past the house, its tires squealing as it turned the corner and blasted away down the street. The noise woke and unnerved everybody.

Fortunately for Maura and me, the loud intrusion diverted attention away from us cowardly campers. But before we could get settled into our beds, red squares of light began flashing on our bedroom walls. Soon, the whole family was standing at the front window watching a police car move slowly down the street and come to a stop in front of our house. Now, ours was a tiny, rural Wisconsin town. Nothing exciting ever happened here. I was tempted to go out and see what all the commotion was about, but my wife's common sense kept us all inside. Soon the squad car was gone, the neighborhood was quiet, and we were all in our safe, warm beds.

The next morning, I discovered tire tracks running across my neighbor's lawn and onto mine. In the tracks' wake, several young trees my neighbor Bill Reed and I had planted earlier that spring were lying flat, broken off just above ground. The tracks swerved into the street leaving me one last, lonely tree. I questioned Bill about it, but he had slept through the entire commotion and knew even less than I did.

Just before noon, I received a call from the police wondering what I had seen. I told them the little I knew. They told me a neighbor across the street had heard the screeching tires and called them. They had no suspects, but another lady farther down the street described seeing a red, cloth-top jeep in the neighborhood about that time.

That brings us back to Matthew.

The Sunday he appeared at my house I was watching the Packers' game with my family.

"Matthew," I said as I opened the door. Then I noticed the dour look on his face and quickly added, "It looks like things aren't going so great. How can I help? Come in."

"No," he replied, not looking at me. "I can't come in. The cops sent me here to pay for your trees."

Then he stood there while a big tear splashed onto the concrete step, just missing his right foot. Matthew crying?! That was as unbelievable as his running over my trees.

"Matthew," I replied, "are you saying you ran over Mr. Reed's and my trees?"

"No, I didn't run over them!" he said emphatically. "You can trust me ... I give you my word ... I didn't do it! But the cops think I did and they said if I paid for them, nothing would go on my record. But honest, I didn't ..."

He couldn't get the rest of the sentence out; he was too upset. And so was I. Why would they do this to Matthew?

"Matthew, I believe you," I immediately assured him. "I know you well enough to know you wouldn't do a thing like that. If you had, you would admit it and not lie about it, so why do they blame you?"

"Well, somebody saw a Jeep like mine in this neighborhood that night, and when the cops stopped me, there were leaves under my front bumper. I explained to them that I picked up the leaves when I drove near the creek to get dad's cows and ran over some bushes. My dad even told them that, but they won't believe us. Finally, Dad said, 'Just pay it and get it behind you!' So I guess that's what I'll have to do. It's not fair though."

"Sorry, Matthew, I can't accept any money from you. And I'll make sure Mr. Reed won't either. Let me call the police and tell them I believe you."

"Do you think they'll listen to you?" he asked.

"I'm sure I can convince Mr. Reed of your innocence, and together we can convince the police. Bill Reed is a lawyer, you know; it's good to have him on our side."

"What should I tell the police and my Dad?" Matthew asked.

"Don't worry about either of them. Give me your phone number and I'll call your dad right after I call the police."

Matthew heaved a sign of relief. "Thanks, Doctor. I

feel better now, and I wasn't even sick," Matthew replied, trying to make a joke.

"Let me know how it goes," I called to him as he ran to his Jeep. "And call me if anybody gives you grief."

As Good As Their Word

I knew I could trust Matthew. He had given me his word. I had known him for years. I also knew his dad and his wrestling coach and mentor, Don Kreuser. If either of them gave you his word, you knew it was the truth. So I called the police and talked to the detective on the case.

"Doc," he advised, "don't be a fool! You can't believe what that kid says."

"Sorry to disagree with you," I said. "I make my living believing what kids tell me. And I believe Matthew is telling the truth."

"Well," he snapped, "I make mine NOT believing what they tell me."

I realize that a lot of parents would agree with the detective. That's a consequence of this age of pessimism. We believe the worst because in a few recent events, like Columbine, we've seen the worst. But the Matthew I knew was worth trusting.

After talking to Bill Reed and Matthew's dad, we waited; but we didn't have to wait long. A week later I got another call from the detective.

"You were right," he began. "We picked up Charley Bradson and he admitted to running over the trees. Seems Bill Reed was representing a fellow who Charley allegedly beat up, and Charley wanted to get back at Reed. Your trees just happened to be in the way. Luckily, he didn't do anything worse. He confessed as soon as we brought it up. He'll be calling you to make amends. Let me know if he gives you any trouble."

Trust First

Matthew's story illustrates the question that ultimately confronts every parent or adult who deals with teenagers: "How much should I trust them?" You can't avoid this conundrum—it will always find you. So be prepared to respond with a set of values that measure what trust means to you, as well as what you want it to mean to your child.

The *Capital Times* in Wisconsin recently reported on using the Global Positioning System (GPS) to follow teens. An October 12, 2007, article said, "Transmitters can be planted in teenagers' cars making it possible to track the car's movements on a computer screen map. The block-by-block progress of the car can be watched live (real time), or recorded on a computer chip and downloaded and viewed later."

Proponents of using the GPS contend that it allow parents to know where their teens are at all times, as well as keep an eye on their driving habits. They say it gives parents peace of mind and most importantly, ensures the safety of their children. But at what price to the child's emotions and character development? Teens are constantly seeking trust from their parents and this surveillance would call that trust into question. Kim Allen, a father of two teenage boys, was quoted in *The Tennessean* as saying, "If you are tracking your teens, you are saying to them, 'I do not trust you to make the right decisions.'" In the same article, 16-year-old Mia McIntyre said the GPS "would be like my baby-sitter. (It) would make me feel like I'm not an adult almost, and it would disappoint me."[7]

Let's pray that surveillance will not be the future of parenting because spying is based on distrust, and distrust can be as harmful to a child as it is to an adult. Imagine how we would feel if our bosses placed monitors over our work stations. Would that engender belief in ourselves and our ability to do the work required of us? Or would it make us edgy, angry, and less capable of creative thinking? The answer is obvious. We might even start looking for another job.

Honesty Is for Parents Too

Parents and kids need to realize that trust is not given, it is earned. We begin to trust kids in small ways in early childhood. Then as they mature and prove themselves trustworthy, we trust them in larger ways. Thus, trust grows as kids make more and more good decisions and erodes if they make bad decisions. Trust builds their confidence (and ours) in their ability to make good choices. Distrust leads to diminished self-assurance, resentment of authority, cover-ups, lies, and general distrustful behavior. To answer the GPS advocates: if you cannot trust your teens, you should not let them get a driver's license. It's as simple as that!

But there's more to trust than kids making good decisions. Parents need to be willing and able to trust. Some people are never able to trust others because they have been hurt by someone they trusted; others know they are not trustworthy themselves and consequently figure no one can be trusted.

The ability to trust (or not trust) can even run in families and cultures, passed on from parent to offspring by emulation. Distrust is often based on ignorance, hatred, and fear. Prime examples are the prejudices between Arabs and Christians; blacks and whites; Jews and Palestinians; Serbs and Bosnians—I could go on and on. But the distrust had to start somewhere, and it usually starts with bigoted parents who want their kids to share these negative values. However, education and experience can slowly change these perceptions.

How can we trust our kids if we are not trustworthy ourselves? What is a parent teaching when he or she says:

"If the phone is for me, tell them I'm not home."

"If the boss calls, tell him I'm sick."

"Tell your teacher you had a stomach ache and couldn't get your homework done."

How can we expect children and teenagers to tell the truth when their parents are teaching them to lie?

When Sean, my oldest son, was 13, he and his friend went with his friend's parents to a local sporting event. When he came home, he was excited to tell us about the game they'd watched. At the end he added, "And we saved money because Mr. Montgomery said if we slumped down in the car when we drove in the gate and said we were 11, we could get in for free. So we did, and he didn't have to pay for us."

Giving myself time to think, I asked, "Sean, do you think that was the right thing to do?"

Sean hung his head and didn't look at me. "No, Dad. "But, I didn't know what else to do."

"You're right, Sean, it wasn't the right thing to do. But if I'd been in your shoes, I wouldn't have known what to do either. It wasn't fair of Derrick's dad to ask you to lie, and it put you in a real bind. There was nothing you could have done at the time, but I tell you what. Next time something like that happens just say, 'Oh, that's okay, I brought some money,' and pay for your own ticket."

"So, you're not mad at me?" Sean asked, embarrassed.

"Sean," I replied, slapping him gently on the shoulder, "of course I'm not mad at you. You did the best you could in that situation. Let's just make sure you don't get in that situation again. Okay?"

My wife Mary and I made sure there wasn't a next time with Mr. Montgomery. If Sean and Derrick wanted to go some place, we took them.

Honesty is the foundation of character. I knew that Matthew was being honest when he told me he didn't run over my trees, but I never really knew what it meant deep down to Matthew for me to

HONESTY IS THE FOUNDATION OF CHARACTER

trust him. I know what it meant to me. It reaffirmed my belief that teens can be trusted. They are worth the risk of trusting, whether we are proven right every time or not. Trust cannot be an act of blind faith, however. It is an exercise that comes from extensive experience: how often and how long we talk to our teenagers, how they answer our questions, and how they show respect—these are all telling signs. Sex, drugs, drinking, Internet usage, friends, and smoking are some of the many topics upon which trust often runs aground. Yet it is our behavior as adults which shows kids the right path. The fact is, they will do as we do, not as we say.

Matthew taught me that honesty and trust are issues that remain first and foremost in the adult ballpark. Our kids will never get a hit in that park unless we first set an

TRUST ME, I GIVE YOU MY WORD

example of honesty. Then we'll know that great feeling when we hear the words, "Trust me, I give you my word," and see a good teen like Matthew hit a home run.

THE FAMILY MEAL

Sharing food with another human being is an intimate act that should not be indulged in lightly.

M. K. Fisher, 1949

*R*ICK WAS A burly 17-year-old with dark hair and a heavy beard that framed his face. He had the intimidating appearance of a college linebacker. His looks and gruff attitude would have made any high school running back cut for the sidelines to avoid a collision. But Rick did not play football, or any sport. He was a bit of a loner, most comfortable when he was thinking and writing.

In these post-Columbine days, loners sometimes scare us. We often worry about kids when they keep to themselves and hold things in. We're afraid they might explode one day and consume themselves or our children, like the young man did at Virginia Tech in the spring of 2007. Most times our worry is unfounded, and I wasn't worried about Rick. His goal was to be a philosopher or a poet or perhaps both. His father, however, was another story.

I had known Rick's family for a number of years. His dad was a machinist who worked long hours and tended to be controlling with his family. I don't mean "control" in the sense of every father's role in providing a sense of direction on rules and relationships; he micromanaged them. Although many parents may act differently at times because of outside events, like September 11 and Virginia Tech, our children will respond in the same manner to changing pressures and perspectives that occur inside the home.

Time to Be Together

Rick was healthy and like many teens, he did not smoke, drink, or use drugs. As we proceeded with his health evaluation I asked him, "How often do you have dinner with your family?"

The answer to that question is usually indicative of how far today's families have shifted away from spending time together. Many family members are constantly on the go. Both parents may need to work to make the kind of living they desire, to fulfill their career goals, or in many cases, just to survive. Their children are on the go, too, with soccer, dance, gymnastics, and all their other activities. For the family, that means added pressure on schedules to transport, deliver, and pick up kids; find time to buy groceries and cook meals; and somehow get everyone to sit down together and eat. Many teenagers also have jobs that begin after school and don't end until late at night. Sometimes parents are already in bed when their kids get home. They become like ships passing in the night, and their lack of communication makes it easier for unfortunate and sometimes tragic events to occur.

With these thoughts in mind, Rick's answer about the frequency of dinner with his family was unexpected. He said, "Every night, if possible."

His enthusiastic response made me wonder if something more was going on, so I continued. "And how often is that possible?"

"Usually five or six nights a week."

"That's good," I assured him, backing away from my suspicions.

"Not good," he corrected. "Great!"

"Great? Why great?"

"Well, I think you should have dinner with your dad every night because he's not mad when he's eating. You see, when Dad comes home from work, he's mad until we eat. Then he gets happy and laughs and talks about everything. He even asks about my friends. We always have a good time at dinner. But as soon as it's done, he sits down in front of the TV and grumbles if we say anything. Even if he's not watching TV I can't talk to him without him yelling that I did something wrong or forgot to do something. Sometimes he's upset because my hair is too long or my room's a mess or I need to do more sports or my friends are rude. Anything will set him off. It's like he's a psycho. Some of my friends say their dads are the same way. Why do dads get so crabby all the time?"

"I don't know," I mused; this aloof young man had really been doing some remarkable thinking. "Maybe they have a lot on their minds, or maybe *their* dads were always mad, and they're following that example."

"Well, I'm not going to be like that when I get to be a dad ... if I ever do," Rick replied.

"Good for you. You can be whatever kind of dad or person you decide to be. I'm just glad you're such a great guy now."

We talked more about the influence of fathers on the behavior (both good and bad) of their children as adults. Although children often pick up bad habits from their parents, the encouraging news is that they pick up good habits, too.

Benefits of the Family Meal

Too many parents, dads especially, only talk with their teenagers when they're reprimanding them for something they did wrong. Luckily, it's hard for people to be angry when they're eating. John O'Sullivan in his book *The President, the Pope, and the Prime Minister* quoted Pope John Paul II as having said, "Difficult problems can often be resolved over a meal."[8] Rick never read that book—it was published a decade or more after I saw him—but he was still quick to pick up on the importance of a family meal.

When questioning teens, I found that those who ate

fewer than five family meals per week were twice as likely to use drugs or alcohol or have sex while still in high school as those who sat down more frequently to eat with their family. Other factors may have been involved, but a study of 527 kids in Cincinnati showed that those who ate five or more meals per week with their family were better adjusted and less depressed than peers who ate fewer than three family meals a week. Furthermore, the kids who ate family meals did better in school, were less inclined to use drugs, and had better social skills.[9]

Joseph A. Califano, Jr., chairman and president of Columbia University's Center on Addiction and Substance Abuse, studied the association between family meals and drug abuse and concluded in their September 2007 quarterly report that "... preventing America's drug problem is not going to be accomplished in court rooms, legislative hearing rooms, or classrooms, by judges, politicians, or teachers. It will happen in living rooms and dining rooms and across kitchen tables by the efforts of parents and families."[10]

Researchers aren't sure what accounts for the difference, but suggest that family meals may help kids learn to deal with the pressures of life and maintain a close relationship with family members. Sharing stories about the day's events and hearing how other family members deal with their stress may be the tools that help prevent adjustment problems.[11]

On the other hand, research conducted by Martha Marino and Sue Butkus of Washington State University found that sharing food and conversation around the dinner table might occasionally backfire if the parents are too controlling and dysfunctional. These researchers questioned college women who were being treated for bulimia neverosa about their family meals held a dozen years earlier. Some of the women remembered their parents being too controlling or in others ways demonstrating dysfunctional behavior (using food to control behavior, expressing hostility toward the children, dominating conversation, and belittling the girls).[12]

Certainly this type of mal-parenting can have a negative effect on children; it does not incriminate the meal, however, but the parenting. This study stands alone in its criticism of family mealtime. Furthermore, it was a retrospective study asking individuals with known psychopathology what they remembered. Every scientist knows retrospective studies are the poorest form of inquiry and rarely discover any reliable or reproducible results. Many, many studies have found family meals a very important part of a child's development; no other studies have found agreement with this 1993 study.

Fortunately for Rick, his father was able to make mealtime enjoyable by suspending his controlling nature while the family ate together.

Scientists have also noticed that the positive effect of eating together was diminished if the family watched television during dinner. They found that families who watched television while eat-

HAVE DINNER
WITH YOUR FAMILY
EVERY NIGHT

ing ate more junk food, fewer fruits and vegetables, and drank more caffeinated beverages.[13, 14] But watching television while eating is not the only thing that decreases the intake of healthy food. A young man named Zach was well aware of another problem that was just as important and even more common.

Dangers of Junk Food

Zach was a skinny, 13-year-old boy with wavy blond hair, freckles on his nose and cheeks, and a contagious smile that never quit. If you knew Richie Cunningham from "Happy Days," you knew Zach. I had known Zach and his family for some time, so seeing them was like greeting old friends. His grin broadened when I entered the exam room and said, "Zach, my son, how's it going today?"

Mom smiled and nodded, but before she could respond with a greeting, Zach replied, "A little good and a little bad."

"Really?" I said. "What do you want to talk about first, the good or the bad?"

"Well," he said, "let's get the bad out of the way first."

Mom had a look of disbelief on her face. She was visibly concerned with Zach's comment. He had always been a model child, as carefree as any boy could be. But she kept quiet and let him talk—something many parents say they can't get their teens to do.

"It's not a big deal," he assured us calmly.

I sat down next to Zach and said, "Okay, Zach, if you're ready to tell me about the bad things going on in your life, I'm ready to listen."

"It's three things," he began. "McDonalds, Wendy's,

and Burger King. I know I shouldn't eat junk food because it's not good for me. I'm trying to be an athlete, and I need good food; but every time we get close to a take-out, I insist on a cheeseburger and fries. Mom doesn't always stop, but usually I beg until she gives in. I know I need to stop eating that junk so I don't get fat and lazy."

Mom seemed relieved as he told of this "trial," and I felt relief, too.

"Zach," I said, "we'll discuss some ways to keep fast foods from becoming a habit. I think you're very wise to see this as a problem."[15]

We all know Zach is right, but just how right is he? A 15-year study of the eating habits and health of 5,000 volunteers between the ages of 18 and 30 began in 1985 and concluded in 2000. The subjects from four major U.S. cities were seen for health evaluations, blood tests, and extensive interviews of dietary habits six times during the study.[16] The study showed that eating fast food over several years resulted in the increased likelihood of both diabetes and obesity. The average participant, excluding white women, ate fast food two or more times each week; white women ate fast food somewhat less often, only 1.5 times a week. Furthermore, those who ate more than twice a week gained almost 10 pounds more during those 15 years than those who ate only once a week.

The Bogalusa (Louisiana) Heart Study, which followed 1,379 young adults for many years, showed that coronary artery disease, hypertension (high blood pressure), and heart abnormalities such as ventricular enlargement begin in childhood.[17] These problems were more common in adults who had diabetes and high blood pressure, diseases associated with obesity. Lead Investigator Dr. Gerald Berenson said, "Obesity is the only consistent factor predicting cardiac enlargement in adults. It also predicts adult vascular stiffness." Vascular stiffness, also known as hardening of the arteries, is a major cause of hypertension.[18] He didn't mention fast foods, but as the other studies cited have shown, fast food consumption leads to obesity and diabetes.

I might have blamed Zach's mother for taking him to Mickey D's, but Zach didn't. Neither would Dr. Thomas Robinson, director of the Center for Healthy Weight at Stanford University's Packard Children's Hospital. He noted that even though parents hold the keys to the car that goes to the fast-food restaurants, they're not entirely to blame. In 2007, both the Federal Trade Commission and the Kaiser Family Foundation released studies on the effect of advertising on children. They found that children between the ages of two and eleven are exposed to about 5,500 food advertisements every year. "Parents don't choose for their children to be exposed to this type of marketing," Dr. Robinson said.[19] "Parents have a very difficult job. It may seem easier to give in to their child's plea to go to McDonald's than to give in to the many other hundreds of requests they get during a day."[20]

I'm not as willing to let parents off the hook. From my experience, I feel parents need to restrict their children's consumption of television, where most of these ads are seen. They need to learn how to say "NO," and they must limit their own exposure to fast food. There are more than 250,000 fast food restaurants in the United States. We all must be enjoying them or they would not proliferate.

It's only fair to note that over the past few years the fast food industry has begun to offer more healthy foods, including fruit, yogurt, and salads. However, almost all restaurants continue to offer food too high in fat, salt, and sugar, and rarely serve veggies and fruit.

So listen to Rick and Zach: eat dinner with your family as often as you can; eat nourishing food; turn off the television set and talk; ask questions and laugh. Food nourishes the body, conversation nourishes the mind, and togetherness nourishes the soul. These are things money can't buy.

Influencing Future Generations

I did not realize how much good a family dinner can do until last year when our daughter Maura, now in her mid thirties, wrote a piece for our family reunion (which we call a symposium). At the symposium dinner, which in this instance was held at our home, each member has to present a short paper on a pre-announced topic. That year the subject was food. Here's what she had to say:

> When we were kids, almost all of our meals were eaten together, as a family, at this table. I have come now to realize, as I sit with my own children around my family's table, that meals aren't really about food; they are about the people who come to break bread together. Through our

everyday meals, we learn about each other and from each other. When we were growing up, at our meals we discussed not just the events of each person's day, but also the social and political issues relevant to the times. We learned how to think, how to feel, and how to love. Now I can see that family meals help to build community. Each member makes time for the meal, sacrificing other duties, other work that could be done, to make time for each other. We bless each other ... and honor each other through this sacrifice. Most times we do so willingly since we feel responsible to each other as members of a family community. ...

Today, we come to this table to celebrate our symposium meal. We look at the beautiful feast set on the table before us; Mom and Dad have said, 'Eat and drink, we made this for you.' The food is here for us to enjoy, to strengthen us, and to let us know how much they love us. Yet, this family meal is about more than just our family, for it is within the family structure that children learn that love and justice are connected. The love shared between parents and the love they have for their children must flow outward from the family into social, civic, and political commitments. Families must first gather as communities of love in their own homes before they can be communities of love for the world. ... It is our calling as a family.

Wow! Who knew my kids were taking so much from a meal their mother and I took for granted. My daughter knew, and so did Rick and Zach. A lot of good things can be passed on to our children through family dinners.

CHAPTER 4

IN PRAISE OF MOTHERS

The foundation of our national character is laid by the mothers of the nation.

Josiah Gilbert Holland, c.1875

EOPLE WHO SAY eyes are the windows to the soul must have met Olivia. She had the biggest, brownest, most inquisitive eyes I had ever seen. At 14, she was already an attractive and refined young woman. She was, I concluded some time ago, a copy of her mother.

Mothers Save Lives

Olivia was as full of questions as she was of life itself, and neither her parents nor I ever tired of her curiosity. She started as soon as I opened the exam room door.

"Hi," she began as I greeted her. "There are a couple of things I want to ask you before I forget. Does chocolate actually cause pimples, and do they really get worse if you touch them? Oh, and should I be taking vitamins? And how much sleep do you think I need?"

Olivia continued her questioning throughout the exam and even during the habit review. (I looked twice to see if she had a written list in her hand.) But it was a joy to see her enthusiasm for life and health, so I didn't mind answering her questions—even though I was getting a bit behind in my schedule.

When I finally got to ask how she was getting along with her mother, I thought I knew what her response would be. I was surprised by the story that followed, however.

"I just love my mother," she said. "She's the best mom anyone could have. I try to be just like her. Did you know she saved my big brother's life one time?"

"No," I replied. "I didn't know that. Tell me about it."

"Well, when my brother Fred was about six or seven months old, he was sleeping in his crib and he had a 'cow jumping over the moon' mobile above his head. Somehow, he was able to reach one of the stars and pull it off and put it in his mouth. Mom just happened to poke her head into his room and see him choking on it. He was all blue and just limp, so Mom ran to him, picked him up, and saw that he was not breathing. She didn't panic or anything because she knew just what to do. She turned him over and patted him really hard on the back, and the star came flying out of his mouth. He started to cry and in a few seconds he was just his normal self, but if Mom hadn't known what to do, he would have been dead in just a few more minutes. At least that's what the doctor told her when she called him a little while later. So Mom is Fred's hero and Fred is my favorite brother, so she's my hero too."

"Wow!" I exclaimed. "No wonder everybody loves your mother. I hadn't heard the story about Fred before."

"It happened before we moved to Atlanta, so you wouldn't know about it," she explained. "Besides, Mom is too humble to talk about it."

"It's amazing what mothers can do, isn't it?" I reasoned.

"Oh yeah, that's why I think that ..." Olivia paused and hit me with those brown eyes, "that mothers save more lives than doctors."

MOTHERS SAVE MORE LIVES THAN DOCTORS

I have to admit, I had never thought about it that way before. Mothers *do* save more lives than doctors. Not all mothers perform CPR on their kids, but think of the accidents mothers prevent by carefully watching their toddlers, or the lives they save by making and enforcing rules of behavior for children and adolescents (I think teenagers need parents as much as infants do, some would say even more).

Keeping Tabs on Teens

In a December 15, 2005, column in *The Tennessean,* Dwight Lewis was talking about saving kids' lives when he asked, "If you're the parent of a child between 10 and 18 years of age, do you know where he or she is at this exact moment...? Knowing where your child is could help save his or her life. ..." He goes on to quote Nashville Metro Police Lieutenant Danny Driskell:

In this age where we all have cell phones, it won't hurt for a parent to call up his or her child and say, 'I'm just thinking about you. I wanted to see where you are and what you're doing and who you're with.' A parent needs to know the names of a child's five closest friends or who that child is out with. I have a 19-year-old, and I'm nosey. I want to know what my child is doing and who he is out with.[21]

If you don't know where your child is or who he or she is with at all times, Driskell says you need to "change your way of thinking even if your child thinks you're a nuisance."[22] And Lt. Driskell knows what he's talking about. He's the one who has to knock on the door and tell parents their child has been injured, arrested, shot, or killed.

I would expand Dwight Lewis's advice: you should know the whereabouts of all the children living in your home, regardless of their ages. Find out where they are going before they leave and establish a time for them to return well in advance of their leaving. This knowing does not mediate the amount of trust we have in them. We're not dictating where they can go or who they are with, but as caring parents we have the responsibility to help them make good choices in friendships and entertainment. After we know they are capable of accepting that responsibility, we give it to them, and then give them the trust they have earned. Then, by merely keeping track of where they are in case they need us—or we need them—we have peace of mind and they know we love them enough to be concerned about their welfare. As President Reagan said, "Trust but verify."[23]

Mothers in Society

There are many other ways mothers save lives. On May 3, 1980, 13-year-old Cari Lightner was killed by a drunk driver who had three prior drunk driving convictions and was out on bail from a hit-and-run accident two days earlier. Turning Cari's tragic death into something positive, her mother, Candy Lightner, founded MADD (Mothers Against Drunk Drivers). MADD's mission is to stop drunk driving, support the victims of this violent crime, and prevent underage drinking. Due to efforts by MADD and other programs to reduce drunk driving, alcohol-related traffic fatalities have decreased from more than 30,000 in 1980 to about 17,602 in 2006.[24] This saving of more than 300,000 lives alone validates Olivia's claim that mothers do indeed save more lives than doctors.

A mother in England, Lucy Cope, founded Mothers Against Guns after her 22-year-old son was killed by gunfire on July 29, 2002.[25] Two years later, Vanessa Hyman and Delroy Elliott joined Mothers Against Guns in an attempt to get kids with guns off the streets of England after the bullet-ridden body of 17-year-old Anton Hyman was found in the River Brent in London.[26] His killers have not been caught. These mothers are concerned about the approximately 100 gun-related deaths each year in England and Wales. What would they do if they lived in the United States? There were 97 murders in Nashville, Tennessee, alone during the first 11 months of 2005, and most of them were gun related. Maybe it's time for Nashville mothers to band together to fight gun crimes like the mothers in England did.

Hero Moms

In April 2006, an especially vicious tornado roared through Sumner County, Tennessee, destroying hundreds of homes, killing nine, and injuring scores of others. We were living in the area at the time, and the tornado missed our home by less than half a mile; but Amy and Jerrod Hawkins weren't so lucky. Their home was totally destroyed: ripped from its foundation and pulverized into a pile of rubble. Fireman Jerrod was at work watching the storm on local radar. As soon as the storm passed, emergency vehicles were sent into the area. When rescue workers arrived at what was left of the Hawkins' house, they found Amy lying on top of her sons in what was once the basement of their home. Using her body as a shield, she had covered Jair and Cole and prevented them from getting crushed by bricks, lumber, and other debris. But in the few seconds of the storm's wrath, she suffered punctured lungs, multiple rib fractures, a serious head injury, and permanent paralysis from

a fractured vertebra. Mrs. Hawkins had sacrificed herself to protect her family. Her sacrifice didn't go unnoticed. In October of 2006, she and her family were on national television. "Extreme Makeover: Home Edition" sent them to Disney World while Ty and thousands of Tennessee volunteers built them a new, wheelchair-accessible home.[27]
Another amazing show of courage occurred on September 4, 2007. Angela Silva of Fremont, California, threw herself between her infant son and a 60-pound pit bull. She received multiple bites which shredded the muscles of her arms and opened her forearm to the bone. Her screams alerted workmen at a house across the street. They were able to get the pit bull off of Angela and save her and the baby. Had she not been willing to sacrifice herself, her baby would surely have been killed.[28]

Not all mothers are called upon to risk their lives like Amy Hawkins and Angela Silva did, but they sacrifice in many other ways. Ask around; you'll frequently hear inspirational and heart-warming stories about the sacrifices mothers have made for their children. Olivia isn't the only child who loves and honors her mother.

Setting the Tone

Mothers set the tone of a home, and if the father is a single parent, he needs to be sure his kids have a woman to act as a surrogate mother. Their grandmother often volunteers, but an aunt, a neighbor, or even a good sitter can fill this position.

Furthermore, there is scientific proof that a mother's

mood can determine the mood of her children. According to a 2006 study in New York, children whose mothers were depressed had a two to three times greater risk of being depressed, anxious, or acting out violently than children whose mothers were not depressed. Treatment of the mother with antidepressant medication resulted in resolution of the children's symptoms within three months.[29]

Another recent study showed that women who were stressed during pregnancy had a greater risk of having a baby with colic.[30] Believe me; a screaming infant who cannot be comforted is very stressful. I'm not sure if a constantly crying baby is the result of the mother's tension, but a colicky baby can prolong anyone's anxiety—dad and doctor included!

In the South they say, "If Mama ain't happy, ain't nobody happy." Lindsey O'Connor[31] has a book by that name, as do Kris and Brian Gillespie.[32] These books show how mothers can find joy and happiness in ordinary living and thereby provide a family with a positive attitude. The Gillespies list 52 rules Dad should follow to make sure his wife is happy. It strikes me that if Dad determines mother's happiness, then it's Dad who sets the tone; but that's not the message the Gillespies or the O'Connors deliver. They indicate that while Dad's role in setting the family's mood is important, the home will more likely reflects the attitude of the mother.

Psychologists tell us that women are usually more emotional than men;[33] that they use their emotions to make decisions while men seem insensitive, calculating, and driven by reason. Because a mother's emotions are more visible, it stands to reason that her children will pick up on her emotional state as well. We all know families with happy, outgoing mothers whose kids have the same attitude. Likewise, unhappy mothers frequently yield unhappy children. The next time you are at the airport or any other public place, watch the people. You will commonly see sad, frowning women with sad, frowning children by their side and smiling mothers with smiling kids.

Dr. Kyle Pruett is a prominent child psychiatrist at Yale Child Study Center and is considered one of the top experts on fatherhood. He and his child psychologist wife, Dr. Marsha Kline, have written *Partnership Parenting, How Men and Women Parent Differently and How it Helps Your Kids.*[34] Among other things, they suggest you and your spouse learn how you are different because it won't take long for your kids to figure you both out: "Mom gives better hugs, but Dad gives us more candy." They suggest, among other things, that you occasionally have "Opposite days" where Mom acts like Dad and Dad acts like Mom. The kids will love it, and it will help both parents be more aware of the difficult role the other plays. Just one of their conclusions states: "Knowing that their parents feel and act differently, but that they will support each other on all the big issues and expect certain behavior, helps your child feel prepared for the world out there." So instead of feigning disgust with those who acknowledge male and female stereotypes, we should celebrate these differences in the sexes and see how much fun life can be.

The Influence of Mothers

I consider mothers one of God's greatest creations. It may sound sacrilegious, but God could have done it differently. He could have made mothers more like dads, or in some way made them less influential in our lives—but he didn't.

In her commencement speech at Wellesley College in 1990, Barbara Bush said, "Your success as a family ... our success as a society depends not on what happens in the White House, but on what happens inside your house."[35]

> OUR SUCCESS AS A SOCIETY DEPENDS ON WHAT HAPPENS INSIDE THE HOME

Commenting on Mrs. Bush's remarks, colmnist Cal Thomas said, "Home, not Congress or the White House, is where ultimate power lies."[36] I would add that this power in the home lies with the mother. Mothers have the opportunity to shape their families and their communities. In a poem published in 1865, William Ross Wallace summed up the feelings of many of us when he praised motherhood by stating, "For the hand that rocks the cradle is the hand that rules the world." Few of us may remember Mr. Wallace, but this line from his poem has become a well-known adage.

Olivia and I continued to talk about the importance of mothers until Nurse Kathy knocked on the door. "Time's moving on," she whispered. "You're getting behind."

I asked Kathy to send Olivia's mother in and I told her how much I enjoyed all her children—especially this wonderful girl.

As they left my office I found myself thinking that if only the mothers of the world knew how important they were in their children's lives, maybe more of them would have the kind of relationships that Olivia and her mother enjoy. I can't imagine anything that could make the world a better place than that.

PETS ARE FAMILY TOO

*I had rather hear my dog bark
at a crow than a man swear
he loves me.*

Beatrice.
Much Ado About Nothing
Shakespeare, 1598

I BECAME ACUTELY AWARE of the worth of pets while I was at work one summer day. It was the most perfect day God ever created, and I longed to be outside where the air was clear and the birds were singing. The golf course, my garden, and the stadium all called to me. But I was stuck in the office feeling sorry for myself, attending to dull, boring, routine cases that only yesterday had seemed interesting and exciting. How could I stay inside for the rest of this glorious day? I needed inspiration.

When I finally finished the long morning schedule, I carried my lunch to the office patio and munched my sandwich. A mocking bird serenaded from a nearby wire as I watched the cotton clouds make pictures in the sky. The other doctors and all the staff had stayed inside to escape the heat; so I was alone to enjoy the summer sunshine, contemplate what a good life I had, and feel bad that I had to go back inside.

"Hey, Dr. Donahue!" a voice interrupted my reverie. "Do you have a second?"

I looked up to see a pleasant young girl walking toward the patio. When I recognized her, I stood and answered. "Hi, Emily. Good to see you. Come and sit down."

Emily was a 16-year-old patient of mine. Her short hair was bleached from the sun and the pool, and she wore white tennis shorts that accented her tan. I thought I should tell her to be careful of the sun and use more sun screen, but I reminded myself that she didn't come for a lecture.

"I came over with Mom to pick up her prescription and hoped you would be here," she said cheerfully. "I want you to meet someone." She gestured to the dog she had on the end of a short leash. "Remember, I told you about him the last time I was in."

I pretended to remember. "Sure, but I forgot his name."

"Ogley."

"You're a right handsome fellow, aren't you Ogley?" I said, petting the top of his head. "How did he get that name?"

"Well, both my parents teach at Oglethorpe University

and we got him from one of my mom's friends there. Ogley is his nickname. His real name is Oglethorpe."

"How long have you had him?"

"I got him for my birthday when I was ten." She sat down under the market umbrella and took off her sunglasses. She lifted Ogley to her lap and rubbed his neck. He kissed her on the lips. "I suppose you think that's unsanitary," she said without embarrassment. Then added, "It's better than kissing a dumb boy!" Her mood shifted abruptly and tears welled up in her eyes.

"Sounds like you broke up with your boyfriend," I suggested.

"Who told you?"

"Ogley."

"Well, I did, or I should say he did." Now the tears were really starting. Ogley went to work. He gazed at her as she talked, then he nudged her

PEOPLE SHOULD BE MORE LIKE DOGS

neck. He licked away her tears as they formed, all the while nuzzling her on the neck. Then, when he thought she had cried long enough, he nibbled on her ear lobe. With that she giggled and pulled herself together. Finally she looked at me and said, "I just can't stay sad or mad when Ogley's around. He always understands. People should be more like dogs."

"Want to tell me what happened, or should I ask Ogley?"

"I really just wanted to show you Ogley, but since you ask, I was just sitting in math, the last class of the day, and

Jason passed me this note saying, 'Let's break up!' I just shrieked. All the kids looked at me, but I couldn't keep from crying. When the bell finally rang I ran to him, but he wouldn't even talk to me. I even cried on the bus. As soon as I got home, Mom was all over me with, 'Why are you crying?' and 'What's wrong?' and everything. So I told her we broke up and she was like 'Oh, I knew you would. Can you get your laundry done before dinner?' or something weird like that. I just kept crying and ran to my room. Luckily, Ogley followed me. I told him the whole story. He listened to every word and looked at me like, 'I'm the one who loves you.' Then he made me laugh, got his ball, and wanted to play.

"I know my mom loves me, but she just doesn't understand the way Ogley does. It always feels so good to play catch with him. Jason wouldn't ever play ball with me. 'Girls aren't good enough to play ball with boys.' He actually said that. Now I'm glad we broke up. But I wouldn't have been able to get through it without Ogley."

"Boys can be mean, can't they? Sure is good you have such an understanding pet."

"Having Ogley is like always having a best friend around. I can tell him everything and he listens and understands. He never interrupts, never gets mad at me, never tells me what to do, and is always there when I need him."

> HAVING A DOG IS LIKE ALWAYS HAVING A BEST FRIEND

Emily knew what she was talking about. Dogs show compassion, loyalty, and unconditional love. Sometimes, having a dog or other pet can be even *better* than having a best friend.

Benefits of Owning a Pet

Studies have shown what pet owners have always known; having a pet helps us stay healthy. Doctors have discovered that adult pet owners live longer, recover faster after an illness or injury, and are happier than adults who do not have a pet.[37] Kids who have a close relationship with a pet have an easier time coping with the stresses of life.

The American Academy of Pediatrics (AAP) in a February 2009 statement about ways to love your kids said, "Owning a pet can make children with chronic illnesses and disabilities feel better by stimulating physical activity, enhancing their overall attitude, and offering constant companionship."[38]

A study in 2002 showed that infants who are exposed to dogs and cats have fewer allergies as children.[39] The finding was completely at odds with the "old doctor's tale" that families with a history of allergies should not have pets. Interestingly, further studies,[40] including one published in February 2008, have supported this finding.[41] The medical profession now knows that the presence of a dog or cat in the home decreases the risk of allergies and asthma.

Psychologists and psychiatrists have discovered that pets can help their patients get better faster. It seems that people seeing therapists are more comfortable talking about sensitive issues while holding, petting, or just being near a pet.[42] Many therapists have dogs in their offices and use these dogs to help their patients relax. The grandmother of our family dog Belle works with a psychiatrist in Hudson, Wisconsin. I haven't met Belle's grandmother, but if she's anything like Belle I'm sure she's an excellent therapist.

Margaret Pepe, the mental health officer for the American Red Cross relief operation after the September 11 World Trade Center disaster, worked with some 100 therapy dogs and 3 therapy cats. She was quoted as saying:

> I oversee 175 counselors, psychologists, and social workers, and I wish they all had four feet. The dogs are incredibly effective. I'm jealous of the four-footed therapists and their ability to engage and relax people in a matter of minutes.[43]

Pets help with physical illnesses as well. Dr. Karen Allen, a research scientist in Buffalo, New York, showed that having a pet helps decrease heart rate and blood pressure. She divided highly stressed stockbrokers into two groups; one group was treated with the usual high blood pressure medicine while the other group was given the same medicine plus a pet dog or cat. After six months, the pet group had a much lower response to stress than the group treated with medication alone. "Petting a dog has a dramatic and significant effect on a person's blood pressure,"[44] she said.

Pets, especially big dogs and horses, encourage their owners to exercise. Exercise, as we all know, has many health benefits; it reduces the incidence of obesity, decreases the risk of heart attack, and helps control blood pressure. Running advocate Jeff Fisher of The Mental Health Association of Middle Tennessee claims it helps control emotions. "[Running] helps me concentrate better at work, sleep better at night, and maintain a positive outlook on my life."[45]

My neighbor, marathon runner Jack Curran, used to take his golden retriever with him when he ran. She provided companionship for him as well as protection.

Some dogs can even help kids learn to read. My grandsons go to a school that has a yellow dog named Dusty. He is a border collie/golden retriever mix with black spots on his feet. He loves to sit and listen to the kids read. He is never critical of the reader and is interested in anyone who pays attention to him. Consequently, the kids love to read to him. By reading more the children improve their reading skills, which results in a boost to their self-confidence.

One group of psychiatrists in Knoxville, Tennessee, helped delinquent boys get dogs from the pound. The boys lived with, cared for, and soon learned to love their dogs. In turn, the dogs taught the boys structure, responsibility, and discipline.[46] Now, many homes for delinquents have in-house pets to help the kids grow into responsible adults.

All in the Family

Dogs and cats are not the only pets people acquire: birds,

fish, turtles, guinea pigs, hamsters, horses, and even snakes are kept by families as pets. When I was a seven-year-old, we lived on a farm in Minnesota where, among other things, we raised sheep. One year, for reasons unknown to me, a baby lamb was abandoned by her mother and no other ewe (mother sheep) would accept her. At about the same time, another ewe had twins. But she died the next day.

Dad did what any caring shepherd would do and brought the three babies into our house. He placed them in a box in the kitchen and assigned us four older kids (ages five to ten) to care for them. After he purchased some black nipples from the farm store, we attached them to used syrup bottles and nursed the babies many times during the day and night. We grew to love these lambs, but Mom didn't! I suppose she wasn't happy sharing her tiny house with three four-footed creatures. Fortunately, a couple of weeks later the weather warmed and the lambs started sleeping through the night, so we moved them outside.

We also had a big mutt dog named Shep who slept on the porch in the warm weather; but he could turn the latch on the front door. Since there were no locks, he could come in whenever he wanted. One summer Sunday when we went to church, a thunderstorm came up and frightened Shep. He opened the door and invited his friends—Whitey, Blackie, and Bucky (names we had given the three sheep)— in out of the rain. When we got home from church, most of the family broke into fits of laughter at the sight of almost full-grown sheep in the living room. Mother, however, was *not* amused.

Our family has told this story hundreds of times and it never fails to send us into fits of laughter. Now, more than half a century later, Mom finally sees the humor in it. The point of the story is that pets of any kind provide material for conversation and laughter as well as instruction in responsibility and compassion.

My mother would not forgive me if I didn't say a word about pets as members of the family. She frequently got upset when she saw families who seemed to give more attention to their pets than they did to each other. "It's a shame that people spend so much on a dumb animal when there are so many starving kids in the world," she would say. And I agree with her, to a point. If a family is neglecting their children (whether they have a pet or not), they should be referred to the county's Department of Family Services and get the help they need. But the truth of the matter—even if Mom doesn't like it—is that people do have pets, pets do help families and kids in many ways, and 87 percent of families consider their pet to be a member of their family.[47]

If you own pets, you know that they frequently help you and your family laugh more, converse more, develop better attitudes, and have more fun.[48] Kids easily identify with them since animals are non-judgmental and see people for what they are, without any pretense—qualities families can emulate. James Serpell, director of the Center for the Interaction of Animals and Society at the University of Pennsylvania, writes, "Companion animals may teach a child responsibility, encourage caring attitudes and behavior, provide companionship, security, comfort, amusement, or an outlet for affection."[49] And there's always the likelihood that as a child matures, because he or she cared for a pet that provided unconditional love, they will learn to love and care unconditionally as well.

Give a Little Love

One of our basic needs is to touch and be touched. Babies who are not touched do not develop normal emotions, and they often do not grow and thrive.[50] Nurseries that take care of sick and premature newborns have volunteers who come and hold them for just that reason.

Many families are "huggers and kissers," but other people do not feel comfortable being touched, not even by another family member. Yet they still have the emotional need of touch. Victims of sexual abuse especially are reluctant to be touched.[51] These otherwise healthy adults can satisfy this basic, biological need by having a pet. The touch of an animal is considered safe and non-threatening and can be an important part of their recovery. If pets are important in these cases, think how much they would benefit a normal, healthy family.

As much as pets give, they need attention, too. When we give our family a pet, we need to make sure we budget for veterinarian bills, food bills, and toys. American pet owners spent more than $40 billion in 2007 on the care of their pets. Even with that expense, 63 percent of American households own a pet.[52]

If you have a family pet, make sure your kids help care for it and exercise it, just like they help with other chores around the house. Dr. Kris Bulcroft, a family researcher, found that mothers are more often the ones responsible for the children's pets, and dads are usually the ones who take pets out for exercise. If parents do all the work, the children will not learn responsibility.

Emily's words of wisdom sunk in as I watched Ogley patiently waiting for Emily to leave. "You know Emily," I commented, "dogs really are good for people. Our dog Belle is one of more than 400 trained therapy dogs in and around Atlanta. These dogs and their owners visit residents in nursing homes and hospitals. Belle has been chosen to visit the sick kids at Children's Hospital. I wish you could go with her to see how the kids, parents, and staff light up when Belle visits. She is such a sweet little dog, a lot like Ogley, but only about a fourth his size."

As we talked, Emily's mother came out of the clinic with her prescription. "Are you three about finished?" she asked.

"Hi, Mrs. Patracuollo," I said. "We've had a good talk. Emily is a remarkably wise girl. You must be very proud of her."

"I certainly am. Thanks for taking time with her."

I walked Emily and her mom to the car and then went back to my afternoon schedule, refreshed not only by the beautiful summer day, but by another very wise teenager. If you have

WHAT A WONDERFUL WORLD IT WOULD BE IF WE ALL WAGGED MORE AND BARKED LESS

a dog for a pet, you will understand why Emily thought we should try to be more like our canine friends. What a wonderful world it would be if we all wagged more and barked less.

PARENTING TIPS

- *Be the person you want your child to become.*

- *Know where you stand, and let your kids know where you stand. Tell your kids enough about your life that they will know and understand how you obtained the values you have. Establish rules and teach them the consequences of breaking them.*

- *Accept responsibility for your behavior. Make no excuses, and accept no excuses for bad behavior.*

- *Respond to news items—national, local, neighborhood, school, friends, and family—as "teaching moments."*

- *Be truthful and trusting. If you are not trustworthy, you cannot trust others. Nor can you expect your kids to be trustworthy. There is no substitute for always telling the truth.*

- *Anticipate and model good behavior. Kids do not know how to act unless you tell them and show them.*

- *Love and respect your spouse. Show your kids what a good marriage looks like. Even if you are divorced, show respect for your children's other parent and work with her or him to present a unified set of values to your children.*

- *Eat meals together as a family. Having your kids help with the cooking and cleaning up will make them more appreciative.*

- *If you have the time, space, and resources, get your family a pet. Require all family members to take part in the care of their pet.*

The Importance
Of Religion

A cure has been discovered that will turn teenagers into better students and safer drivers. It will make them less likely to be involved with crime, drugs, alcohol, and premarital sex. In addition, it causes them to have better manners, greater self-esteem, fewer mental and emotional problems, and to live happier lives. Interestingly, this miracle has been around for some time but is being used less and less by today's society. What is this miracle cure? Plain and simple: religion.

CHAPTER 6

RELIGION AND HEALTH

Clothes are our weapons,
our challenges, our visible
insults.

Angela Olive Carter

C LAIRE'S MOTHER SHOULD have been upset. I know I was when her teen walked into my office the first time for her annual exam. This was the 90s, and Claire was into grunge: the dress-like-a-homeless-person fashion (or anti-fashion) that emerged from the Seattle-Nirvana-Kurt Cobain music scene. Claire's interpretation, however, just made her look sloppy and screamed, "I don't care what you think of me!"

She wore "nature shoes," the kind with straps and no heels; oversized, shapeless, olive green pants; and a large, loose T-shirt. She had on white lipstick and heavy, dark mascara. Her hair had been dyed so often that it was straight, thin, and fragile. I think it wanted to be brown, but it was blonde with violet and pink streaks. Her fashion statement was even more depressing because Claire was really an attractive girl under all the grunge and makeup.

I was puzzled by the mother's apparent lack of concern. Had Claire been my daughter, I'd have been more than concerned; I'd have been alarmed! But this was the South, and Mom was a soft-spoken, well-dressed, polite Southern lady.

I thought, *My work's cut out for me with this family.* I couldn't tell what Claire was trying to be or what message she was sending her mother, but I was glad she wasn't my daughter.

I was so wrong about Claire!

The Church-Health Connection

In my specialty, I've learned that sometimes you know what a teenager is going to say and other times they surprise you. Claire surprised me—and taught me some very important lessons.

The exam went smoothly and without incident. Claire was bright and alert; she even laughed at my jokes and made some clever one-liners of her own. By the time we got to the health habits review I was starting to like her, despite her fashion taste—or lack of it. However, I couldn't help but wonder what I would say if one of my sons wanted to date her. On the surface, she didn't look like she could be trusted, at least not enough to date my son. I started my review questions.

"How often do you have dinner with your family?" I asked.

"Every night," she replied.

"Do you have any guns in your house?"

"Oh, no!"

"What is your grade point average?"

"I'm not sure, probably 3.7, maybe 3.8."

I didn't know if she was being truthful or just telling me what I wanted to hear. It seemed like she was telling the truth, but she spoke a different language than her clothing did. I wagered with myself mentally that I'd get her on the next question.

"How often do you go to church or temple?" I asked casually.

God and spirituality have always been important in my life, but that's not why I asked this question. If a teen has a firm set of religious principles, I know I can worry less about them having problems coping with adolescence. Knowing if a teen believes in God is also very important in dealing with any crisis that may arise.[53] Parents whose kids are religious are at an advantage all during the teenage years.

I didn't expect Claire's answer. "Every Sunday and almost every Wednesday," she said.

Really? Was I not seeing something about this girl? Trying not to show my surprise, I continued. "How important is religion in your life?"

"Oh, very important!" Claire exclaimed. Then she added her own wisdom. "Going to church helps you stay healthy."

That did it. I was wrong about Claire, or about what her fashion, lipstick, and hair were saying about her, anyway. I *would* like her for a daughter, and she *could* date my son.

GOING TO CHURCH HELPS YOU STAY HEALTHY

Still, I continued to wonder why she dressed the way she did when on the inside everything was so orderly. That question would have to wait. Claire's answer deserved an immediate and emphatic "Amen!" Because sure enough, going to church does help keep you healthy. And it's not just religious propaganda; scientific study proves it.

Addictive Behaviors

A study of adolescents in Dade County, Florida, found that the only significant difference between cocaine users and their non-using peers was that religion was an important part of the non-users lives.[54]

Another study in North Carolina showed that college women with strong religious beliefs consumed less alcohol and were less likely to engage in risky sexual behavior than were female participants with weaker religious convictions.[55] It's not that the non-drinking participants were convinced they'd go to hell for partaking, or that a bolt of lightning would strike the Coors cans right out of their hands. Something to believe in, beyond your own pleasure and the moment, provides direction in life, more so than just following the crowd—which is actually moving in no direction at all.

A study from the University of Michigan concluded:

> Relative to their peers, religious youth are less likely to engage in behaviors that compromise their health (that is, carrying weapons, getting into fights, drinking and driving) and are more likely to believe in ways that enhance their health (that is, proper nutrition, exercise, and rest).[56]

At a National Institute for Health Care Research conference held in May of 1997 in Milwaukee, Wisconsin, Dr. David Larson offered many examples of how people with strong spiritual beliefs benefited compared to those without religious convictions:

- Hip implant patients walked sooner and farther.

- Elderly heart patients were fourteen times less likely to die after surgery.

- Illness and death from heart attack, emphysema, cirrhosis, and suicide were decreased.

- Youths had a lower use of alcohol and drugs.

- Released prisoners were less likely to return to a life of crime.

Medical schools have recognized the importance of religion and its effects on health. Students now look at spiritual issues throughout the four years of medical school, learning practical ways to integrate spirituality into their practices.

Yet despite the evidence connecting religion and health, not all educational institutions are open to religion. In a 2002 article in *The New York Times,* Eric Goldscheider quoted David K. Scott, a former research physicist and ex-chancellor of the University of Massachusetts in Amherst, as having said he feared "that constitutional prohibitions against promoting religion had been used to effectively banish religion from public universities, or at least to 'ghettoize' religion in departments where it can be safely ignored by those who do not study it." Goldscheider went on to say that Scott "would like to see universities revamp the general education requirement to include courses and activities that challenge students to think about 'how to live, how to be with each other, how to be in the universe.'" [57]

It's no longer fashionable to speak of spirituality and religion in our society where the news media and politicians promote a secular faith instead of a personal one. But it's how people, particularly young people, personally apply religious beliefs that make a positive difference in their health.

Making Connections

Too many of today's children seem unable to forget themselves long enough to develop the empathy, compassion, and love of others that is needed to maintain a sensible, caring society. According to the Commission on Children at Risk, children and teens are experiencing a "lack of connectedness ... to other people."[58] The commission said they lack "deep connections to moral and spiritual meaning." This commission, supported by Dartmouth Medical School, the YMCA, and the Institute for American Values, claims that humans were created with a built-in need for close relationships with other people. We "are born with a built-in capacity and drive to search for purpose and reflect on life's ultimate ends."[59]

The need for attachment starts with parents and spreads to other family members; and as the child grows, it extends to the community. But instead of developing this closeness, infants are placed into infant seats, fed in infant seats, and carried in the same seats. I call these "slop-pail babies." I have seen mothers and fathers of four- to five-month-old infants who do not know how to hold a baby. To make matters worse, these same infants are placed in front of the television in their infant seats. This leads to what Child Psychiatrist Robert Shaw calls "... unattached, uncommunicative, learning-impaired, and uncontrollable children." Furthermore, Shaw says this denies children "the connections and rituals and nurturing that are so necessary to children's healthy development."[60] These connections are the basis of loving. Through them we learn to care, share, have compassion, and love.

Kids of every age seem to be disconnected. They sit beside each other and watch television or a movie; they text message rather than speak face to face; boys especially give a "high-five" rather than a hand shake, pat on the back, or hug; they line dance or do a twist type of dance, gyrating in front of others without touching or connecting with anyone, and many "dance" alone (perhaps that is why they feel the need to connect sexually—they substitute sexual intimacy for emotional intimacy). Many teenagers feel lonely and unloved. Consequently, they do not know how to love.

However, Robert Shaw went on to say that there are worse mistakes parents can make than failing to provide "connectiveness" for children. One of their biggest mistakes according to Shaw is "not conveying to your child—through both actions and words—the moral, ethical, and spiritual values you believe in (or not having moral, ethical, and spiritual values in the first place)."[61] And I agree. Kids who are not taught these values are left with a moral vacuum that is quickly filled with the amoral and sometimes immoral flotsam and refuse perpetrated on them by the media and secular society in general.

The only answer is to get yourself involved in a religious community long before your first baby is born, practice that religion, and when your first baby is born, introduce him to

WHAT YOU DO IS MORE IMPORTANT THAN WHAT YOU SAY

that religion at once. Live your religion and, as St. Benedict is quoted as saying, "Preach the gospel all the time, but use words only if absolutely necessary." Although that quote has also been attributed to St. Francis of Assisi, it doesn't matter who said it. It tells us once again that what you do is more important than what you say.

Your religious community should fit the definition

established by the Commission on Children at Risk as "a social institution that is warm and nurturing; establishes clear limits and expectations; is multigenerational; has a long-term focus; reflects and transmits a shared understanding of what it means to be a good person; encourages spiritual and religious development; and is philosophically oriented to the equal dignity of all persons and to the principle of love of neighbor."[62]

If you don't belong to a religious community, talk to a respected neighbor, friend, or relative and ask them to sponsor you into their church, and get studying so you can help your children grow and thrive.

When getting little children involved in religion, remember that kids like to have fun. Use arts and crafts to illustrate a point. Teach them how to pray, morning and evening and over meals, and demonstrate through your own prayers how they can pray for others and for things that may be troubling them or their family.

Blessings

A handsome Jewish boy once taught me that a blessing is another form of prayer. For a number of years, Aaron was just "the little brother." I didn't know his family well, although I had taken care of his big brother, Adam. I was not seeing younger children at the time. Adam was a scholar but not much of an athlete; he was nothing special to look at and very quiet. But he was a pleasant high schooler and I happened to like him a lot; so I was looking forward to meeting Aaron.

When Aaron turned 13 and made his Bar Mitzvah, he came to me for his health exam.

"So glad to finally get to meet you," I greeted as I offered my hand. "I've heard so much about you from Adam."

Aaron stood, grasped my hand firmly, looked me square in the eye and replied, "The pleasure is mine, Sir."

During the habit review he told me about his devotion to his religion, and I praised his involvement.

"Aaron," I said when we were through with the visit, "Your folks must be proud of you, and I'm sure your Rabbi is, too. I wish I were your Rabbi so I could bless you."

"Thanks," he said, as his face blushed at the compliment. "But, you don't have to be a Rabbi to give me a blessing. Anybody can bless anybody, any time."

> ANYBODY CAN BLESS ANYBODY, ANY TIME

"You're absolutely right. Could I bless you before you leave?"

"Okay," he said. "I'd like that."

"May the God of ...," I began as I placed my hands on his head.

"Don't touch my hair!" Aaron interrupted, letting me know he was a typical teenager who didn't want his hair messed up.

I blushed. "I'm sorry," I said, letting my hand come to rest a few inches above his head. "Let me continue. May the God of Abraham, the God of Moses, the God of all our forefathers bless you today and every day of your life," I prayed.

"Amen," Aaron answered. Then with a wink of his eye he added, "Thank you. You might make a good Rabbi after all."

To some people my blessing Aaron may seem unusual, but when someone sneezes, most of us offer even a stranger a blessing with "God Bless You." In Tennessee, many people offer a blessing as a greeting. "God bless you," they say, and a friend echoes "and you, too." We're accustomed to blessing our food, our guests, our family, our work, and even ourselves; but other than at mealtime, how often do we think to bless others?

Even though I have often told parents that I would pray for them or their child (and more than once have prayed with them), I never thought to actually offer them a blessing until I met Aaron. I'll admit, many of us would feel strange holding our hands over another's head and blessing them. But a blessing does not need to contain a physical sign; merely saying "God bless you" is blessing enough for most people. It tells the receiver that you really do care about them and are thinking about them.

In the late 1970s, I attended a sick newborn in the hospital. He was not the usual red color of most newborns, which is what tipped me off that things were not right with him. Instead, his skin was pale and his lips and fingers were gray. Cyanosis we call it. When I listened to his heart he had a murmur, and I was left to tell his still jubilant parents of the new baby's problems. After explaining the condition to them and answering their questions, they asked if I would call and ask their minister to come and bless the baby. I did, and in a matter of minutes Pastor

Castels was at my side in the nursery. He, Dad, Mom, and I prayed for the baby and then for the family. The baby went on to have heart surgery and survives to this day.

It seemed strange to me that the parents and pastor thought it was special that I prayed with them, especially since we were of different faiths. I feel it only natural to pray (silently or aloud) with anyone who wants to join me. Why not ask God's blessing on His children? After all, isn't that what religion is about?

Establishing the Habit of Religion

In addition to praying with children, parents need to teach dependence and reliance on God. Every kid loves to decorate for Christmas or Hanukkah or other religious holidays. Even if kids are a bit messy, the fun of letting them help more than makes up for any "irregular" decorations. When they get older, let them light the Hanukkah candles or the Advent wreath. Make religion a part of their lives. Tell stories about your family going to church when you were a child. Kids of all ages love to hear family tales.

As children get older, be sure to take them with you to religious services and teach them the behavior proper for church. They need to learn to sit quietly, listen, and pay attention. That is not always as easy as it sounds. Many years ago my seven-year-old son misbehaved quite badly during Sunday Morning service. Although he didn't disrupt the service, he made it difficult for me and others near us to concentrate with his whispering, laughing, and moving around. After the service was over, I asked my wife to take the other children home as Brian and I would walk home after the next service. Brian was well behaved the second time and every time since. It worked so well for Brian that one Sunday evening years later, while we were talking on the phone, he told me that he and his kids had just returned from evening service. "We went this morning," he explained, "but the kids misbehaved, so I took them back tonight." He assured me they were much better. Not that going to church is a punishment, but it demands respectful behavior!

Amanda L. Aikman in the September 1995 issue of *Reach,* a magazine for Unitarian Universalists, relates recollections from her traditional Christian childhood:

> I loved sitting in the eighteenth-century stone church with the adults and feeling very serious and grown-up. ... I don't suppose I understood a tenth of what was going on in those services but they must have had some impact on me, because I remembered to pray when I had the worst crisis of my life. I remember falling to my knees on the tiles and thanking Jesus for letting me live.[63]

Kids generally learn more and remember more than we think.

Claire and I continued to talk about her health habits, goals, and ambitions. The more I got to know her, the more I liked her. She was a model teen with a delightful sense of humor—but a mysterious dress code. Although I wanted to quite badly, I did not ask her about her clothes; I had to remind myself that I was a doctor, not a fashion consultant.

Her mother returned to the room and I congratulated her for having done such a great job with Claire.

"We're so proud of her," Mom beamed, looking at Claire with delight and satisfaction. Then she added, "Did she tell you why she's dressed like this today?"

Claire's face flushed as she flashed an ear-to-ear smile, showing off her glistening teeth. I thought to myself, *Please tell me, I'd like to know; I need to know! Please.*

"Do you want to tell him?" mother asked daughter.

"No," Claire giggled.

As they left the room, Mom laughed and bid farewell with, "Teenagers, don't you just love them?"

I sure do. They make the world a wonderful, surprising, and yet mysterious place to live, where the faulty fashion of the moment on the outside can't touch the healthy faith of a lifetime on the inside.

The more I think about Claire the more I think she really taught me two lessons that day: the importance of religion in one's life; and (much to my embarrassment) not to prejudge on the basis of appearance. So thanks, Claire. I promise I'll be more thoughtful and less judgmental in the future.

(And Claire, if you're reading this chapter, would you *please* write or call and tell me why you were dressed like that that day? I would really like to know.)

CHAPTER 7

RELIGION AS A MORAL COMPASS

*I don't think anybody can
be a truly successful parent
without a commitment to an
established religion.*

Corrie Lynne Player

S OME PARENTS THINK there is a disease—or at least a
syndrome—that many kids get around 17 years of age
called senioritis. They say it must be some kind of infection of the frontal lobe of the brain, the part that controls
attitude. It strikes these soon-to-be adults quite suddenly
as they enter their senior year of high school. Fiendishly,
the infection destroys all the brain's worry neurons and
boosts chemical levels of mellowing and confidence,
building serotonin to abnormally high levels. Serotonin
is the Alfred E. Neumann of brain chemicals. Alfred is,
of course, the kid on the cover of *Mad* magazine whose
motto is "What, me worry?" As an agent of senioritis, this

chemical encourages teens to disconnect, have some fun, and take advantage of their youth because after this year, their future consists of becoming boring adults and either getting full-time jobs or going to college.

Somehow, though, Nicole and Maria avoided contracting senioritis. In fact, they elevated their attitude to a higher level and knew some lessons that many adults have difficulty grasping. I learned all this over lunch one beautiful summer day.

Influence of Religion

Nicole and Maria were daughters of friends of mine, not patients. I had enjoyed watching them grow up and since they were now between their junior and senior years in high school ("rising seniors" we call them in the South), I looked forward to treating them like adults. They were working as volunteer candy stripers at Children's Hospital that summer and at the time, my office was only a short distance from Children's; so I promised to buy them lunch one day if they could get to my office.

As it would turn out, the girls were much more mature than I had expected. Don't misread me here. I'm not using the word "mature" the way the media often does. That connotation is usually associated with teens doing reckless things with their bodies and futures; things like alcohol, drugs, truancy, and all kinds of sexual activity; things that can leave them scarred, dead, or taking a guest spot on "The Jerry Springer Show." The maturity I'm talking about is the character-building grit that makes parents proud and more hopeful that the next generation can avoid the just-stated kind of "maturity" that is eating away at so much of society.

The day began with a beautiful sunrise, which pleased me since we planned to eat at the Lake Side Patio Cafe across a small pond from my office. But I was disappointed when a sudden summer shower came up just before noon. In spite of the weather, the young ladies showed up on time and announced themselves to my receptionist.

"Please tell Dr. Donahue that Ms. Marvin and Ms. Brice are here to take him to lunch," stressing the "Ms." in order to say that they were no ordinary high school girls. Then they laughed in unison and turned to sit down. They hadn't seen me enter the lobby so I startled them when I said, "I'm sorry it rained. Now we'll have to eat inside."

"Who cares?" laughed Nicole. "A little rain can't keep us from being hungry. If we race to the café, no one will get really wet," she teased.

I accepted the challenge. We darted across the footbridge, jumped a small puddle, and dashed into the cafe. "Damn!" Nicole gasped when we got inside. "I got my shoe filled with water!" she exclaimed as she shook the rain from her auburn hair.

Maria flashed horrified brown eyes at Nicole. "Watch your language," she chastised. "There are adults around."

Since observing teens was my profession, I knew Maria wasn't really shocked with Nicole's use of a four-letter word. I'm sure they knew, and probably used, more. Kids usually emulate the language they hear in their homes or at school. Still, I thought I'd ask about it.

"Is that a bad word, Maria?" I asked.

"Well, my folks don't like it, and my youth pastor is against saying words like that, and I don't think he uses them," Maria answered.

"Well," I replied, playing Devil's advocate, "aren't youth pastors and churches against almost everything?"

"Oh sure," Maria replied with resignation. "But, they say it's best for you."

"Listen," Nicole interrupted with authority in her voice. "Most things churches say we shouldn't do aren't good for us anyhow."

> MOST THINGS CHURCHES SAY WE SHOULDN'T DO AREN'T GOOD FOR US ANYHOW

Nicole's comment impressed me. "Like what?" I asked.

"Well, take four-letter words. If you use them a lot, some people, especially adults, will think you're crude and they'll look down on you. Some even think it means you're a slut, and that can get you in trouble. It's like our minister preaches: we're supposed to live in moderation. If you eat like a glutton you'll get fat, and you know how bad that is for your health. Then there's sex," she added without blushing.

"What about it?" I asked, intrigued by Nicole's confidence and conviction.

"Our parents and ministers say we should wait until marriage to have sex, and if we don't, you know what can happen: AIDS, STDs, cancer, and pregnancy." Then she looked me squarely in the eyes and added, "Did you know that if you have an abortion you have an increased risk of breast cancer?"

"Yes, I knew that," I answered, "but I'm surprised you did. It's not a well-known fact. It may not even be a fact. Scientists are still studying it."

I really was surprised that Nicole knew about the abortion-breast cancer connection. Scientists have been wondering about it since the early 1990s when a study concluded that women who had one abortion had a 50 percent increased chance of getting breast cancer.[64] Women who had multiple abortions and a family history of breast cancer were at even greater risk.[65] Of 33 worldwide studies, 27 showed this connection while five were inconclusive, and one study in Denmark showed no relationship.[66]

A Harvard study in 2007 was hailed as putting an end to the controversy. It showed no increase of breast cancer in women who had had abortions.[67] However, Dr. Joel Brind, a researcher at City University of New York's Baruch College, and others criticized the study for a number of reasons.[68] First, the investigators surveyed women who had had abortions as well as those who had had breast cancer. Women who had died of breast cancer were thus excluded. To confuse matters more, the survey referred to miscarriages as spontaneous abortions—the correct medical term, but not one with which many women are familiar. Brind also noted that the average age of women in the study was 42, whereas the average age of diagnosis of breast cancer is 61. Furthermore, the investigators only followed the women for ten years and did not include the

399 cases of carcinoma in situ, the earliest form of cancer.[69] That's like following a high school kid who smokes for ten years and then saying that smoking does not cause cancer. The abortion-breast cancer controversy is far from settled; cause-and-effect relationships are not always easy to establish.

Well-documented studies do show that depression follows many abortions. David Reardon, the American director of the Elliot Institute and a pro-life activist, in association with Jesse R. Cougle and Priscilla K. Coleman, compared data for women from the National Longitudinal Survey of Youth and concluded that women who have aborted a first pregnancy are 65 percent more likely to experience depression than those who carry a pregnancy to term.[70] This study and others like it have also stirred controversy. But even if abortion is found not to contribute to breast cancer or depression and in no way affects a woman, it has a fatal effect on the pre-born, developing baby whose life it takes. In this case, it is well to remember what Nicole said, "Most things churches say we shouldn't do aren't good for us anyhow." The operative word here is "us"; she didn't say "me" or "you," but "us." And "us" includes all of God's children, both born and pre-born.

Know Your Religion

It is no surprise to anyone that kids begin to question authority during the mid-teen years. That's why it is so important for teens to understand as well as know the tenets of their religion. To help them understand, make it a practice to question your teens about why your church teaches what it does. Questioning helps them to think and, like Maria and Nicole, they will realize that religion is one of life's greatest allies. Opportunities to discuss religious beliefs (or lack of them) arise often from television programs, articles in the newspapers, and through ordinary conversation. When parents take advantage of these opportunities, they pass their faith on to their children. But this is not possible if they or their children lack basic knowledge of their religion. Insist that your teens attend religious education programs whenever possible.

When I was practicing in Alpharetta, Georgia, I was impressed by the Mormon kids who began every school day with seminary (religious education) at five in the morning. These kids sacrificed early morning sleep to learn about their religion.

At the 2006 Memorial Day 10K run in Hendersonville, Tennessee, I saw a group of junior high and senior high school boys wearing T-shirts exclaiming, "I can do all things through Christ who strengthens me." The T-shirts were a project of their Sunday evening religious class conducted by their youth minister. These kids, like their Mormon brothers in Georgia, will have an easier time living a moral life because they understand their faith and have supportive friends. Youth ministry is very important in educating high schoolers in the tenets of their religion and in giving them a connection with kids who have similar beliefs.

The Role of Youth Ministries

A very comprehensive National Study of Youth and Religion concluded that "religion really does matter" to teens.[71] In this study, investigator Christian Smith found that devout teens hold more traditional sexual and other values than their non-religious counterparts. They have fewer emotional health problems, greater academic success, and more community involvement; they show greater concern for others, trust adults more, and are more likely to avoid risky behavior. On most of the measured criteria, Mormon youths were the most engaged in practicing their faith, followed in order by evangelical Protestants, black Protestants, mainline Protestants, Catholics, and Jews. Catholic youths were described as fairly weak "on most measures of religious faith, belief, experience and practice." The problem is attributed largely to ineffective youth programs and "the relative religious laxity of their parents."[72]

As a practicing Catholic, I have long been concerned about Catholic youth education programs. Most Catholic parishes end all formal religious instruction when kids get to high school and replace it with Sunday night teen Mass followed by pizza, basketball, and other social activities. Social activities are important as they are the reason many youth attend church, but they cannot be a substitute for formal study. Many denominations have developed very successful education programs combining fun with learning. Smith's study confirms that teenagers need more instruction. Unfortunately, many Catholics are not getting it.

Finally, the study confirmed once again the importance of parents in teaching values. Lax parents lead to lax teens! If you want your kids to go to church or temple, you must go. If you want your kids to be fervent in their faith, you must be fervent. If you want your kids to have high moral standards and avoid promiscuity, you must emulate these qualities. There is no substitute for good leadership!

If your church has an ineffective youth program, whatever your religion, you owe it to your kids and to the community to step in and get things going on the right track. I am not a cleric nor a theologian, but as a parent and a physician who has seen many, many well-adjusted youth, and too many teens in trouble, there are some things I believe every youth group should provide: didactic religious instruction in the tenets of faith; advice, especially by example, on how to pray; upstanding adult and peer role models; supervised social interaction with peers and adults; volunteer work in the community; group discussion and the opportunity for one-on-one discussions with a youth minister or other trained adult; and last but not least, a place for safe relaxation, recreation, and fun. I am sure religious educators would enlarge this list. This may seem like a lot to accomplish in the time available, but your kids are worth this and more. Insist on nothing less. Your kids may not like it at the time, but as adults, they will thank you.

Finding Strength Within

Lunch with Nicole and Marie was an eye-opener on several fronts. It was strikingly evident that it helps tremendously to have a friend who shares your moral and personal convictions. Nicole had Maria and Maria had Nicole. This made it easier for the girls—especially Nicole—to speak so clearly and strongly about their beliefs to an adult; even on things like using four-letter words and having sex. That camaraderie also made it easier for these young ladies to talk about these issues with others, particularly those who did not share their beliefs.

"Nicole," I commented as lunch came to an end, "you preach a powerful sermon. I never thought about religion like that before. Have you Maria?" (I specifically wanted to ask Maria that question because sometimes one friend relies on another's strength to get along. And when friends are parted by high school graduation and different futures, the dependent friend can be set adrift in more ways than one.)

"Oh, sure," Maria assured me. "We talk about that a lot. It started after we had a sex education class in school. There are a lot of other things too, like drinking alcohol. If you drink in moderation—as long as you're an adult—you're okay; but if you get drunk you can do a lot of things that aren't good for you.[†] Think, too, about telling the truth or telling lies. Which one is better for you?"

[†] Alcohol is not good for teenagers because it poisons developing brain cells. Adults might benefit from a daily drink since it has been shown that alcohol increases the "good" cholesterol and decreases the "bad" cholesterol. However, the American Heart Association "cautions people NOT to start drinking … if they do not already drink alcohol. If

Religion News Service recently reported on the National Study of Youth and Religion, which has been described as the most comprehensive research ever done on faith and adolescence. Four of five teens in this survey of 3,000 teens and their parents said that religion is important in their lives. And among parents who said religion was *very* important in their lives, two-thirds of their children said the same. Most importantly, the survey said that teens with strong religious convictions are more likely to:

- Do better in school.

- Feel better about themselves.

- Shun alcohol, drugs, and sex.

- Care about the poor.

- Make moral choices based on what is right rather than what would make them happy.[73]

All too soon we had to finish our discussion of Nicole's philosophy and return to work.

"Before we leave," I said, "I'd like to buy you both an ice cream cone—if you won't accuse me of gluttony."

They laughed and agreed. The rain had stopped while

---

you drink alcohol, do so in moderation. This means an average of one to two drinks per day for men and one drink per day for women. (A drink is one 12 oz. beer, 4 oz. of wine, 1.5 oz. of 80-proof spirits, or 1 oz. of 100-proof spirits.) Drinking more alcohol increases such dangers as alcoholism, high blood pressure, obesity, stroke, breast cancer, suicide and accidents. Also, it's not possible to predict in which people alcoholism will become a problem. ... The risk of alcohol addiction is always possible with some personalities and can even run in families." Quoted from http://www.americanheart.org/presenter.jhtml?identifier=4422 , cited October 5, 2009.

we were eating, so we could enjoy our cones in sunshine as we walked back to the office.

"Thanks for the lunch," they said together as we stepped through the doorway. "We had a good time."

"I had a good time too, ladies. Thank you for enjoying it with me; and thanks, too, for the lesson in practical morality. Tell your folks 'Hi' for me, and tell them what fine women they have for daughters."

Now, I know what some of you may be thinking. Perhaps these girls were just telling an old family friend what he wanted to hear. But they had so many elements in their characters that produce good moral decisions and strongly directed futures that it was impossible for me to overlook them. And there is no more important element than faith. All too often we think religion is somehow against us or not on our side; that the rules are arbitrary and make life more difficult for us. Yet as Nicole and Maria discovered, the truth is this: Religious rules are our best guidelines for healthy living. Let me quote a paragraph from *The New Harvard Guide to Psychiatry* that was published in 1988, but is still true today:

> RELIGIOUS RULES ARE OUR BEST GUIDELINES FOR HEALTHY LIVING

Many who have worked closely with adolescents over the past decade have realized that the new sexual freedom has by no means led to greater pleasures, freedom, and openness; more meaningful relationship between the sexes; or exhilarating relief from stifling inhibitions. Clinical experience has shown that the new permissiveness has often led to empty relationships, feelings of self-contempt and worthlessness, an epidemic of venereal diseases, and a rapid increase in unwanted pregnancies.[74]

This paragraph is only related to sexual freedom, but it is a short step from relaxed sexual values to permissiveness in all areas of life. Or does the road go in the opposite direction—from general permissiveness to relaxed sexual values?

Religious rules are guides to curb our behavior and ensure our happiness. Yes, life seems harder at the end of the teenage years, so the need to temporarily disconnect is understandable. But it is far better, more exciting, and a lot easier to simply find a guide to follow and plow ahead. Life is infinitely more enjoyable without the consequences of reckless sex, overdrinking, and overindulgence. Most churches have always known and preached these lessons, but some teens (like Nicole and Maria) just latch onto that wisdom sooner than others their age.

Teens, like people of every age, are searching for meaning in life and may at times get involved in religious fanaticism, cults, superstitions, or other over-the-edge religious fads which abandon common sense, science, and medicine. It is estimated that every month as many as five children die due to the religious superstitions of their parents or guardians. Some diabetics die because their parents refuse them insulin, some die of infections—pneumonia, meningitis, sepsis—because they rely on prayer to the exclusion of medical care. Ron DuPont, one of my good friends in medical school, said it is twice as hard to be good as it is to be bad because good generally follows the middle of the road, and there is evil on both sides. Relying on prayer without using the modern medical miracles which God has provided for us can be as dangerous as ignoring deity and religion altogether.

No, not all is well in the world, particularly with the world of teens. But the increased presence of faith in their lives means that our teens will have an important moral compass that can guide them to happiness and fulfillment, regardless of age or circumstances. Faith will make them stronger, less likely to get a serious case of senioritis, and make us, their parents, even prouder of them.

Parenting Tips

- *Belong to an organized religion and attend services regularly.*

- *Insist that your kids attend with you and are attentive to the service.*

- *Observe your religion's tenets in your home. Read religious books and view religious programs on television.*

- *Make sure your teens attend youth group or other structured high school religious education programs.*

- *Make use of those teachable moments to express your thoughts and your religion's views.*

- *Respect others' religions.*

- *Bless your children, your family, and your friends. It shows them you believe what you preach. Blessing even those who dislike you is even more telling.*

- *Make religion a habit.*

Substance Abuse

When we think about kids and substance abuse, we are usually quick to point out the effect of peer pressure. But just how important is peer pressure in a teen's decision to start using alcohol, tobacco, or drugs? Is peer pressure a reason or an excuse?

CHAPTER 8

PEER PRESSURE

The Child is the Father of the Man.

William Wordsworth, 1802

MY SON RAFE was a bright boy with a GPA of 4.00 to prove it. But more importantly, he was street smart. He played trombone in the marching band, and although he had a lot of fun, he never got in trouble. He knew which kids to avoid and where to draw the line between fun and danger. He was the kind of guy you'd like for a friend, yet he didn't seem to have a lot of friends, just a few close ones who did things the same way he did.

"Tell me, Rafe, how do you deal with peer pressure?" I asked one evening during dinner.

"Peer pressure? What peer pressure?" he answered as if I had conjured the term and the problems associated with it out of thin air. Then he looked at me with his deeply set brown eyes and I noticed for the first time how thin his face was. I'd have to keep a close eye on him to be certain I wasn't just fooling myself, that I wasn't missing some terrible ailment befalling this youngster.

"Well, Rafe," I continued, "I see so many kids who smoke and drink and a lot who use drugs, so there must be some pressure for you to do the same. How do you handle it?"

"How do you deal with peer pressure, Dad?"

"I don't have any peer pressure," I replied, not expecting my well-intentioned query to be turned back on me. I was supposed to be asking the questions, not fumbling for the answers. *This skinny kid is sounding smarter than I am*, I thought, *and I'm supposed to be teaching him and reassuring myself.*

"Sure you do," Rafe said. "I work at the Country Club and I see some of the doctors you work with come in every Friday night and drink too much, then

> PEER PRESSURE IS JUST AN EXCUSE TO DO WHAT YOU KNOW YOU SHOULDN'T

get in their cars and drive home. I never see you do that, Dad. Peer pressure is just an excuse to do what you know you shouldn't."

Birds of a Feather

Rafe's revelation was one of those moments that parents dream about but don't really expect to happen. Real life rarely provides clear moral-building episodes like we used to watch on "Leave It to Beaver" or "The Brady Bunch." It occurred when we were simply having dinner together as a family. Now a sense of urgency surged through me. *I need to tell Coach Larsen about this*, I thought.

Seven years earlier, when our oldest sons started high school, Coach Larsen and I decided that if we expected our kids not to drink, we shouldn't drink either. We both quit, and at that moment it seemed that the decision was paying off. Still, I wanted to draw my son out further to hear more of what he'd learned from my example and perhaps, just perhaps, what he could teach me, his father.

"Rafe, my case is a bit different," I explained in my condescending adult way. "I'm old enough to handle things like that."

"Are you saying that because I'm 16 I don't know right from wrong?" Rafe responded indignantly. "That I can't think for myself or that I can't stand up for my own values? You know I'm right. Just admit it, and pass me some more peas. I hate it when you treat me like a first-grader."

I surrendered the conversational tug-of-war because deep down I knew I had already won an important battle.

"You're right Rafe, and I'm sorry. I know you have a working moral compass, but tell me why all the books and 'experts' are always talking about peer pressure?"

The question was my way of giving my son a sense of victory, too, something all teens long for. And judging from the answers he had already given, he deserved it.

"Well, Dad, experts should start seeing normal kids and stop comparing us to the weirdos. Otherwise, it's like this: If you want to smoke or do something dumb like that, are you going to hang out with people who don't smoke and have them listen to you cough and tell you how dumb you are? No, you're going to find an idiot like yourself who smokes and you'll hang around with him and talk about how cool you look. No one comes up to you and says, 'Smoke this cigarette or I'll break your arm.' They usually don't even say, 'Smoke this or I won't be your friend.' Most of the time people don't care about you, or what you do. They only care about themselves. You can always find friends who want to do what you want—right or wrong."

Rafe may be a little cynical for his age, but his monolog convinced me that he has human nature figured out. And he has successfully applied his almost formulaic truth to an age group most adults don't put forth the effort to understand. Yet, even if I could rent out a lecture hall for Rafe to repeat his truths to benefit those capitulating adults, how many parents would really listen to a 16-year-old with a bit of a smart mouth on him?

But Rafe's is not the only wise young voice out there waiting to be heard.

Peer Pressure or Personal Choice?

In her column, "Fresh Voices," Lynn Minton quotes 17-year-old Trent Collins as saying, "I hate all that 'peer pressure' nonsense. The major reason why I—or any of the people I know—started to do drugs was because we wanted to. Nobody ever talked me into it when I didn't want to."[75]

However, not all studies agree with Trent or support Rafe's theory. A study in the Bronx of 2,500 eleven- and twelve-year-olds indicates that for the younger kids, peer pressure was a significant factor, especially in those kids who had "difficult temperament and poor self-control and deviance-prone attitudes."[76] On the other side, a study of 90,000 adolescents from 134 schools across the United States concluded:

> Youth both pick friends who do what they want to do, and are influenced by those friends' behaviors ... the influence of having friends who smoked was enhanced by risk factors in other domains. This suggests that the association may be at least partly due to the influence of friends.[77]

Let me relate a personal story I'm not particularly proud of. Just before starting my senior year in high school, my family transferred to a new school district. I had been a popular kid in the previous school and was class president there for three years running. Now, as a senior, I knew no one. At the close of that first lonely week, I went by myself to the football game. In this small town, with a population of fewer than 400, our school was only a few blocks from downtown.

The junior varsity played at 6:00 p.m. and was followed by the varsity game. Between the games, the custom was to walk downtown and have a bottle of pop at the drug store. After the J.V. game, I followed the crowd to the drug store, sat by myself at the soda fountain, and drank my pop. Feeling a bit sorry for myself, I did not walk back with the herd, but lagged behind. On the way back I noticed a small group of boys in the alley smoking cigarettes. One called, "Hey kid, come over here."

A sudden rush of adrenaline coursed through my veins. I was not invisible after all! I didn't run to them, but I hurried. As I approached, one of the boys said, "We'll give you a cigarette if you don't tell anyone that we were smoking." Smoking in those days would get you kicked out of school.

"I won't say a thing," I answered, lighting up the cigarette they gave me. We made a bit of light conversation as they filled me in on which girls were available in this school and which ones I needed to leave alone. Then I walked with them to the varsity game, happy that I had found some friends. But satisfied that their smoking would remain secret and that I would not compete for their girlfriends, they quickly dispersed and left me as alone again.

I wish I could say that was the first—or the last— cigarette I ever smoked, but unfortunately, it wasn't. Many months before (while still in my old school) I tried my first cigarette, and that first cigarette came from a friend's pack just like two-thirds of all smokers' first cigarettes do. Eventually I became a daily smoker, like nearly half of the almost 4,400 middle and high school students who start smoking cigarettes each day.[78]

A year later, I began the first of many attempts to quit; I finally managed it some ten years later when my five-year-old son said he wished I would quit so I wouldn't get cancer. I took his advice, threw my pack into the waste basket, and have not smoked since.

Now, some could say I started to smoke because of peer pressure, but I would agree with Rafe and Trent. If I hadn't wanted to smoke, I could just as easily have told the boys that I wouldn't tell, talked with them briefly, and gone back to the school. I started to smoke not because I was lonely, not because of the boys behind the drug store, not even because of my friends at my other school; I started smoking because I wanted to. Almost three decades before he was even born, I proved that Rafe was right.

My excuse is that we did not know then how bad smoking was for your health. It wasn't until 1964 that the United States Surgeon General Luther Terry released the Public Health Bulletin landmark report "Smoking and Health" describing the relationship between smoking and cancer.[79] The success of that report was unparalleled in public health history. Since then, adult smoking rates have dropped in half and millions of lives have been saved. Unfortunately, many still smoke; 25 million Americans alive today will die from smoking cigarettes.

Living Without Peer Pressure

The kinds of truths Rafe and Trent recounted didn't constitute brain surgery. The simple truth is that if your teen's friends are smoking or doing drugs or having sex, chances are good that your child is, too.

Rafe's approach may be simple and a bit tough when it comes to human nature, but perception is reality; and if he and those who think like him don't accept peer pressure, then for them there is no peer pressure.

One last note about Rafe; when I noticed how thin he was, I suspected the worst. But then I realized that he spent more than four hours daily in swim practice and that he was really unable to eat enough calories to replace what he used in the pool. Sure enough, when swim season was over, he replenished his body fat and gained the weight he needed.

Years later I had the pleasure of having dinner with Rafe and his family. While my 15-year-old grandson Harry and I were alone on the patio, I asked him the same question I'd asked his Dad some 27 years earlier. "Tell me Harry, how do you deal with peer pressure?"

"Peer pressure?" he asked. Then he thought for a minute and replied, "I just ignore it."

"Ignore it?" I prodded. "I thought peer pressure was a big part of high school. Isn't that what the experts on teen behavior say?"

Not feeling any pressure to agree, he answered, "Grandpar (that's what he calls me), I suppose there are some kids who do things so other kids will like them, but that's dumb. I just do what I need to do!"

Harry, like his dad, didn't even acknowledge peer pressure.

The old saying, "You're never too old to learn," should be accompanied by another adage: "You're never too young to teach." In our conversation years ago, Rafe became the teacher, and I marveled at him. As parents, we have to take the time to listen to our kids if we are to realize the wisdom they've acquired.

Don't be afraid to talk with your kids and their friends frequently about their goals, values, and habits. Keep communication between you open by not over-reacting to what they tell you. Then let them know your thoughts and values and expectations for them. Believe it or not, most of the time your kids do listen to you; and even if they don't show it at the time, they value your advice.

Sure, peers are important in your child's life, but your influence is so much greater. Use it! Connecting with your teens and their peers (not as a friend, but as a caring, loving parent) is special to them. Make time for them; be watchful of their habits and the relationships they form. And never again accept "peer pressure" as an excuse for bad behavior.

CHAPTER 9

THE INFLUENCE OF FRIENDS

Faithful friends are a sturdy shelter: Whoever finds one has found a treasure. Faithful friends are beyond price; No amount can balance their worth. Faithful friends are life-saving medicine; And those who fear the Lord will find them.

Sirach 14–16

THE NBC-TV SERIES "Friends" was more than a very successful Thursday night sitcom. A big part of the appeal was the model of friendship displayed on the series. It was how Americans wanted their friends to be in real life.

As much as anything else, friends reflect who we are. We pick friends who are most like us, who share our goals, or our lack of goals. Friends can be a sturdy shelter reinforcing our better traits—or our worst enemies who feed our destructive sides. For the years "Friends" ran on television, Rachel, Monica, Phoebe, Joey, Chandler, and Ross laughed together, cried together, and did fun and silly things together. They could act like themselves, say exactly what was on their minds, and still be friends. None of them did anything extraordinary, but they were always there for each other in every crisis.

Dogs and Fleas

Parents tell their teenagers that they'll be there for them no matter what happens, but a friend is there because he or she likes who we are and sees the value in having our well-being tied to theirs. That's an incredible endorsement of who we are as people; everyone, particularly teens, needs that kind of endorsement.

Sharing experiences with someone your age with similar character traits is critically important. We can't choose our parents, but we can choose our friends. Choosing friends is not the simple task I thought it was before I met Marc.

Marc looked older than his 14 years. He was tall and thin with well-developed muscles and a splash of fine black hair on his upper lip. It was not enough hair to call a moustache but enough so that his mother, as mothers do, nagged him to shave.

He smiled (and she frowned) when I told him it looked cool. It really didn't. He knew it and I knew it. But if he shaved, who would know that he was fast approaching manhood and the kind of maturity defined by hair above the upper lip? Ah, manhood—that indefinable fantasy and urgency all teenage males desire and pursue.

"How did your mom ever talk you into a physical?" I asked, knowing that nobody, especially a teenage male, ever comes for an exam without prodding.

"Friday is my birthday, and Mom thinks I need to come in every year, even if I don't want to. And I don't want to," Marc assured me.

"Well," I confided, "nobody likes physicals. I don't mind them when I'm standing on this side of the table, but I'm just like you when I'm the patient. Your Mom is right, though. Men your age need to have a checkup every year. But you don't need to like it."

Then I explained the health evaluation process, a process that has allowed me to gain remarkable access into the teenage mind and the extraordinary thinking going on inside.

"I look at a checkup as having three parts," I explained. "First, we try to find out if you've *been* healthy, then if you *are* healthy, and finally if you're going to *stay* healthy. So, I'll ask you and Mom some questions about your health history, and then I'll examine you from the top of your head to the bottoms of your feet. Finally, to see if you'll stay healthy for the next hundred years, I will ask you questions about your health habits. Can you think of any habits that can help you stay healthy?"

"Sure, that's easy," Marc rapidly replied. "Exercise every day, eat right, and don't smoke."

No surprise there. It seems like all kids know these three, even if they haven't formed the habits. Marc's response was as routine as if he were reciting his multiplication tables.

"Sounds good to me," I told Marc and Mom. "How about some habits kids could form that would make them unhealthy?" I've asked this question often enough to know what his answer would be.

On cue, Marc replied, "Don't exercise, eat bad foods, and smoke."

"That's a good start," I assured him, following my good doctor script. "There are many others: fighting, drugs, alcohol, sex, maybe even arguing with your mother!" I added that quip to make up for the frown I induced from Mom in complimenting her son's mousy-looking moustache. She rewarded me with a smile.

"Let's get on with the first set of questions, then we'll ask Mom to have a seat in the waiting room while we finish the last two parts," I continued. "Remember, the things we talk about are confidential as far I'm concerned. You can talk to anybody you like, but my lips are sealed. The only time I would break that confidence would be if you had a rapidly progressing fatal disease or if I thought you were in danger of shooting a friend, or me, or somebody really important, like yourself. Are you both comfortable with that?"

Mom and son agreed and we proceeded. By the time we got to the third part of the evaluation, Marc was relaxed and talking easily. Now he felt free to break from the script and textbook responses.

"Do any of your friends smoke?" I asked.

"Not if they want to be my friends," Marc answered.

"How much alcohol does your best friend drink?"

"None."

"Do you have any friends who use marijuana or other drugs?"

"No. I have really good friends," he said proudly. "You'd like them." He paused for a moment and then asked, "Can I tell you something?" He leaned over conspiratorially, as though he was about to tell me where Osama Bin Laden was hiding. "If you sleep with dogs, you'll get fleas," he said quietly.

"Hmmm, I guess you're right," I replied, but I really wasn't sure where Marc was coming from with that statement, or where he was going

IF YOU SLEEP WITH DOGS, YOU'LL GET FLEAS

with it. I'm not a vet, I'm a pediatrician. So I repeated, "If you sleep with dogs, you'll get fleas means ...?"

"Well, say you're at a party and everybody is smoking pot, but you're not, and the cops come in," Marc began. "They will take you *all* away and it won't matter what you say. They and everybody will think you smoked too. So you will have their fleas, and no one will believe you're innocent."

Then he smiled that all-knowing smile kids use with adults to say "Gotcha!"

"That's great!" I exclaimed, trying to reclaim face for not understanding initially. I was in awe, too. "I wish I had been as wise as you when I was 14. Too bad all kids don't know that."

"Oh, they do," Marc corrected me. "They just don't want to admit it."

We talked a while about friends and peer pressure and all too soon the interview with this wise teenager came to an end.

The Wrong Kind of Friends

Later that day I saw one of my regular patients, Craig. He was a known troublemaker who had served time in the youth detention center for fighting, drug use, truancy, and who knows what else. I was seeing him for counseling.

I couldn't help but like Craig. With me he was charming and thoughtful. But I knew he could also be cunning, manipulative, and very anti-authoritarian. Perhaps he didn't see me as an authority figure, or maybe he saw me for the softie I am. In any event, we got along well. I saw him a number of times over the summer and by the time school started, he was willing to get back into the classroom. (I wish I could say he graduated with honors and went on to become the governor of Georgia, but he didn't. He did finally get his GED, and the last I heard from him, he was gainfully employed.)

During football season that fall, my sons and I met Craig in the runway leading to the football field.

"Hi, Doc," he said with a smile. "Good to see you get out of the office once in a while."

I returned the greeting and we went on. As soon as we were out of his sight, my 15-year-old son asked in almost parent-like disgust, "Dad, do you know who that boy is?"

"Yes," I said. "He's a friend of mine."

"Well, Dad," Sean replied in the same parental fashion, "You shouldn't have friends like that."

I was taken back a bit, but was able to come up with, "No, Sean, *you* shouldn't have friends like that."

Sean, like Marc, knew the value of having good friends and the danger of having the wrong kind of friend. I guess you might say Sean was worried that I might get "fleas" from Craig.

Yes, Marc had been right; teens do know about the dog and fleas analogy and about choosing the right friends. And they know ignoring that rule can have consequences.

On August 11, 2000, 16-year-old Kirby Cruce of Duluth, Georgia, was killed in a car accident while driving home from a party. Her blood alcohol test confirmed that she was legally drunk. The police raided the party some minutes later and arrested 41 teens for possession of alcohol. Later, in court, 21 of them pleaded guilty and were sentenced. The others entered pleas of not guilty and were given court dates to defend themselves. An article about the incident in *The Atlanta Journal-Constitution* stated: "All claim they were not drinking or even holding alcohol when police arrived. Police have said they charged everyone at the party, whether they were drinking or not."[80]

Just as Marc had told me three years earlier, no one believed these kids were innocent. Most people thought they were drinking, too; they got "fleas" from Kirby and the 21 others who *were* drinking. And poor Kirby lost her life—which is a tragedy no matter how you look at it.

I wish every teenager recognized the fact that they will be influenced by their friends. That's why picking friends who follow the rules is by far the wisest thing to do.[†]

---

† One last thought on the subject of friends. As important as they are, they need to know their place, and bedrooms are not it! Bedrooms are for changing clothes and sleeping, not for entertaining friends. Imagine your kids' reaction if you had another couple over and you and your spouse disappeared with them into the bedroom and closed the door. That should be your reaction if your kids have friends in their rooms. Don't start a habit you will live to regret. I have known many teens who got into trouble in their own bedrooms while their parents were in the home. Your children's friends should remain in the family room, the recreation room, the living room, or any other public part of your home—never the bedroom. And finally, as unpopular as it may sound, I've found that "sleepovers" are a bad idea! Many high school kids have told me they watch porn, drink alcohol, have sex, and some even use illegal drugs in their or their friends' bedrooms during sleepovers.

BROTHER'S KEEPERS

> *All along the line, physically,*
> *mentally, morally, Alcohol*
> *is a weakening and deaden-*
> *ing force ... And it is worth*
> *a great deal to save women*
> *and girls [and men and boys]*
> *from its influence.*
>
> Beatrice Webb, 1917

*D*ESPITE WELL THOUGHT-OUT strategies and careful planning, life-changing communication with children often comes when it is least expected. The only secret is to be there so that when it happens, you can positively reinforce what is being said.

I learned this one day while visiting a high school in Atlanta. The teacher had left the classroom, so I was alone with the students when a girl, a newcomer in the class, stole the show and changed a lot of lives in the process. She did this by answering a question that my mentors and colleagues had been unable to answer—an answer that was helpful to me, her classmates, and many kids I've met since. I'd like to introduce her to you, but I don't know her name or much about her since I only met her that once. For the purpose of this story, however, I'll call her Beth.

A Hard Lesson

I had been invited to talk to the sophomore class at one of the Atlanta area high schools. They were having a career day, and I was to represent physicians. I never pass up an opportunity to talk with students or to eat with them because that's when I learn from them. The invitation included lunch, so I left the office and set out for what was to become an educational day.

After a too-short lunch with a fun bunch of high schoolers, I proceeded to my assigned classroom and commenced my presentation. I only had an hour, so as soon as the short introductions were finished I started answering the many questions the students posed.

"How many years do you have to go to college to be a doctor?"

"Do you really have to get good grades in high school?"

"How long did it take you to get used to seeing blood?"

"How do you deal with people who die?"

"Aren't you afraid of catching something?"

"What do you do if patients cry when you tell them something is wrong?"

"Did you ever have a patient try to commit suicide?"

"Do you ever take care of people who have AIDS?'

"What do you do if patients don't follow your advice?"

And then the zinger from a girl in the back row:

"What should a person do if her friend is using drugs or alcohol?"

She obviously had someone in mind. This would have to be handled delicately; the offender could be in the room and my answer could affect a life, maybe many lives. Unfortunately, there was no one to help me.

"That's an outstanding question," I replied. "Let me ask the class what they think would be the best approach."

The room was dead silent. There was some shifting of feet in the back and a glance from a student on the right, but no hands up yet. Then a boy near the front on the left cleared his throat.

"I guess," he began, "if he was really a friend of yours, you should help him by, maybe, telling him that was stupid and he should quit." Then more confidently he added, "That's what I'd do."

"That's just plain dumb," a blonde behind him criticized. "How much good do you think you can do by telling him to quit? I think you should tell his mother."

"Narc!" someone from the other side of the room called out. It was starting to get interesting. Then he continued. "All you'll do if you tell his mom is get him in trouble and get him mad at you. Then his mom will call your mom and they'll have an argument. So, I say just let him be."

"Joe!" a feisty red-headed girl jumped in. "What kind of a friend are you? You're supposed to help your friends when they're in trouble, not abandon them. I'm glad I'm not your friend." She flushed in anger. "Besides, you're not getting him in trouble if you tell his mother. He already got himself in trouble."

"That's what I meant," the first boy interjected. "If you abandon him you can't help him. But if you're his friend, then you can help."

"How can you help?" a third girl chimed in. "We all know of kids who are in treatment centers and even with lots of counselors and doctors and stuff, some of them still can't be helped."

This discussion continued for quite a few minutes. *Boy, this is good,* I thought. *But how am I going to resolve it?*

Then, from the middle of the classroom, Beth raised her hand. I nodded to her and she stood up. *Strange,* I thought. *She must have been in a private school somewhere before this. I never saw a public school kid stand to answer a question.*

There was something special about Beth. Unlike most of the other girls, she didn't wear makeup. Her pale lips quivered slightly as she began to speak.

"Can I say something?" she asked softly. I nodded and she continued. "Most of you don't know me very well. I just moved here from Maryland two months ago."

She turned and addressed the class. "Let me tell you what I think, but first let me tell you why I moved here. You'll find out anyway.

"When I was living in Annapolis, both of my parents

left for work before I went to school; so I just sat in the kitchen, bored, and waited for the bus. One Monday, after my folks had had a party the night before, I thought I'd try some vodka. It was still sitting on the kitchen counter, so I poured myself a glassful. I can't say I liked it, but I drank a pretty big glass of it, and by the time I got to school I was laughing, and everybody thought I was like a clown or something. I felt like, real popular, so after that I drank vodka every morning before school. It was easy because my folks always had a big liquor cabinet and they never seemed to miss what I drank. This continued for almost the whole year. It got to the point where I couldn't pay attention and would fall asleep in class. Before long, my grades were shot and I was in trouble. My folks didn't know what was going on until one day my friend said she had had enough of me destroying my life, so she called my mom. Then she told my homeroom teacher, and she even called the police."

By now Beth was in tears and the classroom was in a total hush. But she continued.

"The police were at my house when I got home from school. I was so scared I was shaking. If my folks hadn't been there, I would have had my usual after-school drink. Boy, did I need one. I was in serious trouble and I knew it. My folks put me in a rehab center and I was so mad. I swore I would never talk to my friend again; I would find some way of getting even with her! But revenge had to wait while I went to rehab. When I got out, all my former friends thought it was really funny that I had been in rehab. They made fun of me and some even tried to get me to drink again. I mean everyone except the friend who had called my mom. She tried to stick with me and help me, but I was still mad at her and wouldn't even talk to her. The teachers didn't trust me, and I was eventually asked to leave the private school I was attending because the headmaster said I was an embarrassment to the school.

"After a few months of Teen AA, I started to think about what my friend had done. She'd saved my life. I really had messed everything up. That's why I moved down here to live with my grandparents. It

IF YOUR FRIEND IS USING DRUGS OR ALCOHOL, YOU SHOULD TELL HIS OR HER PARENTS, THE SCHOOL COUNSELOR, AND THE POLICE

was really awful; especially the way I treated my friend who really just wanted to help me. Before I moved here, I called her up and went to see her. We both cried for almost two hours. I thanked her a hundred times, and now I call her every night to thank her for what she did. So let me tell you what I think. I think ... no, I *know*, that if your friend is using drugs or alcohol, you should tell her parents, the school counselor, and the police."

Then she broke into big sobs with tears rolling down her face and sat down trembling to a standing ovation from her classmates.

Beth's new friends surrounded her at that point, and I couldn't get close enough to tell her how brave I thought she was. Before I could establish order out of this chaos, the bell rang and the students dispersed, escorting their new heroine out of the room and out of my life. I sat at the desk waiting for the teacher to return, not knowing if I should tell her what had just happened or wait until she heard it through the grapevine. She returned with her usual enthusiasm and stopped in her tracks when she saw me staring into space.

"Were they that bad?" she asked.

"No," I answered. "They were that good!"

Teen Alcoholism

I've thought about what Beth said hundreds of times since that day, and have related the story to many teens. This lesson is one we should all learn because alcohol is no small problem for our school kids and their parents. And even though Beth's problem was alcohol, the same could be said about drugs.

In 1992, Alcohol problems alone cost our nation more than $70 billion.[81] As of this writing, "Alcohol-related problems cost every man, woman, and child in the United States $683.00 each year."[82] With a 2009 population of 307,465,000, that equates to more than $200 billion annually. Alcohol is involved in nearly half the deaths attributed to car accidents, suicides, and homicides—the number one, two, and three causes of death in teenagers.[83] As for drugs, according to recent estimates the total financial cost of drug use disorders to the United States is estimated to be 180 billion annually[84] as well as taking an immeasurable toll on the user's health and general well-being.

Parents significantly underestimate how much alcohol their teens drink. It is estimated that 20 percent of the alcohol consumed in the United States is drunk by minors.[85] A study of 12,352 teenagers in Miami found that 20 percent of them began drinking before the age of 13![86] Too frequently we adults think drinking is only a problem for teenage boys, that girls are somehow resistant to the lure of alcohol. Yet an estimated 4.5 million 12- to 17-year-old girls reported consuming alcohol during the past year. (According to the National Institute on Alcohol Abuse and Alcoholism, 39 percent of ninth-grade girls in 2005 reported drinking in the past month.)

An article in *Girls' Life Magazine (GL)* indicates that "for the first time in history, teen girls drink more than boys. Almost 40 percent of ninth-grade girls have had a drink in the past month versus only 34 percent of boys. And a whopping 45 percent of high school girls drink alcohol."[87] However, the 2007 National Survey of Drug Use and Health showed that, "among youths aged 12 to 17, the percentage of males who were current drinkers [had had at least one alcoholic beverage in the past month] (14.2 percent) was similar to the rate for females (15.0 percent)."[†][88]

The Century Council, a national not-for-profit organization funded by distillers dedicated to fighting drunk driving and underage drinking, commissioned a program called Teenage Research Unlimited and fielded a study of teenage

† This government study did not include 18- and 19-year-olds, perhaps partly explaining the difference from the other study. Additionally, studies have shown that fewer kids are drinking today than in 2004 when the *Girls' Life* article was written.

drinking in 2005. The study revealed that although 30 percent of 16- to 18-year-old girls say they drink with friends, only 9 percent of their mothers think their daughters are drinking.[89] Although adult males are more likely than their female peers to report past-month alcohol use, among 12- to 17-year-olds the reported rate of past month alcohol use was almost equal with females (17 percent for males compared with 18 percent for females).[90]

As horrid as these statistics sound, there is much a parent can do. According to former Congresswoman Susan Molinari, chair of The Century Council, "We parents are the most significant influence in [a] teens' decision to drink or not to drink." The mother of two girls, she emphasizes the need for parents to talk with their kids about drinking as well as drug and tobacco use. Parents, she continued, "need to have the conversation early and often."[91]

A new survey of 1,000 American teens ages 12 to 17 conducted by The National Center on Addiction and Substance Abuse at Columbia University (CASA) found the following:

> [Only] one in four teens in America (27%, about 6.5 million) lives with "hands-on" parents, parents who have established a household culture of rules and expectations for their teen's behavior and monitor what their teens do, such as the television shows they watch, the CDs they buy, what they access on the Internet, and where they are spending evenings and weekends. These teens are at one quarter the risk

of smoking, drinking, and using drugs as teens with "hands-off" parents.[92]

That last sentence says it all, but some adults and parents do not take much of a stand against drugs and alcohol. Fred Hechinger in *Fateful Choices*, a book published by the Carnegie Council on Adolescent Development, states:

> During the 1960s and 1970s, many adults, wanting to be on the youth side of the generation gap, publicly played down the harmful effects of drugs, or even urged their acceptance. Unfortunately, such opinions were widely expressed by certain university faculty members, psychologists, and others who had reputations as experts or otherwise commanded the respect of young people. They contradicted those who warned about drugs' potential dangers and sometimes even pressed the matter of drug use as a civil liberties issue. Such misguided voices have largely fallen silent, but their effect lingers.[93]

Adult Responsibility

Some parents mistakenly think that kids will eventually drink, so why not provide them a place to drink safely? I remember Sharon, a girl I saw for her college physical the day after she graduated from high school. When I entered the room she was sitting quietly holding her head in her hands. She was such a pretty girl that it almost distracted me from the reeking smell of alcohol on her breath.

"Don't talk," she said as I entered the room. "I had too much to drink last night and my head is killing me. Can I just go home and we can do this some other time?"

"That's fine with me," I replied, "But you'll have to explain to your folks why we have to reschedule."

"Duh," she replied, inferring I was some kind of dinosaur. "We had a graduation party. They were there."

I was a naïve young doctor just starting my practice and couldn't for the life of me imagine her dad, a professional, allowing an underage daughter to drink to excess at his party. *Maybe she's not telling the whole truth*, I thought, so I asked, "So your folks had a party and let you have too much to drink?"

She lifted her head from her hands and looked at me through her beautiful but bloodshot, deep brown eyes. She opened her mouth and stared at me, but did not say anything. I'm sure she couldn't believe my incredulous attitude. Finally she said, "The purpose of a graduation party is to get drunk and celebrate. I'm going home."

Fortunately, she did not add "stupid" to the end of the sentence. I followed her to the waiting room where her dad was waiting.

"Dad, I'm sick," she said. "Let's go home and do this some other time." Then she walked out the door.

Dad shrugged his shoulders, smiled, and promised to reschedule. Giving him the benefit of the doubt, I suspect he thought there was nothing he could do to prevent his children from drinking, so he would "keep them safe and let them drink at home." But research suggests otherwise. Parents exert significant influence on whether their kids choose to drink, smoke, or use illegal drugs. And the earlier parents talk to kids about their social problems, the more effective they are. The number one reason teens give for not using alcohol, tobacco, or drugs is that they do not want to disappoint their parents.[94]

An interesting study in 2000 from the *Journal of the American Academy of Child and Adolescent Psychiatry* confirms what we discussed in Chapters 6 and 7 by noting that religiosity as defined by being affiliated with a religious denomination and having a personal relationship with the Divine was associated with decreased use of alcohol, tobacco, and drugs.[95]

So if you have children, start talking to them at age 10 or 11 about alcohol and drugs. Tell them what you expect their behavior to be and bring up the subject again every chance you get. (Hollywood and its stars will provide you with more than enough opportunities.) You might also consider doing what Coach Larsen did in Chapter 8 and be a positive role model. And be sure you and your family are involved in a religious community.

If you or your kids know some teen or preteen who is using alcohol or drugs, remember Beth and do them a favor: tell their parents, the school, and the police. In time, they will thank you.

Parenting Tips

- *Discuss both good and bad aspects of peer pressure with your kids.*

- *Don't accept peer pressure as an excuse for unacceptable behavior. Kids really make their own decisions.*

- *Remember that parental pressure is as influential as peer pressure, if not more so.*

- *Listen to your kids.*

- *Know your kids' friends and their friends' parents.*

- *Re-evaluate your own friendships. Are your friends the kind of people you want your kids to become? If not, it's time for a change.*

- *Keep tobacco, alcohol, and drugs out of your home and away from your kids!*

- *Talk with your kids frequently about alcohol, tobacco, and drugs. Use every opportunity that society provides.*

- *If you use alcohol, use it with temperance and responsibility. If you use tobacco or illegal drugs, QUIT.*

- *Encourage your kids to tell the authorities if they know of a peer who is using alcohol, tobacco, or drugs.*

Teen Sexuality

By the time most parents get around to talking to their teenagers about sex, they already know just about everything. They learn it from TV, movies, teen magazines, their friends, and often from the school sex-education program. But is this information taught from the viewpoint we want our kids to have? Or is it laced with the poison of permissiveness? Kids need to know what is normal and what is abnormal, what is right and what is wrong, what they should do and what they should avoid. The kids in this section know why adults who love their kids "always want to talk about sex." They will show you why teens need to have a moral view of sexual activity and how you as a parent are crucial in forming that moral compass.

CHAPTER 11

MASTURBATION

Whatever is true, Whatever is honorable, Whatever is just, Whatever is pure, Whatever is lovely, Whatever is gracious, If there is any excellence, If there is anything worthy of praise, Think about these things.

Philippians 4:8

I HAVE ALWAYS BEEN uncomfortable talking about sex. In high school and college I found the subject embarrassing and shied away from my friends when they talked about it. I had little knowledge and no experience. Other than anatomic differences, even medical school taught me nothing about sex; so I was red-faced when 19-year-old Airman Wilson came to me on sick call. The year was 1965, and I was a general medical officer in the United

States Air Force. I had treated a number of troops with venereal diseases, but I wasn't prepared for Airman Wilson when he complained, "I think something is wrong with me because all I can do is masturbate." He spoke in little more than a whisper. His face was flushed; his eyes looked at the floor.

Masturbate, masturbate! Did he say masturbate? I knew what it meant, but I didn't remember ever hearing anyone say it aloud. I knew I never had. Remember, this was years, even decades, before Seinfeld held a contest with his friends on his nationally televised series to see who would be "master of his or her domain" and forego masturbation the longest. In today's world, many of the words we used to think vulgar have now become commonplace, even trite. But in 1965, many of us were still Victorian in our vocabulary.

I tried to respond but no words came. My mouth was a desert; I couldn't swallow, let alone talk. I wanted to help this poor airman, but how could I help if I couldn't even talk with him? I knew the only way to help was to face the enemy—my fear—head on. I took a deep breath, forced my head up, and looked directly at him; but our eyes never met. I responded meekly, "All you can do is masturbate?"

I got the word out and nothing happened. I don't think I was expecting a bolt of lightning to strike me, but I didn't really think I could say it in front of a patient.

"That's about it," he answered, sensing I was as nervous as he. I'm not sure if my discomfort made him more or less uncomfortable, but he forced a laugh and continued, "I work in the typing pool and if I make a mistake, I can't get it out of my mind. I become paralyzed until I go to the bathroom and masturbate. Yesterday, I must have done it 20 times. I'm spending more time in the bathroom than I am working. I just can't help myself. Can you help me?"

This was no case for a nervous, green, naïve general medical officer. This guy was addicted to masturbation. He needed to see a psychiatrist, so I sent him off, relieved to see him leave the office. A few months later I saw his name on my sick call list. My face turned red when I picked up his chart, but this time he had a sprained ankle, and I could handle that. As we were saying good-bye he grinned and said, "Thanks for sending me to see Dr. Rifkin. I needed him, and boy did he help."

Masturbation Mythology

Wilson was just the first of a long line of patients I would see with problems or perceived problems related to masturbation, but I hadn't given it any more thought until I finished examining Joshua some years later. Josh was a plain-looking child of 16, but nature had not been good to him. He was physically the size of an average 13-year-old and had just started puberty. Had I not examined him closely, I would not have noticed that his testicles were just starting to enlarge. I was completing my note on his chart when he finished dressing and came out from behind the privacy curtain. He sat down next to me and quietly asked, "Can I ask you a question?"

"Sure, go ahead."

"Do you know what whacking-off is?" He spoke so softly I almost didn't hear him.

"Yes," I replied confidently, "I know what that is. Medically, it's called masturbation, though most boys call it whacking-off or jacking-off. It doesn't matter what you call it. What about it?" I asked matter-of-factly, proving to myself that I had become less intimidated by such questions.

"I can't do it. You know my friend Bernard, don't you?"

I assured him I knew Bernard.

"He does it all the time, but I just can't do it, no matter how long or how hard I try. Something must be wrong."

I explained that even though Bernard and he were the same age, Bernard had already finished puberty. "I'm sure you noticed he has to shave."

"Yes," Josh assured me.

I explained that puberty starts when the testicles begin to enlarge and that his puberty was starting and that most likely by next year he wouldn't have anything to worry about. He left happy and told me on the way out that Bernard had referred him to me to answer that burning question.

Next came Carlos, a 16-year-old, handsome, dark-skinned Hispanic boy. Before he moved from South America, his uncle told him that if he wanted to have a big penis he had to masturbate a lot. "Well," Carlos confided, "there must be something wrong because I've done it five times every day for the past two years, I don't think I missed one day, and it's not any bigger than it was when I left Brazil." I explained to Carlos he had a perfectly normal sized penis and masturbation wouldn't make it grow any bigger. I'm not sure if he was comforted or disappointed.

Russell was 14 and in such a panic that he asked his mother to bring him to see me. He immediately asked her to leave the room and explained that he was worried that he was over-sexed as he had masturbated 18 times the afternoon before. He explained that his parents had gone shopping and left him home alone. He found one of his older brother's porn movies and watched it over and over all afternoon, masturbating the whole time. He said he would have done it more but, "My penis was so sore I couldn't touch it." Now he was worried he had damaged his precious organ. I assured him that it would heal, but that the porn movies were not good for him. His problem was that his mind was being "brain washed" by pornography and he should find other, more wholesome things to do with his time. We talked more about the problems with porn, and I saw him a few weeks later by way of follow-up. He had discarded the porn tape, which greatly upset his brother, and he seemed to be doing well.

Over the years it became obvious to me that if these boys had enough concern to talk to me about masturbation, there were other boys who were worried but not brave enough to discuss it. That's when I started asking kids about masturbation, as well as their other health habits. Some years later, I was talking with 16-year-old Joe during his health evaluation.

"What kind of problems do you think masturbation causes?" I asked, finally comfortable talking about such a taboo subject. I had seen Joe twice before for his annual evaluation; he was waiting with a reply.

"All it causes is a soft penis and a sticky hand," was his quick answer. "I know lots of kids who worry about it and some who say they never do it. But I have other friends who say they do it, and I'm sure it doesn't cause any problems."

I assured Joe that he was right; it doesn't cause any physical problems. But I added (as I always do) that many religions do not think it is the right thing to do. Then I started to think maybe Joe was teaching me a lesson; but if so, I really didn't like it. I needed to think more about this.

"What do you think?" he asked, interrupting my reverie. "Do you think it's a sin?"

"Well," I began, "remember, I'm a medical doctor not a theologian, but I think in the long run it's not the right thing to do. I suppose a guy might try it once or twice to be sure everything works, or to see what it's like, but then he should get on to other things. I have seen boys become addicted to it. I know of boys who think they have to do it or their penises won't grow, and some boys who think it will make you blind or crazy. None of those things are true. What kind of a sin it is, or even if it is a sin, I don't know. I think it can become sinful; but questions about sin should really be addressed by pastors, priests, rabbis, or parents."

Joe thought a while and then said, "I guess you're right, but I couldn't ask my parents or my pastor about it. My pastor acts like he wouldn't know what it was and I would have to explain it to him, and my parents would probably figure out I was doing it and get mad." He was pensive and less cocky now. "I wonder who I could talk to about it?" he added, telling me he was more concerned than he let on.

"Well, Joe, I know your pastor, and I agree he would be difficult to approach. But I also know your church has a youth minister. I've met him many times and I bet he would welcome a conversation with you. Don't you belong to your church's youth group?"

"Nah, I never joined. My folks said I should, and some of my friends belong, but I never felt like going. Maybe I will though."

"Would you do me a favor?" I asked.

"Okay, what?"

"I really would like to know what your youth minister says. If I asked him, I might get a different answer than you would. So, why don't you join the group and after a few weeks, when you feel comfortable, ask him about it. Then give me a call and tell me what he said. That would help you, help me, and maybe even help some other guy who has a problem with it. Could you do that?"

"You want me to be a spy? That'll be fun! I'll do it!"

"You don't have to think of it as spying; but I agree, it could be fun. I'll put your name on my calendar and if I don't hear from you in two months, I'll call you. Is that a deal?"

"Heck yes, but you won't have to call me. I'm on a mission."

Joe left the office resolved to join his church youth group and find out what Pastor Schmidt had to say on this subject. As he left, I got to thinking about how important youth groups really are to teens.

A Chance to Refocus

Joe's opportunity for a one-on-one discussion with his youth minister turned out to be a blessing. But before Joe called to tell me what he learned, I saw another boy, Caleb, who was about Joe's age. I had seen him a number of times before, and like Joe, he was ready when I asked what he thought about masturbation.

"I don't like it," he said, "because masturbation keeps my mind stuck on sex and there are so many other worthwhile

MASTURBATION KEEPS YOUR MIND STUCK ON SEX

things to do and think about." He went on, "It's a lot like porn, only the movie is in your head instead of on the TV. Think of that, your head filled with porn. Isn't that kind of disgusting?"

Before I could answer he added, "Besides that, we learned in Sunday school that sex is supposed to be giving to another person, and the only one who gets anything from masturbation is you. So I guess it's selfish, too."

Father Joe, in Tony Hendra's book by the same name, would agree. He says selfishness is really the only sin; all others are some variation of it.[96] But I really wasn't thinking about Father Joe, selfishness, or even sin. I was once again awed by a right thinking teenager. What a straightforward, outstanding lesson!

"Caleb," I commented, "You are 100 percent right. Sounds like you spend a lot of time thinking and some time in religious education. No wonder your folks are so proud of you."

Caleb was not an exceptionally bright boy. He was from a poor neighborhood where he lived with his folks and three sisters in a small apartment. They were hard-working laborers whom I saw every Sunday in church. And here was Caleb, a poor, working-class, "C" student teaching me a moral lesson. What a treat to have patients like Caleb.

Joe called back before his two months were up and made an appointment to see me about his acne. We discussed skin care and I gave him a prescription. Then he explained what his youth minister had said about masturbation. Before he left I told him about Caleb, although I did not tell him Caleb's name.

"I think he's right, don't you?" Joe said. "He agrees with what Pastor Schmidt said. I wonder if he's in our youth group."

Then Joe told me how much he was enjoying the group and how much he was learning. "You know, after talking to you and Pastor Schmidt, I hardly ever do it. I'm not sure why. I guess I just don't have time to think about it. And, like your other patient said, who would want to have his head filled with porn? I'm glad you told me about him because I never thought about it that way before."

I hadn't thought about it that way either, until I met Caleb. Isn't it funny how teenagers can get you to analyze things from a new perspective? That's one of the reasons I love caring for them. And there are a lot more Caleb's and Joe's out there than there are delinquents. We can have even more of them if we beef up our religious education programs, put ourselves into our religious culture, listen to our kids as much as we talk to them, be forthright with them about the do's and don'ts of sex—including mastur- bation—and continue to be the best adults we can be.

CHAPTER 12

PREMARITAL SEX

> *For every action there is an*
> *equal and opposite reaction.*
>
> Sir Isaac Newton, 1686

A NUMBER OF YEARS ago, Karen Shideler wrote a Knight Ridder[†] article picked up by *The Dayton Daily News* titled, "Youthful Health Mistakes That Will Come Back To Haunt You."[97] For the article, she interviewed Dr. Donna Sweet, who is chair of the board of governors of the American College of Physicians. Dr. Sweet discussed the health consequences of "drinking through college"; "smoking like a chimney"; using marijuana, LSD and other drugs; "sleeping around"; and other less than healthful activities. It was a short, interesting sermonette filled with information all primary care physicians

---

† Knight Ridder was an American media company specializing in newspaper and internet publishing. Until it was purchased by The McClatchy Company in 2006, it was the second largest newspaper publisher in the United States. (Wikipedia)

know. Unfortunately, many college and high school students aren't aware of these consequences to their behavior; or more likely, they think they are somehow immune and that it "can't happen to them."

Staying Smart about Sex

Shideler's story was published in August 2000, some years after I heard the same lesson from 16-year-old Luke. Luke was a handsome blonde boy who played French horn and the piano and had his heart set on becoming a scientist. I had known Luke for a long time and knew of his special interest in lemurs. Each time I saw him, he was quick to tell me he planned to get his Ph.D. in biology and go to Madagascar to further his study of the ring-tailed mammal.

One summer day I saw him for his health evaluation, and as we progressed past the lemur to his habit review, I realized once again why his mom was so proud of him. I shared her admiration and respect for this fine lad. He was a good student, and he didn't drink, smoke, or chew tobacco. Nor did he have any of the other bad habits we adults are so quick to ascribe to our teenagers. Yet, he was not the least bit geeky or nerdy.

"No, I've never had sex," he replied to the obvious question. "And I don't plan to until I get married." Then he added, somewhat out of character, "I tell my friends, the screwing you get now is nothing compared to the screwing you'll get later."

He waited a minute for my response and since I wasn't sure what to say, I was silent.

Thinking perhaps I was kind of dull, he asked, "Do you get it?"

"I'm not sure exactly what you mean," I admitted.

"When a guy has sex he thinks he's really something great and goes around and tells everybody, 'I got screwed last night! Boy was it great,' and other dumb, bragging stuff like that. But I tell him wait

> THE SCREWING YOU GET NOW IS NOTHING COMPARED TO THE SCREWING YOU'LL GET LATER

until he gets an STD or AIDS, or gets a girl pregnant, then he'll really be screwed. And if he has to marry her, things will probably get worse because she'll most likely divorce him. Then he will really, really be screwed.

"Kind of funny how one word can have so many different meanings isn't it?" he added. Again he waited for my response while I wondered if this was a prepared script, and if so, why?

"There are a lot of words with several meanings," I responded. "Some people take offense at using "screw" to mean sex. Why is that?" I wondered aloud.

"Heck, I don't know," he answered. "But I do know it's better to say it than do it. At least that won't get me in trouble."

I wasn't about to let this valuable lesson go without understanding how he came to know it at the age of 16, so I said, "I've heard many, many people talk about the consequences of premarital sex, but I never heard it put so succinctly. How did you come to develop such a mature concept?"

He thought a while, obviously unprepared for the question, or perhaps wondering if he should tell. Finally he sighed and began. "It all started when I was only about 13 and my neighbor was about three years older. One night he and I were down in our basement playing pool and he started bragging to me about all the sexual things he had done and how great it was. He made me really nervous, because I hadn't even thought about girls and sex at that time. I didn't even have any—I guess you would say—puberty. I was kind of shocked. After that, every time we got together he told me about his sex life, bragging about all the girls he had and everything. Then, when I was 14, all of a sudden he got married."

Luke paused, took a deep breath, and then continued at a rapidly increasing pace. "It didn't seem like a very happy wedding though. And next thing they had a baby and he didn't get to go to college and every time I saw them, his wife was crying and he was swearing at her. And then they got a divorce. Now every time I see him he tells me how hard he has to work to earn enough money to pay for the baby, and his ex-wife is trying to go to college and he has to pay for that, too, and he can't even go to college himself. He said his baby will probably graduate from college before he does. Funny thing, though, he never talks about his sex life anymore. He screwed himself real good and he's only 20."

He hesitated, then was quick to add, "Don't tell Mom I told you this, because she gets real upset whenever anybody talks about her 'wonderful neighbor boy.' Except for the sex thing, he was a nice guy and Mom always liked him. I did, too."

I sometimes wonder if the kids know I'm an easy dupe and they try to see who can tell me the biggest one and get me to swallow it. This sounded like Tom Cruise in *All The Right Moves,* except the movie had a happier ending and Luke was hardly old enough to walk when the movie came out. *Well,* I thought, *even if he is making this whole thing up, at least it sounds like he learned from it.*

Yet somehow I knew he was telling the truth, so I responded, "Luke, you're incredibly lucky to have had a friend make the mistakes for you to learn from. I heard once that if you learn from someone else's mistakes you have knowledge, but you have to make your own mistakes to have wisdom. Sounds like you proved that wrong. You obviously have developed wisdom from your friend's mistake. I congratulate you for being so sharp."

"Thanks," he said, accepting the compliment. "But don't you think that makes a lot of sense?"

"I sure do!" I affirmed. "I think it's a saying that should be published in the school newspaper and everywhere that kids, I should say people, congregate. Adults can learn from it, too, you know."

In his lesson, Luke implied that young people who get married because the girl is pregnant have a high rate of divorce. That may or may not be true, but the overall divorce rate for first marriages is around 50 percent, and those who co-habit prior to marriage are even more likely to divorce. A study by the National Center for Health Statistics found that 49 percent of couples who lived together before marriage ended up divorced in five years, compared to 20 percent of those who didn't live together prior to marriage.[98] And yet, when I looked in the local paper recently, more than 60 percent of the couples applying for marriage licenses listed the same address. They were living together—very likely increasing their chances for divorce.

Risking STDs

I didn't intend this to be a sex-ed chapter, but there are some things about sexually transmitted diseases (STDs), also called sexually transmitted infections (STIs), that are misunderstood—yet are so important. Many young people and adults, too, think that all STDs, except AIDS, are curable, and thus are becoming rarer. But the incidence of STDs (concurrent with the so-called "sexual revolution" and perhaps *because* of it), is increasing rapidly. And so many of these diseases, while treatable, may go undiagnosed and have significant long-term consequences.

Gonorrhea and chlamydia are treatable with antibiotics and can be cured if treated early. However, many men and some women have "silent" infections, which produce no symptoms and go undiagnosed. Years later, many of these women find they cannot get pregnant because their "tubes are plugged" as a result of silent infections. Today, plugged tubes are the primary cause of infertility in women.[99] The Centers for Disease Control (CDC) estimates that there are almost three million cases of chlamydia in the United States each year and that 75 percent of the infected women and 50 percent of infected men have no symptoms.[100] Condoms are actually quite effective in preventing this disease, but abstinence is far better.

Syphilis, which in its early stage can be cured with an- tibiotics, can also cause long-term problems as it spreads to the heart, brain, and almost every other tissue. William Osler, the father of modern medicine, said, "Syphilis mim- ics every disease." Syphilis does not stop with infection of sexual partners, but can infect a pregnant women's baby with drastic, sometimes fatal results. What a terrible birth- day present from a baby's mother!

The Link between HPV and Cancer

Perhaps the most significant gynecological discovery in recent times is the link between cervical cancer (cancer of the lower part of the womb) and human papillomavirus (HPV), a sexually transmitted disease. This virus causes genital warts in some individuals, no symptoms in most, and cancer in others. More than half of all sexually active people reportedly have this virus. The CDC estimates there were more than six million new cases of HPV in 2004, and about 10,500 of them will go on to develop cervical cancer, which will kill about 4,000 women.[101] Pap smears, done at the time of pelvic exams, have greatly re- duced the death rate from cervical cancer. They can find pre-cancer which can easily be destroyed. A Pap smear is the only way to diagnose active HPV in women. Both men and women can be tested with a blood test for antibodies to HPV to see if they have, or have had, the infection. But because most men have no symptoms, men who harbor the virus just go on giving cancer to all the women with whom they have sex. Since HPV can appear on parts of the genitals not covered by condoms, condoms have only a limited role in prevention.

Fortunately, scientists have developed a vaccine for HPV which became available late in 2006. All girls should get this vaccine! Some believe giving their daughter this vaccine is giving her license to have sex, but in truth, giving a girl this vaccine will protect her if she is raped, makes a foolish decision to have sex, or if she marries a man who has had previous sex partners and harbors the human papillomavirus. Every good parent and thinking adult would argue that sex should be saved for marriage, but cervical cancer is too high a price to pay for indiscrete sex. In 2010 the vaccine was approved for boys as well as girls. It will prevent most cases of venereal warts and reduce the spread of HPV—cancer—to girls. This vaccine will prevent about 80 percent of the cases of cervical cancer, so the best prevention is still to avoid sex or have a single partner who has not had sex with anyone but you. Obviously, the best choice is to save sex for marriage.

Additionally, scientists reported in May 2007 that people who are infected with HPV are 32 times more likely to develop oral cancer (cancer of the mouth and throat).[102] It is possible that the HPV vaccine for cervical cancer will also prevent oral cancer, but confirmatory studies have not yet been done. About 11,000 Americans develop oral cancer caused by HPV and spread by oral sex each year. Tragically, this cancer, like cervical cancer, strikes young adults.

Genital Herpes and Hepatitis

Another STD that "keeps on giving" is genital herpes. Herpes is a common infection. Once you have it, you are subject to painful outbreaks of genital sores lasting about two weeks and recurring approximately six to eight times the first year. After the first year, the recurrences usually become less frequent. There may be months or even years between eruptions, but it is still possible to spread herpes at any time. There are medications that will reduce the frequency of these attacks, but there is no way to eliminate the Herpes virus. The CDC estimates that 25 percent of American women over the age of 12, and 20 percent of men, are infected with herpes.[103] Like syphilis, infants can get herpes from their mothers. Neonatal herpes can cause encephalitis, which often results in severe brain damage or even death.

Just a brief word about hepatitis—a viral infection of the liver that is responsible for most cases of liver failure, primary liver cancer, and more than 5,000 deaths annually in the USA. There are at least five types of hepatitis; all types can be spread through sex. Since a vaccine was developed for type B in 1982 and given to almost all infants, the rate of infection has dropped by about 70 percent. But there are more than 1.2 million carriers of hepatitis B in the United States. A vaccine is also available for Type A, but none exists for the other types. Condoms can be helpful in preventing spread, but because viral hepatitis is not curable, relying on a condom is foolish.

AIDS and HIV

Everyone knows the worst STD of all is AIDS—the Acquired Immune Deficiency Syndrome caused by the human immunodeficiency virus (HIV). There are approximately 1.5 million people in the United States infected with HIV, with about 40,000 new cases and just under 20,000 deaths each year. In some parts of the world, the disease is even more prevalent. In Sub-Saharan Africa there are some 25 million people with AIDS, and 2.2 million die each year. Two countries in Africa, Botswana and Swaziland, have more than 25 percent of their populations infected.[104]

The worst part of this whole picture is that all of these cases, with the exception of the few who had been infected by contaminated blood or blood products, were caused either by illegal IV drug use or by sexual activity. In other words, they were caused by events that were done voluntarily and could have been avoided. AIDS is a completely avoidable and preventable disease! The CDC recommends two easy methods to avoid AIDS:

- Abstain from sexual intercourse until ready to establish a mutually monogamous relationship within the context of marriage.
- Refrain from using or injecting illicit drugs.[105]

Could the prevention of such a fatal, frightening, and common disease really be that easy? What about blood transfusions? It is true that in the early days of the AIDS epidemic, blood and blood products did spread HIV. Of the 1,200,000 cases in the United States, 20,000, or about 1.6 percent, were due to blood transfusion.[106] Today, it is virtually impossible to get HIV from blood as all blood is tested multiple times before use. Of the more than 3,000 cases reported in Georgia for the year ending in March 2007, not one case was caused by blood products.[107]

There is good news on the horizon as researchers are now testing a vaccine for AIDS. If successful, medical science can chalk up another win against a uniformly fatal disease. (There is a lot more about vaccines in Chapter 15.)

Take Precautions

Many people, adults as well as teens, practice oral sex as they believe it is safe sex, but there is no such thing as safe sex. Most of the diseases described above—including herpes, syphilis, gonorrhea, HIV, HPV, and most cases of oral cancer—can be and are spread through oral sex.

For those who do not choose to abstain from sexual intercourse, oral sex, or illegal IV drugs, the CDC reminds them that there is no such thing as safe sex or safe drug use and that, at the least, people who choose to have promiscuous sex or use drugs should:

- Avoid sexual activity with anyone who is known to be infected, who is at risk of being infected, or whose HIV infection status is not known.

- Use a latex condom with spermicide.

- Seek treatment if addicted to illicit drugs.

- Not share needles or other injection equipment.

- Seek HIV counseling and testing if HIV infection is suspected.

One teen told me avoiding AIDS is easy. She said, "Just live right, don't have sex [except with your spouse], and don't do IV drugs." It's as easy as that.

Premarital Sex and Divorce

Much of today's society considers sex as another form of recreation. In January of 2006, Rev. Joseph Nolen wrote: "Some think of a sexual relationship as another form of friendship having no meaning beyond the pleasure it brings. The sexual relationship strengthens the marriage bond and is meant to do so. A sexual relationship is one of the privileges of marriage and it is wrong to enjoy that privilege without the commitment."[108] (Too bad no one taught that message to Luke's friend.)

As mentioned earlier, the divorce rate for first marriages is around 50 percent, but even higher among those who get married because of pregnancy or who co-habit prior to marriage. Divorce is not only tragic, it is also expensive. I was surprised to find that according to *smartmoney.com*, the average cost of a divorce is between $15,000 and $30,000.[109] That's just in legal fees. It doesn't include alimony, child support, or any of the other on-going expenses. Furthermore, it does not take into account the emotional cost to each partner, the children, or the parents of the couple. Any way you look at it, divorce is costly; consequently, couples should do everything they can to avoid anything that will likely lead to divorce.

Exercising Self-Control

I would be remiss if I didn't say a word about sex hormones. Many adults and teenagers think the rush of hormones is more than teens can resist. The truth is, hormones don't rush! Even if they did, sex hormones are secreted into the blood in 24-hour cycles and are highest in the hours just before dawn, and lowest in the late evening. Yet most promiscuous sex occurs at night. Sure, hormones play an important role in one's sex life, but they do not cause people at any age to do things against their will. Don't make excuses for unacceptable behavior!

Finally, Luke's lesson is about more than premarital sex. It applies to every action we take: smoking, drinking, eating dessert; even studying, doing homework, or going to work. Before we act, we need to know the long-term as well as the short-term effects of our actions and evaluate what we do based on knowledge of what will happen. If the short-term effect is pleasure at the expense of long-term pain—for ourselves or for others—then we really should ask, "Is it worth it?" Or to paraphrase Luke, "Is the pleasure I get now worth the suffering I'll cause later?"

You can also turn Luke's lesson on its head to make better decisions. Sometimes actions that lead to long-term pleasure require short-term pain. Example: Stay in and study now (pain) and ace the exam next week (pleasure).

However you use Luke's lesson, thinking about short-term and long-term rewards and consequences can help all of us make better decisions and avoid serious problems that may occur later, even years later.

THE CONDOM HOAX

*Abstinence is saying yes to
the rest of your life.*

Teen-Aid, Inc.

T HE CONCEPT OF "cool" has survived the past half-century pretty much intact. Almost 50 years after James Dean's *Rebel Without a Cause,* teens still see "cool" as the ultimate in peer acceptance.

There are a few tried-and-true ways to gain membership in the exclusive club of teenage coolness. The star jock is a shoo-in because he or she can do something most other students cannot. Crowds cheer him and school spirit gets a giant boost. The cheerleader with her good looks and vigor is considered the ultimate in femininity, and she usually dates the star jock or his buddies, which also gets her in the club by virtue of association.

Far away from the athletic field is the guy with the fast,

sleek car, a sort of maverick when it comes to risk taking, hairstyle, fashion, and other cultural characteristics. Finally, there's the guy who seems to have everything figured out on a topic that stirs and stumps most teens: sexuality. Among the teen set, these Don Juans are believed to have warped ahead of everyone else maturity wise when it comes to relations with the opposite sex. They seem to know everything about something teens think a lot about. And the thing they regularly flash as their membership card in the cool club is a round and usually transparent item called a condom.

Not a lot of thinking is associated with the condom. Couples are often in such a hurry when they break open the package that they don't take time to think. The University of Minnesota did an interesting study of high school boys who had not had intercourse and measured their knowledge of condom use and effectiveness.[110] They also asked the boys how *certain* they were that their answers were correct. One year later, the boys were interviewed again. Of those who had had sex during the year, 40 percent had used condoms—with one notable exception. Of the boys who knew little about condom use and efficacy, but were nevertheless *sure* of their knowledge, only 18 percent used a condom.

This statistic proves once again that those who don't know, and don't know they don't know, are the most dangerous. Still, when young males congregate to idolize its most frequent user and his stories of conquest and lust, no one wastes time explaining how to use the darn thing properly. Joe Cool just slips it out of his wallet and explains to his buddies how he's going to use it tonight on his date with so-and-so. To some teen boys, that's really cool; but one young man named Jeff felt differently.

Concerns with Condoms

I met Jeff in the heat of summer in "Hotlanta" when he came to see me because of a sprained ankle. He sat in the exam room with his mom, dad, and two younger sisters. It was the first time I had met this family, and I knew I was being tested. They had just moved to Atlanta from "Up-North," that mythical fifty-first state I, too, had left. Up-North-Mom was as over-protective as any Southern mother; and Dad, while he was careful not to disagree with anything she said, was also careful not to baby his blossoming athlete son. His sisters assumed the role of protecting Jeff lest the new doctor hurt him.

I took a careful history, examined his ankle, and developed a treatment plan to get him back to baseball. Before they left I asked, "When's your birthday, Jeff?"

"I'll be seventeen in November," he said.

"Good, I'll see you then for your annual health evaluation. I guess you would call that a physical, okay?"

"Sure," he said. "I'll be able to drive in by myself." Then he cast a quick look at his dad and added, "Won't I, Dad?"

"If it's okay with the doctor, then it's okay with us," Mom answered for Dad.

"Sure is okay with me," I replied. "Just be sure to have

his old medical records sent in and be near a phone so I can call you if we have any questions. I like to see kids by themselves as they get older. I think it helps them develop independence." I then explained my confidentiality policy and assured them Jeff and I would call one of them at the end of the visit.

"I'll see you on my birthday," he reminded me as he left. Then he turned and added with a laugh, "If not before."

Jeff came on his birthday. I wish I had remembered it so I could have brought a piece of cake to share, but I had forgotten. Anyhow, it was a cold, rainy day; so cold in fact that several parents called and rescheduled their appointments, leaving me with an unusually quiet schedule. Thus, I was glad to see Jeff's name on my list.

"Good to see you, Jeff," I said as I entered the exam room and extended my hand.

Jeff took my hand, looked me in the eye and said, "Remember, you said it was okay if I came by myself, so I did. And it's my birthday. You did remember that, right?" he teased.

"Of course I remembered," I kidded. "Didn't you see the Red Corvette I left in the parking lot with your name on it?"

We both laughed and I added, "Sorry, Jeff. Next year I will remember. Now let's get started."

We were soon finished with the history and the exam and sat down for the health-habit review. We talked about school, friends, drugs, alcohol, smoking, sex, and all the usual stuff. The more we talked the more I became convinced that Jeff was the sharp boy I initially thought and not a stooge who did not even know that both his grandmothers had diabetes. After a brief discussion of sexually-transmitted diseases I asked, "Jeff, what do you know about condoms?"

He cast a quizzical, long look at me as if to say, "What's there to know?" He thought a moment and said, "Condoms are smart things for stupid people."

Now the quizzical look must have been on my face, so he added, "If you're stupid enough to have sex with someone you're not married to, then a condom is a smart thing."

> CONDOMS ARE SMART THINGS FOR STUPID PEOPLE

I just sat there and nodded. Happy with having the podium, he went on. "You see, a condom can break or come off, and you can get some STDs even if you wear a condom. I think it's like getting on an airplane that has a 95 percent chance of making it to England and a 5 percent chance of ditching in the ocean. I'm not stupid enough to get on an airplane like that. I can't risk having sex, so I don't need any condoms. To me they're stupid."

"That's as good an answer as I've ever heard," I said, once again amazed at what comes out of these kids.

Before I could say any more he asked, "Don't you agree?"

"One hundred percent!" I answered. "Wouldn't it be great if everybody thought like you do?"

"That would be nice, but it isn't the way it is. I have friends who carry condoms 'just in case' they need one. One kid I know says his dad gave him some for his birthday! I think that's awful. I try to tell them to just be sure they don't need one, but they laugh and say I'm weird. Do you think I am?"

"Do I think you're weird? Good grief, no! I think you're about the smartest, most normal kid I've seen in a long time. You have good knowledge and you're using it to keep yourself healthy. What's weird about that?"

"Sometimes I think it would be easier and a lot more fun to be like some of the other guys, and see how much sex I can get; but the boys I know from my church teen group are a lot of fun, and they think like I do," Jeff said. "To tell you the truth, I really would like to have sex, just once, or maybe twice, to see what it's like."

Then he quickly added, "But don't tell my folks that!"

His face was bright red now. He thought he'd said more than he should have, and it caused his platinum blond hair, which had looked dull and dirty before, to glow against the dark exam room wall. "Jeff, if you didn't want to have sex, I'd think there was something wrong with you," I replied, wanting to drain any embarrassment out of his extraordinary display of honesty. "Sex is part of life, you know. Don't you think that's the way God created it?"

"Yeah, I guess. But, remember don't tell my folks," he answered, still embarrassed by his normal feelings.

We talked a while longer. When it was time for him to leave, I handed him my card and said, "Call me any time, or make an appointment. I'm always here. And don't forget to pick up the keys for your new Corvette from the nurse."

He shook my hand, gave me a light hug, and we laughed together as he walked proudly out the door.

False Security of "Safe Sex"

I must agree with Jeff that condoms are smart things for stupid people. If couples correctly use condoms each time they have sex during a year, then the risk of pregnancy drops to 3 percent compared to 85 percent if condoms are never used. But they're not a perfect protection, especially for disease. There is no such thing as "safe sex."

Heather Boonstra from the Alan Guttmacher Institute, a nonprofit group that researches reproductive health issues, is quoted in *The Tennessean* newspaper as saying: "They [condoms] do not provide 100 percent protection, but for people who are sexually active, they are the best and the only method we have for preventing these diseases [STDs]."[111] In the same article, conservative Senator Tom Coburn, a physician from Oklahoma, was cited as one of a group of people who want to make the condom package label "medically accurate." Users need to know that condoms are not 100 percent effective. While condoms do reduce the risk of HIV infection by about 80 percent and gonorrhea by more than 50 percent, the National Institute of Health[112] reports that for STDs (besides AIDS and gonorrhea), the evidence on protection is unclear.

In June of 2007, the *American Journal of Public Health* reported a study of 2,932 healthy men and women aged 18 to 27.[113] The study showed that 1 percent were infected with a relatively new STD caused by Mycoplasma genitalium. Although none of them had symptoms, previous studies have shown that Mycoplasma genitalium does cause urethritis,[114] infertility, arthritis, and infection in newborns. More than 4 percent of the group carried Chlamydia, and 0.4 percent were infected with gonorrhea. Interestingly, the prevalence of Mycoplasma genitalium was four times higher in those who used a condom the last time they had vaginal sex, and increased by 10 percent for each additional sexual partner. In a review of the article, Matt Barber, policy director for cultural issues for Concerned Women for America, said, "The study revealed the flaw in promoting condoms as the 'safer sex' answer."[115]

HIV and Other Sexually Transmitted Diseases

An article in *The Week* from January 24, 2003, says it all:

> In the 1990s, Uganda's government promoted abstinence, faithfulness, and condom use and saw a "nearly miraculous reduction" in HIV infections. Meanwhile, the African countries with the highest rate of condom use—Botswana and Zimbabwe—have the highest infection rates. The "condom orthodoxy" may not like these statistics, but abstinence is the best policy.[116]

We discussed STDs in Chapter 12, but let me mention here that in the United States, more than three million teenage girls contract a new STD every year, which means

365 girls get an STD every hour.[117] More than one-third of American women are infected by human papillomavirus (the virus that causes cancer) by the age of 24. As much as condoms are promoted, the rate of STD infection is increasing; but abstinence can prevent all STDs!

While there is no doubt that abstinence is the only sure way to prevent pregnancy and STDs, too often sex-education programs place the emphases on condom use rather than self-control. Cal Thomas in his December 18, 2005, column said:

> Though true abstinence-only programs have been effective in altering sexual behavior, the "sex education" programs in government schools do more to promote sex than prevent it, giving lip service to chastity while spending most of the class time teaching kids how to use condoms.[118]

Abstinence only programs came under attack in a government study conducted in April of 2007.[119] It indicated that kids who attended the programs were as likely as those who did not attend to have premarital sex.

Of course there was no difference. A program has to do more than demonstrate how to put condoms on bananas. In order to make a difference, a sex education course must be comprehensive, teaching both abstinence and protection. It should also include a course on social skills—especially decision-making skills—and assertiveness training for boys as well as girls. Kids of either sex need to know how to resist pressure from a date or companion. Too many people think of sex as a form of recreation and not as part of a committed relationship. As long as television, movies, music, and videos continue to promote casual sex and drug and alcohol use, our kids will be tempted. They need comprehensive, continuous, and repetitive educational programs in school, in church youth groups, and in the home. The operative word here is "repetitive." Frequent discussions about moral behavior, sexual and otherwise, have been shown to be much more effective than the one "big talk" parents are encouraged to have with their teens.[120] Dr. Michael A. Carrera of The Children's Aid Society agrees when he says: "Repetitions of these messages, throughout their development and daily adult role modeling, will provide the needed emphasis on the specific view a parent wants to convey to their child."[121].

Victor Strasburger, an adolescent medicine specialist at the University of New Mexico, commented on this problem in the April 2006 issue of *Pediatrics*:

> Everyone (pediatricians, parents, teachers, the entertainment industry, and state and federal governments) must share some responsibility if we are to be successful in helping teenagers delay the onset of sexual intercourse until an age at which they can be more responsible about relationships and birth control. ... If parents and schools do not provide sufficient information to satisfy teens, the media will pick up the

slack, and American media are most decidedly not abstinence-only.[122]

Peter Millet, a psychologist at Tennessee State University, reported on a study of 1,400 sixth-graders conducted by the National Center for Health Statistics. It claimed that 30 percent had had sexual intercourse prior to the beginning of the school year, and an additional 5 percent had done so by the end of the year.[123] A study by the CDC released in March 2008 found half of all African-American girls and 20 percent of white girls aged 14 to 16 tested positive for at least one STD. Even more telling, 20 percent of teen girls who had had only one sexual partner had an STD.[124] They did not test teen boys, but they obviously are also infected. With these grave statistics, we need to do everything possible to teach our kids right from wrong!

But in spite of all the programs, some teens will choose to engage in sex. They—and all people who are not in a monogamous relationship (that means married)—should use a condom every time they have sex. Pregnancy, HIV, and other STDs are too serious not to use everything that might reduce the risk.

Benefits of Abstinence

An *American Journal of Public Health* article notes that teens who have sex after drinking or smoking marijuana are two to three times less likely to use condoms.[125] I suspect Jeff would say these people are doubly stupid. Unfortunately, drugs and alcohol increase the likelihood of many risky behaviors, including fighting, reckless driving, and casual sex.

But wise teens and wise people of every age will be like Jeff and not need to worry about the effectiveness of condoms. They know that the best way to prevent pregnancy and every STD is abstinence: it's the right way to live. And like Reverend Jerrode Keys of Bogalusa, Louisiana, said: "A condom does not protect you against a broken heart."[126]

When Jeff left me after his health evaluation, I thought he had something else on his mind and would call in the next day or two. But he never did. I saw him early the next spring with a sore throat and after I took a throat culture, he smiled and said, "I still have your card."

He still had it when I saw him the following November for his health evaluation. He was doing great, and I bet he still is. He knows the secret of coolness is not in a condom, but the wisdom to know who you are and why the pleasure of the moment is not worth a lifetime of woe.

PARENTING TIPS

- *Get comfortable using proper terms when discussing sexual issues. It will make things easier when talking with your kids.*

- *Talk with your kids' personal physician and their youth minister about their teaching attitudes regarding teens and sex.*

- *Insist that your teens attend and participate in your church's youth program. If your church does not have a youth ministry, START ONE!*

- *Discuss your values regarding sex and other risky behaviors with your kids at every opportunity. Capitalize on the behavior of others—friends, television and movie characters, and news stories—to demonstrate your attitudes regarding sexuality. These teachable moments are much more effective than the one "big talk" parents are encouraged to have.*

- *Have that "big talk" anyhow.*

- *Don't accept hormones as an excuse for unacceptable behavior.*

- *Make sure your kids, boys as well as girls, know and understand your expectations regarding sexuality and/ or abstinence.*

- *Give your teens the HPV vaccine.*

- *Contrary to popular belief, living together (Dr. Laura Schlessinger calls it "shacking-up") leads to an increased divorce rate. Don't do it.*

- *Be firm in your dogma and in your teaching, but remain kind and loving enough that your teens will come to you if they or their friends get in trouble of any kind.*

Adolescent Medical Issues

In many ways, teens are less healthy than they were ten, twenty, or thirty years ago. This decline is seen across every social group—rich and poor alike. Kids from every part of town smoke cigarettes, abuse drugs and alcohol, get pregnant, become depressed, attempt suicide, murder or are murdered, have developmental disorders, and become disabled or die from accidents. Adolescents are the most medically underserved segment of our population. If we are to change this bleak picture, it is imperative that each teenager has his or her own doctor who will give them an annual health evaluation. They need a physician who has the same values their parents have, and they need a "Medical Home" with a compassionate, understanding practitioner who knows and uses the Guidelines for Adolescent Preventive Services (GAPS).

CHAPTER 14

TELEVISION AND OTHER SCREEN ADDICTIONS

She sat among us, at the best,
A not unfeared, half-welcome
guest, rebuking with her cul-
tured phrase, our homeliness
of words and ways. ... she
blended in a like degree, the
vixen and the devotee.

John Greenleaf Whittier

I N THE FALL of 2005, I became aware of a Sunday night television show called "Gray's Anatomy." Having extensively studied the book *Gray's Anatomy* almost half a century earlier, my curiosity was piqued; so I turned on the "half-welcome guest" most people call a TV.

The show opened with a young glamorous couple bursting into a bedroom in a passionate embrace while he rapidly undressed her and fell on top of her onto a waiting bed. As this scene fortunately faded from view, it was replaced by another beautiful couple similarly embraced and rushing to an open bed while the woman in a passionate fit undressed her mate and they both fell, in prurient pose, onto satin sheets. A third couple competed more successfully as they feverishly undressed each other even more rapidly than either of the first two, but with the same end result. A final, passionately entangled couple entered another room as I clicked them into oblivion.

"What on earth was that?" I asked of no one in particular. But my wife Mary, who had shared the scenes with me, replied, "Welcome to Sunday night TV. Get used to it."

"Well," I replied, "I'll have no part of it. Let's see what's on the History Channel."

As the picture came into focus, we saw a group of archeologists digging in what appeared to be a desert or some sand dunes. Then the announcer intoned, "In search of Sodom and Gomorrah."

"What!" I all but shouted at the television. "Stop digging! Both cities are only a few channels away."

This Sunday night actually happened, just as I described it!

After a glare from Mary, I settled down to thinking. *What irony, looking for Sodom and Gomorrah when we are practically living there. No need to search the desert for those sinful cities when you can see the same salacious activity every Sunday night on "Desperate Housewives." And what have they done to my* Gray's Anatomy?!

I won't go on criticizing this program because I've

never seen a whole show. Instead, I want to tell you about a wonderful, thinking teenager who shares some of my views about our "unwelcome guest"— television!

Turning Off the TV

Darrel was a high school junior in the fall of 1999 when I saw him for his annual health evaluation. I have to admit, he was not the brightest kid I ever met. As a matter of fact, he required some special-education classes; but he had a great smile and a magnetic personality. I found him interesting in a subtle way and over the years I grew fond of him.

He came in this day with his dad, as he usually did. Dad, a quiet and pleasant driver for UPS, was still in his "browns." He stood to greet me when I entered the room.

"Good to see you, Doctor," he said folding the morning paper as he extended his hand.

"Darrel needs his 100,000 mile check-up," he joked. "And probably an oil change as well. He's been running with the cross-country team, and I know for sure his wheels need grease."

Darrel blushed at his dad's attempt at truck humor and extended his hand. "Never mind him," he said. "He tries too hard to be funny."

"I understand," I replied. "I have a dad too, you know, and what's more, I am one. So I know how annoying we can be. But just be glad he cares enough to bring you in to see me."

Darrel's evaluation was rather uneventful and we were soon finished. Dad was back in the room and the three of us were casually talking about the Columbine tragedy which had just occurred. Columbine was the first of too many mass school shootings. On April 20, 1999, two high school boys brought an arsenal of weapons to Columbine High School in Colorado and shot everyone they could see. They killed 12 students and a teacher and wounded 23 others before they turned the guns on themselves.

While I put Darrel's medical record in order I said, "Tell me, Darrell, what do you think can be done to prevent things like Columbine from happening again?"

This was a simple question I had asked dozens of kids before and I knew, like everybody else knew, that there was no answer. But Darrel surprised me when he looked first at me and then glared at his dad and said, "If parents turned off their TVs they could be more involved in their kids' lives."

> IF PARENTS TURNED OFF THEIR TVS THEY COULD BE MORE INVOLVED IN THEIR KIDS' LIVES

My first reaction was to think Darrel was trying to pick a fight with his dad, and in a way he was. He certainly seemed to have his dander up about this one, something I had not seen in him before as he was usually calm and polite.

"You watch your share," was Dad's only retort.

"Not as much as you do!" Darrel shot back.

"Sure, now, but you used to watch a lot. Before you started school you watched it all day," Dad replied calmly.

"Dad! That was ten years ago and doesn't count. I don't have time to watch now. And you still watch three to four hours each night," Darrel said, anxious to make his point.

But Dad was unshakable. "You're right," he said, acknowledging defeat and ending the discussion at the same time.

Having conquered Dad, Darrel turned to me. "It's true. So many of my friends' dads are just like him. We could all be making bombs in our garages and they wouldn't know until they saw it on the TV. Parents should pay more attention."

Darrel is so right about television (and other screen addictions such as gaming and the Internet) interfering with parenting. Most of us are guilty of letting it occupy too much of our time, and time is really all we have to give to our families.

> TIME IS REALLY ALL WE HAVE TO GIVE TO OUR FAMILIES

Television and other electronic media have a way of consuming us. Teens watch an average of three hours of TV each day and grade school kids watch even more.[127] Parents often watch as much or more TV than their teens. Many dads I know turn the set on for the evening news and sit in their chairs and watch until bedtime. I have not found any studies on the effect television has on parenting; all the research seems to be directed to the effect it has on kids, as if adults are not interested in or affected by it at all. But common sense tells us that a parent cannot really interact with a child or learn how his day went or what he and his friends have been up to or help with homework or chores or do any active parenting while watching television. As much as we think we can multi-task, the truth of the matter is, when it comes to parenting, we can't! Kids need and deserve some undivided attention from their parents if they are to successfully learn the skills needed to succeed in life.

Interfering With Life

Television, gaming, and the Internet interfere with more than just parenting. You remember Zach, the boy who worried about eating too much junk food? Well, he was also concerned about TV. He knew too much screen time, like too much junk food, was not a good thing. During his visit he lamented his association with the tube, particularly.

"I come home from school and want to do my homework or my chores or shoot hoops," he said. "I want to play basketball, so I really need to practice everyday. But I can't walk past the TV without turning it on. Then the next thing

TV KEEPS ME FROM DOING THE THINGS I WANT TO DO AND SHOULD DO

I know, two or three hours have gone by and I haven't done any of the things I wanted to do. TV keeps me from doing the things I want to do and should do."

"Do you think you're addicted to it?" I asked.

"Nah, I'm not addicted," he said. "It's just that once it's on it's hard to turn it off. Watching is so easy. I don't even have to think, just relax."

"Do you have one in your room?"

"No, Mom won't let me. I just watch in the family room."

"Good for your mom. She probably knows that kids who have a TV in their room are twice as likely to smoke pot, and more likely to drink alcohol or have sex," I said.[128] "And I'm sure you know that watching TV and playing computer games makes you less active, so you gain weight. I can see that's not one of your problems, but it is a very serious concern for many patients. If you ever watch someone watching TV, you will see that they don't move. I like to say that TV turns people into statues; they just sit and stare. Watch them sometime!"

Too Much TV

The problem with television alone cannot be overstated! Studies show that children under seven years of age spend almost three hours watching TV each day.[129] One-third of all children less than six years of age live in a home where the TV is on almost all the time.[130] Those between eight and thirteen have an incredible six hours a day in front of either a TV or a computer screen![131] Teenagers watch more than four hours of just plain television each and every day.[132] By the time a youngster graduates from high school, he will have seen more than 200,000 episodes of violence and witnessed about 8,000 murders.[133] No wonder our society has become immune to the presence of real violence

Even if television had a neutral effect on kids, just think

what they could do with all that time. Sadly, adults spend almost as much time watching television as their kids.

An April 2008 study in the *Pediatrics* journal noted that teen boys who have a television in their bedrooms watched more TV, had lower grade point averages, ate less fruit, and had fewer meals with their families than teen boys who did not have a bedroom TV. Likewise with teen girls: the ones with bedroom TVs had lower grade point averages, exercised less, ate fewer vegetables, and participated in fewer family meals.[134]

The American Academy of Pediatrics recommends that teens *not* have a bedroom TV, but this advice has fallen on deaf ears as the study found that 68 percent of teen boys and 57 percent of teen girls have a TV in their rooms.[135] And an incredible 26 percent of infants under two have a bedroom TV,[136] even though the AAP recommends no TV or video viewing for babies this age.[137] What about infant learning videos like *Brainy Baby* or *Baby Einstein?* A study of 1000 parents and infants from Minnesota and Washington concluded that children who watched these videos were no smarter; as a matter of fact, they had less engagement with others and fewer words in their vocabulary.[138]

A recent editorial in *The Wall Street Journal* noted that parents are failing to police their kids' media consumption.[139] It cited a new study from the Kaiser Family Foundation that found technological additions like DVDs, videos, music, the Internet, computer video games, etc., have resulted in the average eight- to-eighteen-year-old getting 8.5 hours of screen exposure every day. Furthermore, many kids are entertaining themselves in "the privacy of their own bedrooms." That's real trouble.

"The most startling revelation in the Kaiser report is that for a majority of kids there are no rules in the household about media use," the *Journal* reported.

> Where there are rules, often they aren't enforced, or they apply only to how many hours children watch TV, not to what they watch. So what explains the absence of rules and parental supervision? Perhaps it's the huge effort involved. Busy parents have to muster the energy to learn how to use V-chips, ratings systems and computer filtering. They have to make sure that the songs kids download are the "radio," or cleaned-up, versions. Maybe some parents are ambivalent about playing the role of censor. Monitoring and enforcing are never-ending tasks.[140]

A Zogby poll in March 2007 found that 79 percent of viewers thought there was too much graphic sex, bad language, and violence on television. Yet 88 percent did not know how to use the V-chip, or knew but hadn't used it.[141] Kelli Turner discussed a poll by the Parents Television Council in an article in *The Tennessean*. She said that "of shows containing sexual content, 63 percent lack the 'S' descriptor, 42 percent of shows containing violence lack the 'V' descriptor, and 44 percent of shows containing foul language lack the 'L' descriptor."[142] Essentially, despite the good intentions of the ratings system, programs are being rated incorrectly.

The Truth about TV

A lot of today's parents were raised with television—cable television to boot. They think, "Well, look at me. I turned out all right. All this worry about TV viewing is just a bunch of hysteria from experts who don't have anything else to get worked up about." Like other parents, they want what is best for their kids; they believe kids, even infants, can learn by watching TV. But research has documented that even "educational" shows and videos, while they may teach catchy rhymes or even the ABC's, have an overall negative effect on learning.[143] Let's look at the facts.

In reviewing medical literature the past few months, I made a list of some of the possible harmful effects associated with watching too much television:

- Delayed vocabulary acquisition in children ages 8 through 16 months[144]

- Shortened attention span[145]

- Increased risk of Attention Deficit Hyperactivity Disorder[146]

- Sleep problems—trouble going to sleep, increased waking during the night, and increased tiredness during the day, difficulty waking in the morning[147]

- Increased consumption of caffeine[148]

- Increased consumption of snack foods[149]

- Increased fat in diet[150]

- Decreased physical activity[151]

- Obesity[152,153]

- Increased risk of smoking[154]

- Increased risk of using pot or other drugs[155]

- Increased use of alcohol[156]

- Younger age of initiating sexual activity[157]

- Increased aggressive behavior[158]

- Increased delinquency[159]

Before we go any further, let me point out that it is often very difficult to assign causality just because two things occurred together. However, the above evidence is enough to make parents and doctors concerned that TV viewing contributes to many, if not all, of the above. And, what harm can come from *not* watching TV?

Certainly a show or two each day may help children and adults relax, but more than that steals valuable time better spent in other activities. Some ask if kids who spend a good deal of time playing video games may develop better manual dexterity and might be faster at learning some of the fine handwork needed to maneuver real life objects such as fighter planes and robotic surgical equipment. This effect has not been established and even if it were, it no way balances the time lost to the pursuit of worthwhile social interactions. Dr. D. A. Christakis from Seattle Children's Research Institute states: "No studies to date have demonstrated benefits associated with early infant TV viewing."[160]

Other than David Kleeman, Director of the American Center for Children and Media,[161] and a number of bloggers, I can find no scientific articles showing any real benefits of children watching TV.

Because of the above adverse effects of television viewing, and perhaps other consequences not yet elucidated, the American Academy of Pediatrics has made the following recommendations:

1. Limit children's total media time (screen time) to no more than 1–2 hours of quality programming per day.

2. Remove TV sets from children's bedrooms.

3. No TV for children under 2 years of age.

4. Monitor the shows children and adolescents are viewing.

5. View TV programs along with your children and discuss the content.

6. Use controversial programming as a stepping-off point to initiate discussions about family values, violence, sex, and drugs.

7. Use the videocassette recorder wisely to show or

record high-quality, educational programming for children.

8. Support efforts to establish comprehensive media-education programs in schools.

9. Encourage alternative entertainment for children, including reading, athletics, hobbies, and creative play.[162]

Other Ways to Spend Your Time

There are so many alternatives to sitting and watching television, gaming, or surfing the Internet. One winter in Wisconsin we had a week-long ice storm that got many of us thinking. Because the electricity was off for the whole week (and in some homes, for almost two weeks), lives changed. People with gas stoves cooked for their neighbors who had electric, they heated water for those with electric water heaters, and people shared extra blankets and coats. Neighbor helped neighbor.

School was out, the stores were closed, and the state closed the roads into and out of our little town. By some act of fortune, the hospital and our house had underground wires from another community, and we had electricity! The hospital served as an oasis in the storm, housing as many people as could fit inside. The staff used snowmobiles to transport patients. We had extension cords running from our house to our neighbors' to power their furnace fans. Two families of six lived with us for that week. It didn't take long to empty our freezer, but the other families had food thawing in theirs, which they brought over and cooked. We did dishes and laundry all day for seven straight days, but there was always a game of Monopoly, Ping-Pong, or Pit going on somewhere in our crowded house. In short, it was great fun!

It seems everybody in town had a good time in spite of the difficulties. For weeks after, everyone talked about how they played games, did puzzles, and read aloud to each other under candlelight—all because there was no electricity to power TVs. When the lights came on, many families decided to stop their cable service because they realized how much television intruded on their lives, and the fun times continued. But gradually old habits returned, and soon the town folks were watching the tube again and ignoring each other.

It is possible to limit your use of screen media and that of your kids. I often advise teens like Zach, who want to decrease their TV consumption, to make a list of all the shows they would like to watch. Then, pick out their favorite one-hour of TV each school day and two hours for each weekend day to watch, remembering that any computer game time must fit into that same hour. Then they write that TV show in their homework assignment book, cross if off the homework list when it's over, and then turn off the television set. Many families are surprised that this simple act really works.

There are lots of ways to control TV in your home and add some fun to your family's life while you're at it. Kimberly Daly in an article in *The Tennessean*[163] suggested a

"Family Game Night" as a useful tool for spending quality time with family members. What a great idea! Plan one night each week to turn off the TV and other electronic media and play games with your family. Make it a priority! Put it on your calendar! Respect that night like you would your bowling night, tennis night, or your Bunko night. Your kids—guaranteed—will enjoy it because according to the 2005 Horatio Alger Study of Our Nation's Youth, almost half of our teenagers admit that they want to spend more time with their families.[164]

Wouldn't a game night be a great way to spend that extra time? Think of what kids can learn from playing games. Even preschoolers can learn honesty, counting, color recognition, and waiting in line. As games get more sophisticated, kids learn spelling, math, teamwork, perseverance, patience, good sportsmanship, honesty, strategy, and goal setting. Many games have opportunities to teach how to make choices and to live with the consequences of those choices. Kids can learn many of these things from computer games as well, but relating to a computer and relating to a family member must never be considered equivalent. Kids need time to socialize, and family is the very best place for socialization.

Most importantly, games are fun. They promote togetherness and build the family bond. When you think of your childhood, do you remember the movies you saw on TV, or the fun you and your family had playing some game or doing something many may even consider foolish? Family Game Night is when memories are built.

An additional benefit is that games provide many

opportunities for teaching values to your children. These opportunities are the conversations where values are transferred and where character develops.

Even short and simple games can be fun. Last Christmas, my daughter and her family spent the holidays with us. One evening, before we cleaned up the kitchen, we sat at the table and played "I went on a picnic and I took along ..." This is a game in which each person around the table adds something in alphabetical order to the picnic basket, and the next person in line has to name all the things in the basket and then add a new item. All the kids, seven to fifteen, and the adults of every age enjoyed the game and each other. "Let's play it again!" Maria, the youngest one, declared. "The next time, we eat." So we did.

But television isn't the only "half-welcome guest" we entertain. How often do we see a young parent driving down the street talking on a cell phone while the children are in the back watching some video? I contend that travel time can be turned into quality time by talking with the kids, or playing travel games.

Electronic media entertainment is everywhere and involves everyone. At the YMCA recently, I saw an older man listening to his iPod while working out with the free-motion equipment. Somehow, he managed to get the wire from the iPod to his earbud entangled with the weight machine's cable. I didn't laugh (though I was tempted) as I helped him extract himself from his entertainment.

Every day I see runners and walkers go by my house with their ears plugged with some entertaining, electronic gadget. Just last week my wife and I were out for a walk and saw a woman walking on the other side of the street with two school-age children. I presume they were hers. The boy, who looked to be about 12, was lagging behind the two women, so I called to them, "Hey, he's gaining on you. Don't let him catch you!"

All three of them reached up and extracted their ear-buds. "Pardon?" they said in unison (probably the only thing they had done together all day). Here was an opportunity for some high-quality family time and they were wasting it listening to who knows what.

Take a look around your house and see if you have too many half-welcome guests. Ask yourself if some of them have worn out their welcome and need to be replaced with some quality family time.

Television Viewing and ADD

One last note as I think about Darrel. When I first met him he had been diagnosed with ADD (attention deficit disorder). I wondered if all the television he had watched prior to starting school had anything to do with his developing ADD. Recently, researchers in Seattle observed the television viewing habits of over 2,500 youngsters and concluded: "The likelihood of a child being diagnosed with attention deficit disorders increases to 10 percent for those who watched one to two hours [of television], 20 percent for those who watched between two and three hours, 30 percent for children glued to the set for three to four hours."[165] From their findings, it is apparent that the problem gets bigger depending on the amount of television being consumed.

Exactly why this happens is not known, but the frequent change of scenes and the rapid sequence of events typical of most TV shows may, in the researchers' opinion, "permanently alter normal brain development."[166] Apparently, studies of newborn rats show that an over-stimulated environment causes the structure of the brain to change. People aren't rats, and we can't always compare laboratory animals with people, but at least this is a start as scientists try to understand ADD.

ADD and ADHD (ADD with hyperactivity) perhaps have multiple causes, including a genetic factor. Likewise, there are many possible treatment options, including family and individual counseling, alternative parenting styles, changes in sleep and bedtime routine, increased exercise, more time out of doors, limited TV, and last of all, drugs.

I do not like using drugs for ADD or ADHD unless the symptoms are extreme and other treatment methods, including behavior modification, have failed. A study reported in May 2005 from Oslo, Norway, concluded:

[W]hen the environment supplies clear rules for conduct, immediate and frequent reinforcers and predictable consequences of misconduct, there is no difference between children receiving medication and those not receiving medication.[167]

Often, altering the environment by increasing the

amount of sleep, decreasing television time, and increasing the amount of time spent outdoors is more beneficial than Ritalin or any other drug.

If problems still exist after making these changes— along with behavior counseling and family therapy—I might consider a medication like Ritalin; but as a rule, I do not like to use stimulants or other psychoactive drugs with children.

Darrel had been on Ritalin for several years when he became my patient, but he did not like the way it made him feel and his Dad did not like what it did to his appetite. "He's skinny enough," Dad protested. Ritalin and other stimulants often cause a dull headache, abdominal pain, and decreased appetite. I was in full agreement with stopping the meds. Since then, Darrel has done as well as he was doing on medication, and graduated with his class the following year.

Many parents and physicians, however, do not agree with me, and the use of drugs for ADD has exploded. Medications used to treat ADHD make up three of the five most frequently prescribed drugs for American children. According to the Agency for Healthcare Research and Quality, more than $1.3 billion was spent on these drugs in 2004, the last year data was available.[168] Unfortunately, many parents and doctors find giving a pill easier and quicker than making the lifestyle changes needed to help these kids.

Results of a study published in the May 2009 issue of *Pediatrics* disagrees with me. In a six-year retrospective study, investigators found that the use of medication resulted in a net gain of 0.19–0.29 school years. According to their estimates, these medications cost $2.2 billion per year. However, if the best a year or more of treatment can do is a gain of 6–8 weeks in school at a cost of billions of dollars (not counting the physical side-effects), then perhaps we need to be cautious about how much these medications really help.[169]

I know that television and other screen media are here to stay, and I can't control what is broadcast or who watches what. But I also know that I can control what I watch, and parents can and should control what they and their children view. If there is not enough evidence out there to condemn most television shows today, Darrel and Zach gave us two more good reasons to use discretion in what we watch. We should listen to our kids!

CHAPTER 15

PREVENTIVE IMMUNIZATIONS

An Ounce of Prevention Is
worth a Pound of Cure.

Henry deBracton, 1240

*I*T WAS RAINING one day when I left home for the office, and it continued to pour all that morning. But my spirits were not dampened because I remembered my mother saying, "Rain before seven, clear before eleven." I laughed with the parents who came to their appointments as they struggled with bags and umbrellas trying to keep everybody dry. It was a warm day and the older kids didn't want to wear their hot slickers. Like me, they loved to run in the rain. That's why, after my first appointment, I was happy to carry Mrs. Chapel's diaper bag and walk her and her baby to the car. Tyler, her 11-year-old son, ran along side of us holding his unopened umbrella. "Thanks," she called as I helped her, the baby, and her son into the car. "Look at you!" she said. "Your hair is wet; water's running down your face. You're a mess. Where's your umbrella? You're as bad as Tyler."

"Thanks," I replied, "I'll take that as a compliment." The Chapels were among my favorite patients and I'm sure they all knew it. She laughed and drove away, leaving me standing in the rain.

I dashed to the office just in time to open the door for Tanya Kennedy and her mother. "Shame on you, running in the rain without an umbrella! You'll catch your death of cold or pneumonia," Mother chided.

"Oh, silly me," I jested in return. "Get in here quickly. You're as wet as I am." We all had a good laugh while I kept thinking, *This is even more fun than sunshine.* Tanya and her mother checked in while I rushed to my next patient. My nurse, Kathy, who somehow managed to keep me on time, had Tanya and her mom in the exam room by the time I was ready for them.

Preventing the Flu

"Hi, Tanya, Mrs. Kennedy," I greeted. "Good to see you again."

"Always good to see you, too," Mrs. Kennedy replied. "Even if you don't have enough sense to come in out of the rain."

Tanya laughed with us and grasped my outstretched hand. "Don't pay any attention to her," she said, pointing to her mom. "She loves you and you know it."

Tanya's smile showed off her beautiful white teeth which contrasted with her dark skin. The rain had pulled her curls into tiny, tight ringlets. She was a lovely girl, and I was delighted to know her. "So glad you came to see me on this rainy day. To what do I owe the pleasure?"

WHY GET THE FLU IF A SHOT WILL PREVENT IT?

"Soccer starts in two weeks so I need to have my physical, even though I know I'm healthy. I hate physicals, you know."

"Yes, I know. All high schoolers hate physicals. So does your mom. So do I. So does everybody! That's why I changed the name from physicals to health evaluations."

"Very funny, it's still the same thing." She thought a second and then added, "Isn't it?"

"Yes, Tanya, it's still the same thing, only we talk more about your health habits and lifestyle so we can prevent illnesses and help you live a long and healthy life. But all in all, it's the same thing. Should we get started?"

We did, and too soon we were finished. "Do you have any other questions," I asked, "or is there anything I forgot that we should talk about?"

"Actually, there is. Remember how sick I was with the flu last winter. I need to get a flu shot. I don't ever want to get that sick again."

"I do remember how sick you were, Tanya. But it's only August and the flu vaccine isn't available until October; I'll put your name on a dose. You can come by any time after the first of October and get it. When the new Swine flu (H1N1) vaccine is available you should get that, too, and so should your sister and brother."

"You don't have to convince me. If it were up to me,

there would be lines from Main Street to your door at midnight on September 30, just like there were when Harry Potter came out. The flu shot is a lot more important. Why get the flu if a shot will prevent it?"

"I agree. Let's get your mother in here and tell her what we think."

When Mom came in, she wasn't as convinced as Tanya. "Can't you get just as sick from the shot?" she asked.

"That's what a lot of people think," I answered. "One study showed as many as 38 percent of people think that.[170] But the truth is, you can't. The vaccine is made from dead viruses and there is no way they can make you sick. If you are allergic to eggs, you might have a reaction at the injection site, but I give thousands of shots each year, and I have never seen a reaction."

Though Tanya's concerns echo the concerns of many people, the American Academy of Pediatrics recommends that all children from age six months to 18 years get the flu shot. So should anyone who takes care of children in that age group as well as all medical personal. I am always the first one in line when the new vaccine comes out. Anybody with a chronic disease like diabetes or asthma should get it, too. Anyone, regardless of age or health, who wants to decrease their chance of getting the flu, should be immunized.

I shared this information with the Kennedy's. "You and your husband should have it too," I added. "As teachers you're both exposed to a lot of kids, and you can get the flu from any of them."

Mrs. Kennedy still didn't look convinced. Tanya

noticed it, too. "Mom," she began, "don't you remember how sick James and I were last winter? We both missed a week of school, and so did you. Do you want us to go through that again? How bad can a shot be? Let's just have the shot and be done with it!"

A Deadly Virus

The reality is, every year influenza causes more than 36,000 deaths in the United States, more than 114,000 hospitalizations, and untold days off of work.[171] Depending on the severity of the epidemic, between 15 and 40 percent of school kids get the flu each year, and half of them end up seeing a doctor. Just think of what that costs. What a waste! With most health plans, the immunizations are free.

Unfortunately, in 2004 there was a severe shortage of flu vaccine and many people had to forgo the shots so the high-risk population could be protected. The outcry from the public over this public health crisis stimulated the industry to do a better job. Since then, they have made enough vaccine so that everyone who needs or wants protection can receive it. I wish I could add the good news that the flu epidemic in the winter of 2004–05 was mild— but it wasn't. Many schools around the nation had to be shut down because of sick students and faculty.

Since I talked with Tonya, a nasal mist vaccine has been introduced. This form of the vaccine contains a weakened, live strain of the flu virus. It is unable to live in very warm places, such as the lungs and blood stream; but it can grow in the nose and throat which are cooled by breathing. It has proven to be even more effective in children than the injectable vaccine. I worry that it could mutate and be able to live in warmer places, but the virologists (people who study viruses) assure me that that possibility is extremely unlikely. If you are concerned about that, get the shot instead of the nasal mist; it really does not hurt! So the good news now is that people have a choice to get the flu vaccine by nasal mist or by a regular shot. Personally, I would rather get a shot than have someone spray something up my nose, but some of my grandkids got the spray last year and didn't mind at all. They all agreed it was better than a shot.

In February 2008, the CDC's Advisory Committee on Immunization Practices (ACIP) recommended that all children and young adults through age 18 get flu shots. They noted that 68 youth from the 26 states the CDC monitors died of flu in the 2006–07 season. Through January of the 2007–08 season, 22 more died. The CDC and the AAP have now adopted these new recommendations.[172]

Immunizations Are Smart Medicine

Immunization from any disease, not just the flu, is just plain common sense. Preventive immunizations have changed the whole face of pediatric medicine. Young pediatricians have never seen many diseases that previously killed scores of children. Measles, tetanus, diphtheria, rubella (German measles), and mumps are all practically non-existent in the United States today. Unfortunately, they are still all too common in the developing world.

The MMR (measles, mumps, and rubella) vaccine has saved thousands of lives since it was introduced in the early 1960s, and thanks to the World Health Organization's major international immunization activities, global deaths due to measles alone fell by 48 percent: from 871,000 in 1999 to an estimated 454,000 in 2004.[173]

But contagious diseases that can be prevented with immunizations are not just about life or death. These at-one-time common childhood diseases are fraught with serious complications. Many readers will remember Laura Wilder's book *Little House on the Prairie,* or its television counterpart based on Laura and her family. Laura's sister Mary was blind because of measles. My wife's cousin had measles as a child and became deaf. Any death or handicap from a preventable disease is unnecessary and tragic.

The last case of smallpox in the world occurred in Somalia in 1977.[†] Thanks to the smallpox vaccine, the world is now free from smallpox—a horrible disease wiped out by immunization!

Since 1979, there have been no cases of naturally occurring polio in our entire country. Yet in the 1940s and 1950s, hundreds of thousands of children and young adults contracted polio, killing many and paralyzing many more. My aunt had polio in 1945 at age 25 and spent the next 50 years in a wheelchair. Think how excited she was

---

† "Smallpox outbreaks have occurred from time to time for thousands of years, but the disease is now eradicated after a successful worldwide vaccination program. The last case of smallpox in the United States was in 1949. The last naturally occurring case in the world was in Somalia in 1977. After the disease was eliminated from the world, routine vaccination against smallpox among the general public was stopped because it was no longer necessary for prevention." *CDC.gov*, "Smallpox Disease Overview."

to vaccinate her daughter and grandchildren, and how excited she must have been to see polio all but eradicated from the world. The World Health Organization predicts we will see the world's last case of polio this decade.

When I was in medical school, bacterial meningitis—with a mortality rate nearing 15 percent and serious neurological complications—was a common childhood disease. Since a vaccine was introduced in the mid eighties, the incidence of meningitis has nose-dived. Today, a case of meningitis is so rare it is newsworthy.

Recently, scientists have developed a vaccine for another strain of meningitis, meningococcal, which occurs in teens and young adults. It has a very rapid course and is often fatal. All teens should get this vaccine. Also, the newly released cervical cancer vaccine which we discussed in Chapter 12 will save thousands of young women's lives each year. This really is a good time to be alive.

The Vaccination-Autism Myth

Regrettably, there is a movement by some well-meaning parents to thwart the use of vaccines. A popular myth holds that the measles, mumps, and rubella (MMR) vaccine, or its mercury-containing preservative thimerosal,[†] causes autism. Autism is a serious developmental disorder causing impaired social interaction and general communication difficulties. Unfortunately, its cause is unknown and

---

† Though no link between the mercury in Thimerosal and autism has ever been found, mercury can accumulate in the body and become toxic. Therefore, manufacturers have eliminated thimerosal from infant vaccines.

to make matters worse, it is becoming more common every year. The American Academy of Pediatrics and the CDC have concluded that there is no link between vaccines and autism, yet some people prefer to rely on opinion rather than scientific investigation.

For example, a British study of 103,043 children published in the September 27, 2007, issue of *The New England Journal of Medicine* showed no harmful associations with mercury exposure from any vaccines received in the first years of life. Multiple studies have consistently found no link between vaccines and autism.

There are other immunizations that kids should get, including some just for teenagers. The AAP has a schedule all parents should follow to make sure their kids have all the disease prevention available today. It is included in Appendix C.

The Story of an Epidemic

I recommend that anyone who is opposed to (or uncertain of) vaccinations read *The Great Influenza: The Story of the Deadliest Pandemic in History* by John M. Barry; or *Flu: The Story Of The Great Influenza Pandemic* by Gina Kolata.[174] These books discuss the devastation caused by the 1918 flu epidemic.

John Barry describes the flu virus of 1918 thus:

> It was as if the virus were a hunter. It was hunting mankind. It found man in the cities easily, but it was not satisfied. It followed him into towns,

then villages, then individual homes. It searched for him in the forests, tracked him into jungles, and pursued him onto the ice. And in those most distant corners of the earth; in those places so inhospitable that they barely allowed man to live, in those places where man was almost wholly innocent of civilization, man was not safer from the virus. He was more vulnerable.[175]

The 1918 flu virus began its hunt in Camp Funston, Kansas, (now Fort Riley) in February. From there it spread with U.S. troops to Army bases in Georgia and from there to France. The French troops gave it to British soldiers who then took it to England. In May of that year, 36,473 men from the British First Army were hospitalized. Finally, it spread all over Europe: then to China and Japan.

But disease and epidemics are not always predictable. As fast as the flu started, it stopped. By early August it was over. Millions of soldiers and civilians all over the world (except for parts of Africa, South America, and Canada) had been sick and recovered. This first round was a very contagious flu, but not very lethal. There were few deaths.

As people became complacent that the war against the flu was over and it was safe to concentrate on the "war to end all wars" (World War I), influenza returned with a vengeance. It began in Boston in late August and quickly spread to both the military and civilian populations. In September, more than one hundred troops died each day at Massachusetts' Fort Devens, and approximately 12,000 people died throughout the United States. In October, 11,000 died in Philadelphia alone. In Alaska, entire Eskimo villages were destroyed. Within twenty-four weeks, more people died of the flu than died in the first twenty-four years of the AIDS epidemic. By the time it was over, more than 40 million—and perhaps as many as 100 million—people were dead.

The Ongoing Need for Flu Vaccinations

In 1918, doctors were able to diagnose flu by its symptoms, but they did not know a virus caused it. It would be fifteen years before the first influenza virus was isolated. Soon after identifying the virus, scientists were able to develop a vaccine. However, the flu virus mutates so fast that new vaccines need to be developed each year based on which mutant strain scientists think will circulate. In 2007, scientists were wrong and the vaccine they made was not as effective as previous ones. Nevertheless, it did provide some protection.

Public health authorities are concerned that strains like the "bird flu" may spread to man and produce an epidemic similar to the 1918 flu. If bird flu spreads to humans and is able to spread from person to person, as many as two million Americans could die.[176] As for now, the bird flu has spread only to birds and a rare human, and has not shown the ability to spread from person to person; no immediate threat is anticipated. Hopefully, scientists will develop an effective vaccine before the bird flu becomes the epidemic they predict.

However, in early spring of 2009, the swine flu (scientifically called H1N1) developed in Mexico and spread to the United States and the rest of the world. In June 2009, the World Health Organization (WHO) declared it a pandemic (the CDC and the World Health Organization considers a disease a pandemic if it has spread to all six, naturally inhabited, continents).

Bill Snyder in the *Vanderbilt University Medical Center Reporter* said:

> Since the first cases of a novel influenza strain were reported in California and Mexico in March and April of this year [2009], H1N1 has swept through nearly 200 countries, killing nearly 4,000. By June, federal health officials estimated that more than 1 million Americans had come down with H1N1 flu. Approximately 10,000 people have been hospitalized, and about 600 have died." [177]

By December 2009, the CDC's director, Dr. Thomas Frieden, estimated that more than fifty million Americans had contracted H1N1 flu and as many as ten thousand had died.

Nonetheless, in spite of these numbers, so far H1N1 is a relatively mild flu. As Bill Snyder goes on to explain. "A typical seasonal flu in this country will kill an average of 36,000 and hospitalize more than 200,000—mostly in people over 65, according to the Centers for Disease Control and Prevention (CDC)." Still, H1N1 is an unusual flu in that it seems to affect younger people. The highest hospitalization rates have been in children under 5, and the highest death rates are among people 25 to 49.[178]

In many ways H1N1 is reminiscent of the Flu of 1918. Its unique ability to affect age groups previously thought to be relatively resistant to the disease underscores its potential to develop into a much more deadly strain. What a frightening thought! By comparison, getting a flu shot isn't frightening at all.

By the way, Tanya Kennedy and her entire family, including Dad, showed up on October 1 for flu shots. Like the Kennedys, I strongly encourage everyone to get the flu shot and any other applicable vaccinations.

CHAPTER 16

MAKING INFORMED MEDICAL DECISIONS

Surgeons must be very careful when they take the knife! Underneath their fine incision stirs the culprit—Life.

Emily Dickinson, c. 1859

*R*OBERT WAS A talented high school baseball player that I had known for a long time. Although no athlete delights in the required pre-season physical, Robert relished telling of his accomplishments, knew I had a willing ear, and was not unhappy to see me. He was a small, muscular boy with short brown hair cut close to his head and a smile as constant as his energetic, incessant chatter. He told of his prowess at first base, his batting average, and of the letters he had received from colleges—yet he never seemed a braggart.

He flexed his pecs when I listened to his heart and his biceps when I examined his shoulders. He was proud of his body and himself, and rightly so; he had worked hard to build those muscles and maintain an honor-roll GPA.

The exam and health habits review went quickly since he had answered the questions many times in the past. "Some things never change," he told me.

After we finished the prescribed inquiry, I looked at him and said, "Let me ask you one more question."

"Go ahead," he replied.

"I'm sure you know that most boys your age are circumcised. Did you ever get teased about not being, or did you ever wish you were circumcised so you could be like the other guys?" I asked.

"Heck no," he answered. "I often wondered why some guys had it cut off, but I never wanted to cut anything off my penis! Don't cut anything off that works great, that's my philoso-

DON'T CUT ANYTHING OFF THAT WORKS GREAT

phy." Then he went on, "I asked Mom once why some boys had it done and she said some people thought it prevented diseases. Is that right? There's no real reason to do it, is there? So, why do so many boys have it done?" His questions came as easily as his usual chatter.

"Well," I began, "the Academy of Pediatrics issued a statement in 1971, and reissued it in 1999,[179] that says there are not enough medical reasons to justify routine circumcision. But the Academy is studying the issue again. Most of the boys in the world are not circumcised. The United States is the only Western country where circumcision is routine.[180] Of course, the Jewish and

Islam religions call for ritual circumcision; but today, most Americans circumcise their babies because their fathers were circumcised. It's kind of a social, cultural habit."

"That's dumb," he interrupted.

"There is a slight increase of urinary infections in the first six months of life in uncircumcised boys compared to those who are circumcised, but the Academy doesn't think that's enough to justify putting every baby boy through circumcision. It's pretty painful, you know."

"I bet it is! I'll never have my son circumcised!" he said firmly. We talked a bit more about circumcision, and then the topic changed to his upcoming baseball season.

I have spent a lot of time since then thinking about this issue and the question of medical decisions in general. Barring religious convictions that don't put a child in harm's way, Robert's philosophy is generally sound. Whether or not to circumcise an infant is an example of a medical decision parents regularly make without first fully understanding the matter. To illustrate my point, let's examine circumcision in greater detail.

Circumcision Studies and STDs

I make no apologies for my preference to avoid circumcision, but I respect the world's religions that condone it. My concern is that parents often make the decision to circumcise (as well as many other medical decisions) based on misinformation. For example, the American Academy of Pediatrics and its Canadian counterpart have failed to endorse circumcision.[181] The Canadian policy even goes so far as to say it should not be done, yet Americans continue to circumcise the majority of baby boys. Statistics do show, however, that the rate has dropped in the United States from more than 90 percent in the sixties to about 60 percent in the late nineties.[182] Recent reports showed only 56 percent of newborn boys born in the United States were circumcised in 2003, and the rate has fallen every year since.

Many of the reasons once given for circumcision have been proven invalid. It was once considered a cure for epilepsy, masturbation, and delinquency. It was also thought to prevent cervical cancer. But as we discussed earlier, we now know that a sexually transmitted virus causes cervical cancer.

There is also an ongoing controversy as to whether circumcised men enjoy sex more or less than their intact brothers, or if women enjoy sex more with intact or circumcised partners; but pleasure, especially sexual pleasure, is such a subjective thing that it's hard to really evaluate.

In the United States, circumcision has been promoted as a means of reducing the risk of STDs. Supporting that opinion was a study in 2006 from New Zealand showing that circumcised men had almost a 50 percent lower incidence of STDs than those not circumcised.[183] This study of 510 men conflicted with three earlier studies undertaken in the United States, England, and Australia consisting of over 16,000 men.[184,185,186] None of these studies found a relationship between circumcision and STDs. A recent report, also from New Zealand and published in the March 2008 issue of the *Journal of Pediatrics,* concurred with the larger studies. This study also failed to find any differences in socioeconomic status or sexual behavior that could have confounded the results. By age 32, the statistical rates for all STDs in uncircumcised and circumcised men were not significantly different. The investigators cautiously concluded: "[I]t appears unlikely that early childhood circumcision has a major protective effect against common STDs."[187]

In scientific research, it is not unusual for separate investigators to get different results; rarely is a scientific fact discovered in the first study. When studies show contradictory results, it is a sign that more investigation is needed to arrive at the truth. Sometimes a flaw is found in one of the study designs or in the interpretation of the data. However, if there is a difference in STD susceptibility between circumcised and uncircumcised men in the Western world, it is apparently not great.

Circumcision and AIDS

The confusion of what circumcision medically will or will not prevent is greatest in relation to AIDS. For example, in Sub-Saharan Africa where AIDS is spread primarily by heterosexual activity, as many as 30 percent of the people have the disease. In 2007, two studies from this area showed significantly fewer cases of AIDS in men who were circumcised as adults compared to other study members who were left uncircumcised.[188,189] However, these studies have been criticized.[190,191,192] The investigators' peers have advised caution in interpreting the results because the studies were ended early and thus the results may have been exaggerated.

Another study in these same African countries showed that virgin adolescents who had been circumcised (boys and girls—some African cultures practice female circumcision) prior to puberty actually had a *higher* rate of AIDS than their uncircumcised peers. The authors of this study suggest that this may be due to the unsanitary conditions and non-sterile procedures used in performing ritual infant circumcisions. The investigators concluded that: "HIV transmission may occur through circumcision-related blood exposures in eastern and southern Africa." They further showed that as adults, more uncircumcised males became infected with AIDS than their circumcised peers. They offered several suggestions as to why this may be, but could not come up with an answer they could endorse.[193]

Adding to the confusion, doctors historically believed that uncircumcised men were less likely to contract AIDS from their female partners than circumcised men were. But this historical belief was not borne out when the World Health Organization (WHO) and The Joint United Nations Programme on HIV/AIDS (UNAIDS) concluded that "the efficacy of male circumcision in reducing female to male HIV transmission has now been proven beyond reasonable doubt."[194]

But data from the UNAIDS/WHO 2006 report shows that in North America, where almost all sexually active men are circumcised, approximately 0.9 percent of the population is HIV positive; whereas the Scandinavian countries, the British Isles, and Europe, where circumcision is almost non-existent, have a much lower HIV rate of about 0.2 percent. From this data, one could conclude that circumcised men are more likely to get AIDS than their uncircumcised brothers.[195] However, in all these countries (unlike Africa), AIDS is primarily spread by male-to-male sex and rarely from heterosexual activity, which may or may not account for the differences in the studies' findings.

From these many conflicting studies we conclude that we do not know yet if circumcision helps anyone avoid AIDS or not. Scientists are now testing an HIV vaccine, but there is an obvious and

> **AVOID SEXUAL ACTIVITY WITH ANYONE TO WHOM YOU ARE NOT MARRIED!**

inexpensive solution that makes the question of circumcision moot. Dr. A. Zoosmann-Diskin in the May 2000 issue of the *Journal of Infectious Disease* said, "The mere idea of cutting off healthy erogenous organs of non-consenting minors to reduce the risk of getting a disease that is easily preventable by less drastic means is abominable."[196] By "easily preventable," he is referring to practicing only monogamous sex—sex only with your spouse.

Circumcision Hurts

The Old Testament† informs us that five thousand years ago, the men of Israel took advantage of the severe pain caused by circumcision to slay the recently circumcised

---

† Genesis 34

men of Hamor, an attack precipitated by the rape of an Israelite woman named Dinah. Mankind knew even then that circumcision hurts! But for many years, modern doctors told parents the medical myth that circumcision did not hurt because babies could not feel pain. This was disproved in a study conducted by the Department of Pediatrics at the Hospital for Sick Children in Toronto, Canada, and reported in the major British journal *The Lancet* in March 1997. It concluded that circumcised infants showed a stronger pain response to subsequent routine vaccination than uncircumcised infants.[197] Even four and six months after being circumcised, circumcised boys reacted with more crying and other signs of pain while getting immunizations than uncircumcised boys or girls, suggesting that circumcision increases a boy's pain sensitivity and his reaction to pain.

In the Toronto study, pain was quantified by a commonly used method of scoring the nature of the babies' cries, facial grimaces, and "defensive" body movements. Using this scoring method, neonatal pain of any kind was shown to sensitize a baby's reaction to subsequent pain for months, perhaps even years. Because of these studies, pediatricians recommend that if a baby is to be circumcised, he should have a local anesthetic to numb the penis prior to the surgery. That helps, but circumcised babies still have pain for a week to ten days whenever they urinate, move their legs, or anytime their wound rubs on the diaper.

The American Culture of Circumcision

It is a common belief that circumcision began with God's covenant with the Israelites, but it was actually practiced prior to Abraham. Often it was used to mark slaves; Abraham and his family were marked as subjects (or slaves) of God. Some cultures used (and some still use) circumcision as a rite of passage into adulthood. If the boys could stoically endure pain without wincing, they were worthy to be called men.[198]

However, routine, non-religious circumcision was rare in the United States until the end of the 19th century when John Harvey Kellogg (1852–1943)—the inventor of the corn flake and founder of Kellogg's Cereals—proposed it as a way to prevent masturbation. In his *Treatment for Self-Abuse and Its Effects*, he wrote:

> A remedy which is almost always successful in small boys is circumcision, especially when there is any degree of phimosis [overly tight foreskin that cannot retract over the penis]. A surgeon should perform the operation without administering an anesthetic, as the brief pain attending the operation will have a salutary effect upon the mind, especially if it be connected with the idea of punishment, as it may well be in some cases. The soreness which continues for several weeks interrupts the practice, and if it had not previously become too firmly fixed, it may be forgotten and not resumed.[199]

Kellogg was known as an anti-sex zealot. He was married for more than 40 years and claimed he never had sexual intercourse. He thought that the foreskin was the seat of male sexual pleasure and the root cause of insatiable sexual appetite. Thus, it needed to be excised.

Another example of circumcision entering the American culture occurred in 1870 when Lewis Sayre, a New York orthopedic surgeon, examined a boy who was unable to straighten his legs. Dr. Sayre noted that the boy's "genitals were inflamed." Sayre circumcised him and within a few weeks the young boy could walk again.[200] Because he was a prominent physician and vice president of the American Medical Association, his opinions were highly regarded. He lectured all across the United States and England touting the benefits of circumcision. Soon, circumcision was used to treat (among other things) hernias, bladder infections, kidney stones, insomnia, chronic indigestion, rheumatism, epilepsy, asthma, bedwetting, erectile dysfunction, syphilis, insanity, and skin cancer. This list is not only interesting to the point of being humorous, it shows how quickly opinions unfounded on scientific inquiry can become a part of our culture.

An Expensive and Unnecessary Procedure

Many parents are concerned that if their baby is not circumcised at birth, he will need to have it done later. But studies in England, where newborn circumcision is extremely rare, show only four boys out of 10,000 (0.04%) need circumcision for medical reasons.[201] This includes the rare necessity of circumcision for phimosis, the inability to retract the foreskin by age five or six. Parents should understand that at birth, the foreskin cannot retract and should never be forcibly retracted. In fact, forcing retraction causes pain and scarring that can lead to phimosis. At one time, doctors thought phimosis always required circumcision; but studies in the late 1990s showed that almost all cases (97 percent) of phimosis can be treated successfully with the painless, uncomplicated, and inexpensive topical application of a common steroid cream (often a simple cortisone cream was enough).[202]

The fact is that unless required for religious reasons, circumcision has none of the benefits people once thought it had. It can be painful, leading to increased sensitivity later in life, and it costs $250–$300 per removal. It therefore costs between $525 and $630 million dollars *annually* to circumcise the 2.1 million boys born each year. We can all think of better ways to use that money. So can many insurance companies; and the Medicaid departments in sixteen states—Arizona, California, Florida, Idaho, Louisiana, Minnesota, Maine, Mississippi, Missouri, Montana, Nevada, North Carolina, North Dakota, Oregon, Utah, and Washington—all refuse to pay for routine newborn circumcision.

The particular problem of routine, uninformed circumcision has perhaps reached its climax in a case before the court in North Dakota that seeks to determine if parents even have the right to give a doctor permission to perform an operation that is not medically needed and will result in significant change to the genitalia.[203] All states have a law preventing female circumcision and this case seeks equal protection for boys.

Having said all this, it should be noted that as stated earlier in this chapter, infant males who are circumcised do have fewer urinary track infections during the first few months of life than their uncircumcised brothers. But in both groups, the rate is lower than seen in infant girls. Thankfully, these infections are easily diagnosed and treated and rarely have any lasting effects.

In summary, barring religious convictions and rare medical reasons, and nodding to the possibility that sexually active Sub-Saharan men properly circumcised in early adulthood may avoid AIDS, routine infant circumcision simply doesn't make sense and should not be performed. It hurts, it costs money, and it has been proven to have little health value—yet many parents relying on outdated or false information have their infant sons circumcised every year.

But Robert's admonition to not cut off something that works is about more than just circumcision.

Other Medical Practices to Avoid

Parents need to be alert to other medical and surgical procedures that may not really be necessary or, in fact, that may do more harm than good. Tonsillectomy and adenoidectomy (which most doctors call a *T and A*) is a good example. Once so common it was considered a milepost toward adulthood, "having your tonsils out" is rarely performed today.

Another operation being called into question is placement of ear tubes[204] in kids who have had repeated ear infections. Many studies have shown that these tubes do not change the incidence of hearing loss and rarely decrease the rate of recurrent infection. And yet there are other studies that show tubes may be helpful. This confusion of opinions has made myringotomy (ear) tube placement one of the most frequent operations today. Often, parents or their doctors know someone who got better after having tubes placed, so they rally for tubes. This type of testimony, which should not replace clinical research, has led to many unnecessary operations. Since there is a lack of agreement on this issue, it is important to review each case with more than one expert before making a decision to have tubes placed in a child's ears.

Hysterectomy has also come under severe attack. In the 1950s and early 1960s, many women had hysterectomies for reasons that have since been proven invalid. Consequently, insurance companies have stopped paying for hysterectomies except under very strict criteria, sparing women the pain and inconvenience of unnecessary surgery. I'm certain that the insurance companies' decisions were made for mostly financial reasons, but they first sought advice from expert physicians in cancer, gynecology, and women's health.

Prescription medications should also be considered carefully. It's easy to seek a quick fix for a child's illness in the form of a pill, but our desire for convenience can also lead to medical consequences. In an effort to decrease the development of antibiotic resistant bacteria, infectious disease specialists and the Centers for Disease Control

(CDC) are persuading doctors to avoid over-prescribing antibiotics. Because of their efforts, today's doctors never prescribe antibiotics for a cold, and are debating their use for ear infections. Many pediatricians are choosing to avoid antibiotics in kids who have an earache and a red eardrum unless there is a high fever or other signs of serious disease. Like colds, most of these infections are caused by viruses and do not respond to antibiotic use, and their overuse can cause germs to become resistant to antibiotics. If a doctor suggests an antibiotic for you or your child, ask if there is another option. Likewise, never request an antibiotic if your doctor thinks there is another way to treat your problem.

In the winter of 2007–08, parents were warned that most cold medications for young children were not effective and potentially dangerous. Investigators found no benefit from the use of decongestants. Rather, its chronic use resulted in sleeplessness, rapid heart rate, and hypertension. Cough medicines do not stop coughing. If they did, a patient's lungs would fill up with fluid and no longer be capable of supporting life. We are now back to using honey as a cough suppressant, just like our great grandmothers did.[205]

Some people might think all these changes are confusing. Perhaps they are, but one of the exciting things about practicing medicine is the development of new therapies as science learns more about life, health, and disease. In medicine, the only constant is change.

Do the Right Thing

There are times in all our lives when we need to make decisions: some easy and some difficult. Does something need to be done or should it be avoided? Will a procedure have a good or a poor outcome? Is it time for a new approach or should I stay the course? At those times, remember what Robert wisely said and ask yourself, "Is this like cutting something off that is working well?" The answer may help you avoid doing something that will *not* make things better.

My son Brian, an anesthesiologist, had this to say about making things "better."

"The enemy of good is not 'bad,'" he said, "but 'better.'" He gave as an example an IV that was running pretty well. "But I thought I could make it better, so I removed some tape and advanced the needle a bit before reapplying the tape. Of course, the IV slowed and stopped. I had to start all over with another needle stick. It was running "good," and I thought to make it "better"; but it turned out worse.

When it involves your health or your well-being, remember the first rule in medicine: *Primum non nocere,* i.e.: "First of all, do no harm." If something works well, leave well-enough alone!

OTHER SENSITIVE ISSUES

Man is small, and, therefore,
small is beautiful. To go for
giantism is to go for self-
destruction.

Ernst F. Schumacher, 1973

D R. FRANK PITTMAN in his book *Man Enough* says
one of the greatest sources of masculine shame
is concern over penis size.[206] "It's never big enough," he
says, at least not in the eyes of its owner. I'm not sure
that's a universal worry of boys, but it is more than urban
legend. Bill, who was 15 and depressed, made this point
clear to me. He taught me how this concern can be quite
destructive, even deadly, and how this adolescent worry
can be fed by pornography.

Bill had been hospitalized twice for attempted suicide
and was under the care of a psychiatrist who had him on a

number of anti-depressant drugs. Nonetheless, he was not doing well. His mother asked me to see him and I agreed, but only after she promised to continue his psychiatric care as well. The risk of teen suicide is never to be taken lightly.

Bill came willingly—his mother said he never really resisted doing whatever she asked—but he had a macabre countenance for such a young man. The high cheekbones of his thin, expressionless face cast shadows on his sharp jaw, and his black hair was combed straight back and plastered against his head in thick greasy cords. Moreover, his yellow teeth were covered with heavy brown plaque; he wore a black T-shirt that hung loosely over dirty, black jeans; and when he talked, he mumbled in a monotone, without the use of gestures.

Depressed patients always dampen my mood. Psychologists recognize this, too; it is a helpful tool they use in the diagnosis of depression. But it was getting to me, making me anxious to run out of the room and get to my next case. Nevertheless, I told his mother I would do a complete evaluation, so I trudged on.

He was quiet during the exam, and I was unusually serious in my approach. I did attempt an occasional joke, but I failed to provoke a response of any kind. I finished the exam and the usual inquiry about his health habits and made a note on his chart. Then I looked at Bill and thought I saw a tiny smile force its way onto his face. I wasn't sure it was a smile, but as it grew, it forced me to return the gesture. Now he did smile.

"Bill," I said, "You have a 100 percent perfect body

and are in great health." Then I looked into his big, black, puppy dog eyes and asked, "Why are you so unhappy?"

I never expected an answer, but he stared directly into my eyes, blinked back a tear, and said firmly, "How would you like to go through life with the world's smallest penis?"

I had just examined him and knew he had a normal-sized penis, but I also knew telling him would be more patronizing than reassuring.

I leaned back in my chair and thought for a minute. Then I answered, "Gee, I wouldn't like that at all."

"I don't either!" he answered, now unable to hold back the tears. "And there's nothing I can do about it. Right?"

I thought I'd heard everything—that nothing could shake me—but I didn't know how to respond. I needed more information so I asked, "How big ... or should I say how small is it?"

Without hesitation he replied, "I measured it a thousand times, and it's never more than five and one half inches, even when it's hard."

"Well," I continued, "How big do you think the average man's penis is?"

He started to come alive. He wrinkled his forehead and put on an anxious look. "I don't know for sure, but did you ever see John Holmes?"

"I know who John Holmes is, but I've never seen him or his penis." Holmes was a well-known porn star made famous by his incredibly large penis.

"Don't tell my mom, but I have one of his movies and I

watch it every day. I think his probably is bigger than average, or he wouldn't be in the movies, so I think the average is, ah, 16 inches. Is that about right? Mine is only about a third of that." His face fell.

"Bill, don't you see other boys during showers in gym or after sports?"

"No, I don't play any sports, and nobody takes showers in our school. The only dicks I ever saw were in porn movies." He reverted to the vernacular as he became more comfortable talking with me. "You just can't go around looking at other guys' dicks."

"Come with me, Bill." I left the exam room and he followed me to my consultation office. "Let's look something up." I took a book off the shelf and rapidly thumbed the index. Then I quickly turned to a table of measurements. "Bill, look at this table. What does it say is the average size of an adult penis?"[207]

He stared at the page for a long time and then read in a thin, quaking voice, "'Five and one half inches.' Is that right?" he asked. "Do you think that's right?"

"Yeah, I'm sure that's right," I said matter-of-factly.

"I can't believe it!" He actually smiled. Then he laughed. "I just can't believe it; that means I'm normal! Do you think mine is normal?"

I just smiled and nodded my head slowly up and down. "Yes, Bill, yours is normal. Why don't you think about what you learned today and come back and see me next week and let me know how it's going. And one more thing, throw away that porn movie. It's not doing you any good."

The Dangers of Pornography

Pornography, and its alarming proliferation on the Internet, is doing none of us any good. The Kaiser Family Foundation reported that 70 percent of 15- to 17-year-olds "accidentally came across pornography" while searching for other information online.[208] A study of 1,500 kids reported in the *Pediatrics* journal of February 2007[209] found that 30 percent of 16- to17-year-old boys inadvertently encountered unwanted porn on the net. An additional 38 percent intentionally viewed porn sites. Of girls the same age, 8 percent searched for and watched porn while 38 percent came across porn when searching for other topics. Sadly, 40 percent of these kids thought porn was normal and "not a big deal."

But it is a big deal!!

Steve Walters from Focus on The Family, an American evangelical non-profit organization, says:

> There is a critical period in a child's life where they're developing what you would call the "hard-wire" for their understanding of sexuality—what's normal, what's abnormal, what's healthy, what's unhealthy. If you expose a child to all these obscene and inappropriate images at this point, they'll process it as normal and healthy, because they really don't have the discernment to know better.[210]

The relationship of pornography to child sexual abuse

is compelling. A report to the Canadian Department of Justice noted that, "75% of those who molested boys and 87% of those who molested girls said they were regular viewers of hard-core pornography."[211] And that was in 1983—long before porn was widely available on the Internet. Not that every boy who watches porn will become the next Ted Bundy, an admitted porn addict and a criminal executed for multiple murders, but it does increase his risk of danger. It's not only hard-core porn that is dangerous. Children, especially boys who view soft porn available in magazines, clothing catalogues, television shows, and movies, are at a serious risk for developing emotional problems. Unreal situations, featuring people with unreal bodies having unreal sex without consequences, wreaks havoc on unsuspecting young minds.

Effects of Pornography on the Male Mind

Dr. Gary Brooks in his book *The Centerfold Syndrome* describes five of the most common consequences of boys watching porn.[212]

Voyeurism: Looking at women instead of interacting with them can lead to obsession with visual stimulation at the expense of a healthy psychosexual relationship. It distorts real images of women and trivializes their other attributes.

Objectification: Women become objects for sex. Often, a man will not be able to develop an intimate emotional connection with real women if he has spent most of his psychic energy fantasizing about inaccessible people.

Validation: Beautiful women become necessary to validate a man's masculinity. Men in this situation feel cheated because they were never able to have sex with the women of their dreams.

Trophyism: Today, many successful, middle-aged men have divorced and married young, gorgeous women half their age. They call their new spouse their "Trophy Wife." Many of these men have learned from watching porn that women are trophies to own, collect, and "hang on their wall." They collected beautiful cheerleaders as high school kids, and continue to collect trophies either through serial marriages or extramarital affairs.

Fear of true intimacy: Men learn to substitute sex for intimacy, even though they are badly in need of connection and intimacy.

Perhaps this explains why some men are so reluctant to marry and why others are unfaithful to their spouses. They have not learned to care for another person because they constantly try to satisfy their own needs. Porn addicts are often unable to relate to women in a non-sexual manner and are emotionally unavailable for intimate relationships.[213]

Among other problems, porn exploits and degrades people—especially women and children—and it undermines families and distorts personal and social relationships. Professors Dolf Zillman and Jennings Bryant noted that, "repeated exposure to pornography results in decreased satisfaction with one's sexual partner";[214] and a study conducted by Dr. Reo M. Christensen of Miami University in Oxford, Ohio, found that "pornography leaves the impression with its viewers that sex has no relationship to privacy; that it is unrelated to love, commitment or marriage."[215]

Hypocrisy in the Home

Many media, including the television, video games, and magazines found in many homes, present tantalizing, sensual material as typical teenage behavior. Such media and their soft porn are accepted as normal by much of today's society. What lessons are they teaching our children? Several years ago, my brother-in-law threw the *Sports Illustrated* Swimsuit Edition into his wood-burning stove as he walked from the mailbox. "No reason to let my teenage sons think this type of trash is in any way good for them," he said. And he was right. But how does the rest of the country view this "soft porn" edition of *Sports Illustrated*? How do you?

Cal Thomas in his March 13, 2008, column goes so far as to call all of us hypocrites when he says:

> We watch and tolerate the most salacious television programs; we produce soft pornography to sell in grocery stores, displaying it on checkout line shelves, we post hardcore porn

on the Internet; we feature on magazine covers women who have had babies with sperm donors they call boyfriends, but do not marry them; girls are sexualized at ever-younger ages; we equate shacking up with marriage as equal moral choices and then express shock when members of both political parties behave in ways that emulate what they see the rest of us tacitly approving.[216]

The same can be said of our children who too often adopt the behaviors they see on their televisions every day, the very behaviors we claim to detest.

One thing I will never understand is how our society can refer to porn and its ilk as "adult" or "mature?" What is adult or mature about watching porn? I can find no evidence that mature, healthy adults either need or use porn. On the contrary, watching porn indicates immaturity. There must be a more appropriate name for porn, such as "sophomoric," which means foolish, or perhaps "moronic." But please, let's stop referring to such trash as "adult." Call it like it is—porn is porn!

Sometimes Average Is Good Enough

Bill and I talked a bit more about penis size and porn before returning to the lobby where his mom was waiting. Tears filled her eyes when he laughed and said, "We need to make another appointment for next week."

"I haven't seen him smile in almost two years," She

whispered as she made the appointment. "Thank you, Doctor."

I saw Bill again the next week and the next, and several times over the next few months. At first he wanted to look at the table in the book each time he came in, but his mood rapidly improved, and in a short time his psychiatrist took him off his meds. I saw him for the last time almost two years later. He was a happy, dating high school senior. I'm not naive enough to think Bill's depression was caused merely by concern over the size of his penis; depression is much more complicated than that. But depression can cause a person's thinking to get stuck on one problem (or perceived problem) and prevent healthy thoughts that can lead to recovery.

I learned later that in the South, at least in Atlanta, boys don't shower in school after physical education or sports. During their annual health evaluations, I asked 378 teenage boys if they had ever taken group showers in gym, at camp, at the "Y," or any other place: 252 (67 percent) had not. Unlike the kids I knew from the Midwest, Southern boys are very modest. They wear their gym shorts under their school pants and don't remove anything but their outer pants to "dress out" for gym. I did not know this when I saw Bill.

In 1992, Morris Green, a Professor of Pediatrics at Indiana University Medical Center, recommended a health evaluation history form which included a question that asked girls if they were concerned that their breasts were too small; or if boys felt their penises were not big enough.[217] After seeing Bill, I began to ask these questions.

Since then, I have found many boys who had concerns like Bill's. Some of the boys think the question is funny, but their laughter belies their concern. I kept track of the answers from 215 high school boys I examined in 1997. Thirty-four (16 percent) of them believed that their penises were too short. But when I changed the question in 1999 from how many thought their penis was too small to how many wished it were bigger, 104 out of 174 (60 percent) wished they had a larger penis. However, neither the question nor the answer is important. The important thing is that someone was there to listen to their concerns and tell them what was normal. A quick reassurance of normalcy helps prevent a lot of worry. Only one boy in the ten years I have been asking these questions thought his penis was too big.

Jake, a 16-year old boy I had taken care of for a number of years, summed up the issue nicely. He had heard all the questions before and was prepared when I asked if he had any concerns about the size of his penis.

"No," he said, "It doesn't matter how big it is, as long as you can find it in the dark and don't step on it in the shower."

IT DOESN'T MATTER HOW BIG IT IS, AS LONG AS YOU CAN FIND IT IN THE DARK AND DON'T STEP ON IT IN THE SHOWER

Size really doesn't matter. Even though many boys and men think bigger is better, few know what the average size is. Most boys are too embarrassed to ask their doctor or their dad (even if he would know), and they can't ask a friend lest they appear gay; so they sneak a peek in locker rooms when possible, or more commonly, look at porn stars. And they feel inadequate. Bill made a good point regarding porn stars, but few boys know that the flaccid (soft) penis varies much in length, but the erect size is more uniform. More than 90 percent are less than six inches when erect.

Other Issues of Concern

There are many other issues boys face in their developing sexuality. One winter day in Wisconsin, a junior high boy came in with his mother and asked her to leave the room because he had a "personal problem."

"I think I have VD," he said. "I don't know how I got it. Trust me; I didn't have sex with anybody. I just don't know."

"Gee, I'm sorry things aren't going so well with you," I replied. "How do you know you have VD?"

"Last night I had pus come out of my penis. Isn't that a sign of VD?" he asked.

"Is there any pus coming out now?"

"No," he answered. "It just happened one time."

I asked a few more questions and after examining him, I was sure he did not have VD. He had had his first nocturnal emission, or "wet dream." He didn't know that was normal.

He expressed his gratitude and when his mom came back into the room, he smiled and let out a long sigh. "Sorry, Mom," he said. "There's nothing wrong with me. I'm just normal."

Later that same day another boy came to see me because he was 16 and had never had a wet dream. "There must be something wrong!" he concluded.

Again, after a series of questions and a brief exam, I assured him that he, too, was normal, and that boys who masturbate regularly don't accumulate enough semen to have a nocturnal emission.

Another concern many teen boys experience is a lump under their nipples which may or may not be tender. They often believe they are developing breasts and are rightly worried. More than 90 percent of the time this swelling is normal and goes away by itself, but these boys need to be examined by a doctor to make sure that they are not one of the ones who have a medical problem.

Girls, too, have concerns about their sexuality. I remember a wonderful, thin, athletic girl of 14 whom I had known for many years. When she came for her annual exam, she was concerned because she had not had her first period.

"Don't even ask," she laughed. "I'm not pregnant."

I laughed with her, asked a few more questions, finished my exam, and explained. "Julie," I began, "I'm sure you're not pregnant. Many thin, athletic girls do not have periods. Sometimes they have a few periods, and then stop. You know you need to have a little fat. I think that nature knows you are exercising strenuously and need all the iron you can get. You remember from freshman health, I'm sure, that you need iron to make blood, and you need more blood to carry all the oxygen your muscles need. You remember that, don't you?"

"Right," she replied. "I didn't learn that just so I could forget it." We laughed again.

"The other thing," I continued. "You have enough signs of good health and, even though you're thin, you have enough fat that I'm sure you'll have your period before I see you next year."

"That's easy for you to say," she replied. "I'll bet you a dollar I won't have it before I'm 15."

"That's a bet," I wagered.

Four months later, Julie's dad literally carried her into my office wrapped in a blanket, sick as can be with a high fever, headache, and a sore throat. As he placed her on the table she croaked, "Dad, give him a dollar."

"What?" Dad asked.

"Just give him a dollar and he'll explain everything." Then turning to me she smiled and added, "Won't you Doctor?"

Dad handed me a dollar and I explained the bet to him. After the exam I told her she had mono, explained the disease and treatment to her and her dad, and gave her back the dollar.

On another note, many girls are concerned that their breasts are too small, too large, or asymmetrical. All of these are normal variants and unless a girl's weight is too high causing her breasts to be too large, or too low with associated small breasts, there is not much they can do.

There are many other concerns that boys and girls may have during adolescence which are out of the scope of this book; but these are the most common and show the value of having a good rapport with your kids, a regular doctor, and an approachable youth minister (as mentioned in the section on Religion).

Helping Teens to Talk

Getting back to Bill, my depressed patient. I suspect you're asking how I was able to extract such sensitive material from him when the psychiatrist could not. Part of it has to do with the way psychiatry is practiced today. Many psychiatrists spend little time talking with their patients. They collect enough information to make a diagnosis and prescribe a medication. Then they refer the person to a psychologist or psychiatric social worker for "talk" therapy or counseling. That's what Bill's doctor did. Usually things work out all right doing that, but Bill's social worker was a shy, young, nun-like woman, and Bill simply could not discuss his "problem" with her.

Then there's the way I talk with my male patients. I sit next to them, not across from them in a confrontational mode. It's kind of like the way men sit and talk at a bar or in a golf cart. Girls and women, on the other hand, are more comfortable sitting face to face or across a table or desk, so that's how I interview them.

I try to avoid complicated medical words and use phrases kids know and understand; sometimes, I even use the vernacular. When I talk about sensitive issues like drugs or sex, I ask first about what the kids at school are doing or what they think, then I'll ask about friends' activities, and finally I ask about them. Because they didn't hear me condemn their schoolmates or their friends, they feel comfortable talking with me. They know I want to hear what they have to say because I listen. Then they listen to what I have to say, and I say it without telling them they are stupid or wrong.

Sometimes it's hard to give advice without being judgmental; and too often parents, counselors, and other adults withhold advice for fear of being perceived as judgmental. Kids really want to know what the adults they respect think, so I let them know what I think and they listen—but only after I have listened to them.

Again, one of the really important things in talking to boys or men is sitting shoulder to shoulder. That's when we males talk best, even if the subject is something as sensitive as penis size. We males are strange creatures. If we focused as much on, say, the health of our hearts instead of the size of our penises, we'd probably all live to be 120.

Finally, the thing my other patient, Jake, didn't say is that in a sexual relationship it's not what is between your legs that counts, it's what is between your ears and in your heart. When it comes to brains and hearts, bigger *is* better.

CHAPTER 18

SUICIDE

Alack, what heinous sin is it in me to be ashamed to be my father's child, but though I am a daughter to his blood, I am not to his manners.

Jessica. *The Merchant of Venice*

*P*OPULAR MYTH HOLDS that the holiday season sees the highest suicide rates. All the merriment that abounds simply makes these aggrieved souls more miserable over their depressed state. Even in the celebrated holiday classic *It's A Wonderful Life,* George Bailey is getting ready to take a suicidal plunge on Christmas Eve, contemplating a jump off the bridge in Bedford Falls because by the measure of dollars and cents, he is worth more dead than alive. But as we all know, Clarence the Angel beats him to it, diving into the river and calling upon Bailey's morals to save a life instead of taking his own. Bailey ultimately realizes he has a lot to live for, as do we all. He indeed is the richest man in town, based upon a more lasting measure of friends and family and their love for one another.

Springtime actually holds the infamous distinction for being the season of most suicides.[218] Yet I think society takes suicides much harder over the holidays when so many of us are trying to spread yuletide cheer, cheer that makes the season magical. Someone so far down and so angry that he or she can't celebrate or sense any hope really saddens us. The thought of a teen taking his or her life just a few years removed from believing in Santa Claus is saddest of all.

Near Tragedy on Christmas

It was during one Christmas when my family and I were having brunch in our dining room that I faced this sadness in the season of cheer. In addition to all the usual brunch fare, my wife Mary had made our family's favorite—poppy seed kuchen—and I had just sliced a traditional succulent rib roast. Our daughter Maura and her family were visiting from Ohio. Two sons from Tennessee were also with us, with their wives and kids. Our third son was in Colorado enjoying Christmas with his in-laws. Everybody was dressed in his or her Sunday best. We were having a great time enjoying a day made for a Christmas card.

Then the phone rang. Maura, ever the schoolgirl, rushed to answer, but returned shortly to the dining room with a long face. "Dad, it's for you," she said flatly, throwing me a glare as she handed me the phone. "Why can't we ever have a meal without somebody calling you?"

I took the phone into the kitchen and heard the nurse from the mental health unit at St. Mary's Hospital tell me about Wendy, a high school girl who had been admitted to the intensive care unit the evening before because of a suicide attempt. She had overdosed on two handfuls of pills. After treatment and observation, she was doing well and was being transferred to the "unit," the name hospital staff has for what we used to call the "psych ward." I was responsible for the medical care of patients admitted for psychiatric care, so I had to go see her.

"You don't need to rush in," Nurse Nellie confided. "After all, it's Christmas and she's fine physically, but what a life she's had. You won't believe it. Be thankful she's not your daughter, but you should come see her before dark."

Before I could ask any questions, Nurse Nellie hung up. I knew Nellie well. She ran the ward and when she said "Come," I knew to be there ASAP; if she said, "Come later," I knew things were under control and I could go in later.

"It's no problem," I explained to the family on my return to the dining room. "I won't have to go in until later this afternoon." The table was quiet for a moment as everyone pondered Maura's earlier complaint about why there couldn't be a family meal without a phone call. Inside, they all knew the answer.

We continued with our holiday brunch and our spirits soon lifted. But as much as I enjoyed the food, the conversation, and my family, I couldn't help wondering about Wendy. What kind of a life was she having? Why wasn't she having dinner with her family? Why would a high school girl want to end her life, particularly on such a joyous day when we draw closer to our support system of family and friends?

We finished our brunch with chocolate mousse, cleaned up the dishes, and enjoyed newly opened presents. Still, Wendy was on my mind. When the grandbabies went down for naps, I slipped away.

On the way to Wendy's room, Nurse Nellie began to grumble. "She hasn't eaten a thing all day. She refuses to shower or get dressed; all she does is stare at the ceiling. And all I can say to you is *good luck.*" Nellie was never short with patients and rarely misjudged them, so I wondered what I would find on the other side of Wendy's door.

"Hi, Wendy," Nurse Nellie sang in her usual smiley voice. "This is Doctor Donahue. Remember, I told you this morning he would be coming to see you? Talk with him a few minutes, and then I'll meet you two in the exam room. You'll like him, and I bet you'll even feel better when he leaves."

I knew what Nellie meant by that last remark, but I was sure Wendy thought she sure would feel better after I left—because I'd be gone! Wendy continued to stare at the ceiling and did not acknowledge Nellie or me.

"Hi, Wendy," I said. "Sorry to meet you here on Christmas Day. May I please sit down?"

I stood by the bed for a few seconds, but it seemed like

an hour before she turned her head and said almost with surprise, "You have to ask me if you can sit down?" Then before I could respond she motioned to the only chair in the room and said, "Be my guest." She emphasized "guest" and enjoyed her tone of sarcasm as she paused and heightened the unease by saying, "Would you like me to fix you a drink?"

"No. I'm fine," I said, thinking that I never had a 15-year-old girl offer to fix me a drink before. I wondered what she meant to convey with that remark.

She immediately read the bewilderment on my face. She turned, sat up on the edge of the bed, and laughed a hollow, sad laugh. "I'm sorry," she said. "And please forgive the way I look."

She really looked a mess. The hospital staff had given her something to make her vomit when she came in, and she still had some on her coarse blond hair. The staff followed the vomiting with activated charcoal, which she also vomited, leaving a heavy black ring around her mouth. Streaks of black charcoal were embedded in her hair, which competed with the streaks of black mascara that ran down her cheeks. Apparently ER nurses had also passed a nasogastric tube, too, as there was blood around her right nostril.

"No apology needed," I answered. "I understand you've been through a lot since you came to this place."

She glared at me, rejecting any compassion extended her way. She was intent on keeping her room charged with the anger she was feeling inside.

Then she lashed out, "How would you know? You

were probably home having dinner with your perfect little family. How many perfect children do you and your perfect little wife have?"

Oh, she was trying to be a tough one, but I knew not to take the bait. Not showing any inkling of anger, I replied, "As a matter of fact we were having breakfast when Nurse Nellie called. Since then, I have been worried about you."

"Why would you worry about me?" she asked, incredulous at the very thought of an adult caring about her plight.

"Well, I guess that's the kind of guy I am, and besides, it's my job. Now, can you tell me what you're doing here?"

"I got scared and called 911."

"*You* called 911?" I asked.

"Yes, I didn't really want to die" she explained.

"Goodness no, no one wants to die."

"Well, I did. Or I mean I thought I did. But I really didn't. I guess I'm confused. Do we have to talk about this?"

"No, I could just go home and be with my perfect family and you could stay here and be confused. But before I go, please tell me why a beautiful girl would think about ending her life, even if she didn't want to."

"Well, last night was Christmas Eve, and my boyfriend left me," she said.

"Your boyfriend left you on Christmas Eve?"

"Yes," she was starting to cry now. "He had to go see his children, and he wouldn't take me along. I told him I would be glad to be with him. I had no place to go anyhow."

"Couldn't you have just stayed with your folks?"

"See, I knew you wouldn't understand," Wendy said, sensing in me the apparent trouble she faced in communicating with other adults in her life. "My folks are divorced, and I was living with my mom until she got married this summer. I didn't like her new husband, so I moved in with my boyfriend."

"How old is your boyfriend?"

"Well, he had his birthday last month and he was 35. I bought him a new watch."

"What did your dad say when you moved in with a man almost his own age?" I asked, hardly believing the story that was unfolding.

"He didn't care." Wendy said. "I wanted to live with dad, but he said I couldn't because with his new baby, there wasn't room."

"Your dad didn't care?" I replied, controlling myself to keep from shouting.

"No, he didn't care. Don't you think if you have a daughter you should care about her?"

"I certainly do! How can a man do that to his own daughter? What on earth is wrong with him?" I replied indignantly. I wasn't really trying to take

IF YOU HAVE A DAUGHTER YOU SHOULD CARE ABOUT HER

her side, or convince her of anything. But I have to admit I lost all objectivity. I wanted not to believe this outrageous tale, but I knew something had driven her to try and take her life on Christmas Eve.

"I'm sorry, Wendy," I quickly added, trying to keep the

conversation as open ended as possible. "I shouldn't have said that about your father. Maybe there are some reasons we don't understand. Maybe..." But I could not think of a single reason to excuse this abominable behavior.

"It's okay," Wendy said, trying to console me in my outrage. "That's just the way he is."

It's hard to imagine that teens must face such family situations at a time in their lives when they need parental support the most. I had just come from a Christmas brunch where there were several sets of parents for two generations of children. And this girl, Wendy, couldn't find one parent who cared. And that made her angry and depressed enough to try and take her life.

Teens Need Their Parents

Leonard Pitts, a Pulitzer Prize-winning columnist for *The Miami Herald*, wrote about a "discovery that dramatically reduces the chance that a teenager will use drugs, drink alcohol, smoke cigarettes, attempt suicide, experience depression, engage in violence, or become sexually active at an early age. It's called loving parents."[219]

Somehow this comes as no surprise to any of us. But he was actually commenting on the results of a four-year, $25 million study (using tax dollars) called the National Longitudinal Study of Adolescent Health. This study of 90,000 teenagers showed that "kids who feel loved, [and are] understood and noticed by their parents ... are kids who are more likely to avoid dangerous behaviors that can derail their futures."[220]

Fathers in particular are an important influence, not only so their sons will become well-adjusted men, but so their daughters (like Wendy) can determine what kind of men they want in their lives. The love and approval some daughters cannot get from their fathers often forces them to look for it in other, older males. And the relationship Wendy had with a man more than twice her age shows the extremes to which they'll go to seek this nurturing.

Consider this statement from a 2005 Statistics Canada study:

> Young people who reported that their relationship with their father had increased in closeness, understanding, and affection over time were more likely to have lower scores of symptoms of depression at ages 16 and 17, compared with young people who responded that their relationship got worse.[221]

Another study, this one of almost a million kids in Sweden, showed that children growing up in single-parent families are twice as likely as their counterparts to develop serious psychiatric illnesses such as depression, schizophrenia, and addictions, and were more likely to attempt suicide or succeed in killing themselves.[222]

But we should not delude ourselves into thinking that only kids from bad or broken homes attempt suicide. More than 4,000 youths (ages 10 to 24) kill themselves in our country each year,[223] making suicide a more common cause of death for this age group than cancer, heart disease,

AIDS, and all natural causes combined. Only traffic accidents and murder take more of our young people's lives. Murder and suicide are the number two and three causes of death in this age group, and suicide happens in affluent homes as well as poor ones.

Depression and Suicide

There is an obvious connection between depression and suicide.[†] All depressed individuals should be evaluated by a mental health worker to determine their suicide risk. Depression has always been a major problem, but for some unexplained reason it is increasing in prevalence. Today, 3 to 8 percent of teens and 15 to 18 percent of adults are depressed. Interestingly, if a person's parents are depressed, the risk for a teenager jumps to six times that of a teen whose parents are not depressed.[224] Even more interesting, if the parent is treated with antidepressant medication, it is very likely that the child will get well, too.

There are many kinds of depression, including what psychiatrists call major depression. In Pat Conroy's *Prince of Tides*, Savannah had this type of depression. She was also psychotic, probably with bipolar disease as well. Conroy does an amazing job of describing the hell which exists in Savannah's mind; and consequently, in her life. He also describes the futility of treatment. Fortunately, this type

---

[†] According to an article in the February 2010 issue of *Pediatrics*, 1,771 kids between the ages of 10 and 19 committed suicide in 2006. (Kimberly A. Schwartz, et. al., "Attitudes and Beliefs of Adolescents and Parents Regarding Adolescent Suicide," *Pediatrics* 125 (2) (February 2010): 221–227.)

of depression is not as common as what I call situational depression which stems from a loss or perceived loss in a patient's life.

Dr. Meg Meeker in her book *Strong Fathers, Strong Daughters* says that for many girls, depression is caused by having a sexual relationship, either voluntarily or against her will.[225] When I read that, I thought perhaps she was mixing the cause and the effect; but she quoted an article in the *American Journal of Preventive Medicine* that supported her claim. This is an outstanding article that reported on a study of 13,491 seventh through eleventh graders from all over the United States—and then studied them again a year later. The authors concluded: "Present findings do not support the theory that youth initiate sex and drug behaviors to 'self-medicate' depression," thus disproving a commonly held theory. They went on to say, "Engaging in sex and drug behavior places adolescents, and especially girls, at risk for future depression." They explained that sex and drug use act separately, each of them causative factors, and together they greatly increase the risk. They showed further that the risk of depression increases with multiple sexual partners.[226]

Meeker goes on to call depression a sexually transmitted disease caused by loss of virginity. Like other forms of depression, medication, counseling, and psychotherapy are often needed. Early treatment is more likely to be effective. Meeker's book is also an excellent review of the father-daughter relationship and well worth reading.

One of the tragic things about practicing medicine is that sometimes nothing works; in spite of the best medicine in the best of hands, a depressed patient occasionally finds a way to end his or her life. The needless guilt this places on parents, family, teachers, counselors, and doctors may last a lifetime. While it is not another person's fault, loved ones often can't accept the fact that they are not to blame. They are the true victims of suicide and usually need professional help. Pray for them.

Wendy and I had a long, long talk and by the time Nurse Nellie came to take us to the exam room, we had both been through tears and laughter. The exam went well; physically, Wendy was as healthy as any other teen. We talked a few more minutes and I finally said, "Wendy, I guess we could talk all night, but I must get home to my family. Dr. Johnson, he's the one you called 'The Shrink,' will be in to see you tomorrow, and I'll stop by and see you tomorrow morning, too. If you have any problems during the night, just let one of the nurses know. If she can't help you, have her call me."

I extended my hand, but she threw her arms around my neck and gave me a long hug.

"Thanks for interrupting your Christmas to come and see me," she said, the sarcasm now completely gone. "And I'm sorry I called your family 'perfect,' though compared to me they probably are. I promise I'll shower and look better when you come tomorrow. Have a good night and thanks again."

"Good night," I answered. "I look forward to seeing you in the morning."

When I got home my family was just starting to put

dinner on the table. I gave them each a hug, but I gave Maura an especially long, firm one.

"It's okay," she said as she released her grip. "I don't know what went on with you these past two hours, but I know it was worth it. Thanks for doing what you do."

Social Services reported Wendy's parents for child neglect and found her a home with a foster family. They are also helping her bring charges of statutory rape against her boyfriend (in Georgia, the age of consent to intercourse is 16). I looked in on Wendy each day until Dr. Johnson discharged her a week later.

"Please have your foster mother bring you to see me in a week, but call the office for an appointment first. And promise me you'll not do anything to hurt yourself before I see you again."

"It's a deal!" she beamed as she gave me a parting hug.

Under Dr. Johnson's care, Wendy continued to improve. I lost track of her after a couple of weeks as she no longer needed to see both of us. I don't know what happened to her, but she never appeared in the "Unit" again.

Preventing Suicide

Suicide is a terrible thing; but if it is recognized early, it can often be prevented. As caring parents, friends, and professionals, we should be alert to these signs of depression which usually precede suicide:

- Sad, anxious, or empty mood.

- Declining school performance.

- Loss of pleasure in things meant to be pleasurable (called anhedonia, this is the most common symptom of depression).

- Loss of interest in sports or other social activities.

- Sleeping too little or too much.

- Change in weight or appetite.

The American Academy of Child and Adolescent Psychiatry notes these added pre-suicidal behaviors.[227] A teenager may:

- Complain of being a bad person or feeling rotten inside.

- Give verbal hints with statements such as: "I won't be a problem for you much longer," "nothing matters," "it's no use," and "I won't see you again."

- Put his or her affairs in order: give away favorite possessions, clean his or her room, throw away important belongings, etc.

- Become suddenly cheerful after a period of depression.

- Have signs of psychosis (hallucinations or bizarre thoughts).

If a teen you know shows these signs, get them some

professional help while you still can. Don't wait until they get confused like Wendy and take their life into their own hands; it may be too late. With help, suicide is preventable.

You can educate yourself more on teen suicide by going to www.mentalhealth.org/suicideprevention. It is the Web site for The National Strategy for Suicide Prevention (NSSP) which represents advocates, clinicians, researchers, and survivors around the nation, including the Centers for Disease Control and National Institutes of Health.

Unlike George Bailey from *It's a Wonderful Life*, Wendy didn't need an angel to convince her that she needed to live. This strong girl did it herself by calling 911. And I'm proud of her for that. Yes, her life wasn't wonderful—uncaring parents and a boyfriend way too old for her—but she decided to keep living because she knew she was worth it.

And she is worth it, and so are all the other teens who believe ending their life is the only choice. We can't guarantee them a wonderful life. But we can assure them that like Wendy, things can look very different and life can offer more plentiful choices with professional help from people who care.

PARENTING TIPS

- *Know the American Academy of Pediatrics' guidelines for TV watching and abide by them. Never put a TV in a child or teen's room.*

- *If your child has signs of ADD or ADHD, stop all TV, increase physical activity (preferably out of doors), and seek parenting guidance before ever agreeing to the use of medication.*

- *Do not allow TV, iPods or MP3 players during family time, including mealtime. Use this time to talk with your kids.*

- *Review your kid's immunization records with their physician and make sure they are up to date. Get flu shots for yourself and your kids.*

- *If you have a newborn son, spare him the pain of circumcision.*

- *Seek a second or third opinion before you allow a surgeon to put tubes in your kid's ears.*

- *Do not push your doctor to prescribe antibiotics; but if he does, be sure you understand why.*

- *Do not permit porn in your house. Never refer to porn of any kind as "adult" material.*

- *Know the signs of depression and pre-suicidal behavior; seek medical help if you see these signs in your child.*

- *Show your kids love, approval, and affirmation at all times.*

Living Well

When my son Sean was in the 8th grade, he informed me that he would be Valedictorian when he graduated from high school. He attained that goal. Although the kids in this section never talk about goals per se, they have them. They want to become healthy, happy adults. They want to get into college, control their anger, save some money, and treat people well. Whether they recognize it or not, they have dreams for the future; and as you will see, they are well on their way to realizing those dreams.

CHAPTER 19

THE HABIT OF HAPPINESS

The real world is not easy to live in. It is rough; it is slippery. Without the most clear-eyed adjustments we fall and get crushed.

Clarence Shepard Day

THE 1979 AWARD-WINNING movie *Breaking Away* won an Oscar for screenwriter Steve Tesich, and those who saw it were endeared to the teenage boy who wanted to be Italian. In the film, bicyclist Dave Stoller becomes enamored with the Cinzano racing team from Italy and spends the summer training and "becoming" Italian. He studies Italian, eats Italian food, listens to Rossini and Italian opera, and, much to his dad's chagrin, shaves his legs to emulate the foreign racers. When he meets a college girl, he pretends to be an Italian exchange student to impress her. The filming and screen writing were great, but

· · · 259 · · ·

what impressed me most was Dave's total commitment to becoming something he wasn't—Italian.

The desire to change, to become something they aren't (i.e., adults) is what all teenagers do. And it's what parents, teachers, coaches, and yes, even doctors, are supposed to help them do. For some, it's not an easy task; others seem to zoom into adulthood without the slightest hint of a problem. Many books have been written about the transition trying to explain the plethora of problems that can occur and how to avoid and treat them. Among these authors, Drs. James Dobson, Frank Pittman, David Elkind, and William Pollack come readily to mind; but 17-year-old Eric had an easier solution.

Becoming Who You Pretend to Be

I had seen Eric because of infectious mononucleosis (mono) during his junior year in high school. He was a talented basketball player, but his illness forced him to settle for a shortened season. I looked forward to seeing how well he would do his senior year, as did his coach and fellow students. He had many fans and friends because he was so much more than a basketball player; he was a student leader with a great attitude, and he was about to teach me a valuable lesson.

Early in his senior year he came to see me for his physical. When I entered the exam room he smiled, showing off dazzling white teeth. He rose to shake my hand and introduce his mother.

"Hi, Doctor." Then gesturing to his mom he added, "I

don't think you two have met. Dad always came with me before. This is my mother, Shirley."

Mother smiled with pride as she offered me her hand. "So nice to see you," she said, and then added, "Eric and his dad have told me so much about you. It is a pleasure to finally meet you."

We engaged in a bit of social chatter, reviewed Eric's health, and in due time, Mom retired to the lobby while Eric and I proceeded with his evaluation, which was unremarkable. As we finished I said, "Eric, you seem to be an outstanding young man. I'd be proud to have a son like you."

He thanked me and I asked him one of my pet questions. "Tell me, Eric, how would you like to have a son like you?"

"Like I am? Or, like I pretend to be?" he asked.

"Is there a difference?"

"Yes," he replied. "I sometimes get down and negative, but I try to be happy, optimistic, and positive because I know if you try, you will become the man you pretend to be."

> YOU WILL BECOME THE MAN YOU PRETEND TO BE

"Become the man you pretend to be," I echoed. "What an outstanding concept. And as I think about it, it really is what happens, isn't it?"

"One of my friends says, 'Fake it until you make it,' but I like the way I said it better. It sounds more optimistic. Don't you agree?" he asked.

"I sure do. How did you come up with this ... can I call it a philosophy?"

"I guess it is a philosophy, isn't it?" he answered. "I've never called it that. I just think of it as a way to become a better person. It started when I was in a school play in the seventh grade. I found out the more I acted like the character in the play, the more I became him. I wanted to be a good basketball player, too, so I thought, why not act like a good basketball player? So I did. Then Coach noticed I had more confidence, and he started to play me more, and that's how it started. Then in youth group we always talked about becoming better, and I thought if it works for basketball it should work for other stuff, too. I don't want to brag, and I'm not as good a person as I should be, but I keep on trying."

"Well, Eric, I think you're doing super!" I said. "Your philosophy is so great I want to tell other kids about it. Is that okay with you?"

"What do you mean?" he asked.

"Well, I see a lot of kids who have problems to overcome or who need to make some changes in their lives, and I think it may be helpful to tell them what you said about becoming the man you pretend to be. I wouldn't tell them it's your motto unless you want me to. What do you think?"

"Do it if you think it will help someone," Eric replied. "I know it helps my day go better."

Eric and I talked a bit more about his motto: how it relates to improving one's life and how it might help the transition from childhood to adulthood. Soon, his mom was back in the exam room and I told her how privileged I felt to be able to see and care for Eric. I asked him to discuss his philosophy with her on the way home.

Eric had a great senior basketball season and went on to play NCAA Division II college ball; I went on using his wisdom with my other patients.

The Power of the Positive

Eric's idea is not new, nor is it rare. It's just that I had never heard it expressed like that before. There's an old song from the late 1950s, "Pretend," whose lyrics suggest, "Pretend you're happy when you're blue." The songwriter knew that by pretending, you could become what you want to be.

In C. S. Lewis's *Screwtape Letters,* the devil (Screwtape) says, "All mortals tend to turn into the thing they are pretending to be."[228] Screwtape was a lead devil teaching his devil nephew how to gain control of a man. He was, of course, talking about bad habits, but the same can surely be said about developing good habits.

When my grandson Patrick was being honored as an Eagle Scout, I was reminded that Boy Scouts are "Trustworthy, Loyal, Helpful, Friendly, Courteous, Kind, Obedient, Cheerful, Thrifty, Brave, Clean," and "Reverent." Then I wondered if they really are all these things, or are they becoming all these things by pretending? Aren't they just rehearsing for the future?

Many might call the Scouts egotistical for confessing such virtues, thinking they are just daydreaming or lying to themselves; but professional motivators and coaches call that "visualizing success." Visualizing success causes the brain to believe we are already successful; and this subconscious belief gives us the confidence we need to be comfortable with success. It removes the fear of failure. As we continue to visualize the future and our place in it, our brain gives us positive feedback that prepares us for victory. In short, envision the future, plan for it, execute the plan, and enjoy the success.

Good basketball coaches tell their players to stand on the free-throw line and visualize the ball rising from your hands and dropping—swish— through the net.

Jack Nicklaus, probably the world's greatest golfer prior to the advent of Tiger Woods, says in his book *Golf My Way* that before every shot he "sees" the shot in his mind. "First, I 'see' the ball where I want it to finish. ... Then the scene changes and I 'see' the ball going there: its path, trajectory, and shape, even its behavior on landing. ... The next scene shows me making the kind of swing that will turn the previous images into reality."[229]

In addition to pretending, Eric also mentioned maintaining a positive attitude. Psychologist Donald Clifton said,

> Studies show that organizational leaders who share positive emotions have workgroups with a more positive mood-enhanced job satisfaction, greater engagement and improved group performance.[230]

Isn't that what all employers are looking for in their employees? And don't parents desire something similar for their "workgroup"— their kids? Parents who agree should try to develop positive attitudes and become the parents they know their kids need. We should listen to Eric and visualize ourselves as fulfilling the role of great parents. Then we will have the strength to make a plan to become who we want to be. It is no secret that kids' attitudes are learned from their parents. Parents with an "I can" attitude have children who know their accomplishments can be just short of limitless.[231]

A very interesting 2001 study reported in the *Journal of Personality and Social Psychology* looked at longevity in 180 Catholic nuns, ages 75 to 90, who in their early twenties had handwritten short autobiographies. The researchers found that the nuns who reported more positive emotions in their early bios lived an average of ten years longer than those with few positive emotions.[232] It would seem that a negative attitude is worse than smoking, which shortens the life of a smoker by up to seven years. Now I'm not suggesting that it's better to smoke than to be negative, but it does show the value of a positive attitude. A good attitude is a valuable predictor of longevity.

Visualizing the Positive

Some months after Eric's visit, I was talking with 14-year-old Connor about his health habits. It was the first time I had seen Connor. Mom was in the room as I was explaining how important good health habits are. "The habits you make in junior high and high school will determine how well and how long you will live," I said. And then, before I could ask him if he could think of any habits that would help make him healthy, he interjected: "What you're saying is, boys make the habits and the habits make the man, right?"

BOYS MAKE THE HABITS AND THE HABITS MAKE THE MAN

"Right," I replied, impressed. "Can you tell me more?"

"Nah, it's just what my dad tells me all the time. He's right, too, isn't he?"

I wish you could have seen his mother's smile. It was like a jet stream across the sky. This was Connor's moment and she just wanted to enjoy it, realizing what a great father she had picked for her son.

As Connor and his mom left the office, I got to thinking more about habits. Good habits—exercising, healthful eating, adequate sleep, reading, limiting TV, going to church, being optimistic, being happy—are all habits we make while we're young. So, too, bad habits—smoking, drinking, illicit drug use, deceitfulness, pessimism, disrespect for authority, promiscuous sexual activity, unnecessary risk taking, and aggressive behavior, to name only a few—are ingrained in us before we ever become adults. That's why the teen years are so important in one's life. Too bad so many parents (and society in general) don't understand how important this period of development is.

For a number of years, I taught in medical school. Each year about the beginning of the second semester, many third-year medical students would tell me, "Most of the diseases and problems we see are brought on by the patient." My own sons echoed the same observation when they were third-year medical students.

"Yes," I told them all. "Things haven't changed much since I was in school. We have learned that cervical cancer is almost always a sexually transmitted disease,[233] and now people are giving themselves AIDS; we didn't have that disease when I was a student. But you're right; many of the diseases we see are self-induced." Consider that lung cancer, chronic sinusitis, and bronchitis can all be caused by smoking; and alcohol is responsible for many marital conflicts as well as depression, suicide, cirrhosis, and a host of other physical and emotional diseases. Sexually transmitted diseases, many cases of infertility, throat cancer, and even adult onset diabetes are a few others that come to mind as being caused by bad habits learned in adolescence or before.

But the good news is that habits can be changed. It is not necessarily easy to change a habit, but it can be done. The secret is to visualize yourself without the old habit and with a new habit to replace it. Then make a plan to think like and act like the person you want to be!

Visualizing our new selves is probably the most important factor in making new habits. That is one of the reasons people who are trying to lose weight put a picture of a thin person on their refrigerator. It helps them visualize themselves as thin and boosts their confidence in their ability to stay on a weight-loss diet.

Ian Newby-Clark, an associate professor of psychology at the University of Guelph in Ontario, Canada, who studies habit change, claims there are five steps to forming a new habit.[234]

Work on One Habit at a Time. If you work on changing more than one habit at a time, you run a serious risk of overwhelming yourself and changing no habits at all.

Create a plan. Write it down, and be as specific as possible. Know what you want to do. Visualize it!

Refine your plan. Ask yourself, is your plan realistic? Lay your plan aside for a day or two and come back to it with fresh eyes. Ask a friend to review it to be sure it is a doable habit and not pie-in-the-sky.

Make Mini-Plans. Once your plan is as good as you can make it, break it down into steps or mini-plans.

Repeat! Repeat! Repeat! Repeat your behavior until it is automatic.

It usually takes about three weeks of repetitive behavior to develop a new habit or change an old one. If the habit has been around a long, long time, it may take more repetitions and more time, but persistence pays off and in time, even if there are relapses, the new habit can overcome the old. Many habits are so difficult that it takes much longer to develop them. Just think of how long it takes to become an accomplished musician. The many hours of daily practice soon become weeks of practice, months of practice, and then years of practice. To the virtuoso, practice becomes a habit, a way of life!

Letting Go of Bad Habits

Some of us have a few habits that need to be changed; others have many. We all have room in our lives to become better, to improve our health, to change our way of life. And we can do so by consistently making good choices until we have developed the habit to overcome our past behavior. Whatever our age, we all need to periodically review our health habits; our lives depend on them.

Sometimes developing new habits is, in reality, changing an entire life style. Often, we are forced to change our lives against our will. We might develop a chronic disease, lose a loved one, or move to a new home. How we adapt to these changes will depend more on what is inside of us than on what is happening around us. When adjusting to change, our attitude is always more important than the physical problem.

A patient of mine named Blake knew about bad habits and the need for change. He was representative of the kind of teenager every negative TV news story and movie about young people gone wild exploited. His dad was a pediatric surgeon who had recently moved from Arizona in order to be closer to his extended family and to get help for Blake.

When I entered the exam room, Blake was sitting on the exam table with his head in his hands staring at the floor. I extended my hand to Blake and waited a long second until he took it and gave it a weak squeeze. I did not release my grip until he looked me in the eye. Then I tightened it a bit, smiled, and said, "So nice to meet you. I'm sorry you had to come in on such a beautiful day."

I asked Blake to move off the table and onto the chair beside me. After a bit of small talk, I asked him and his dad about his past history, completed the exam, and began to inquire about his health habits.

"Blake," I began, "I have a few dozen questions I ask all the kids to see what kind of health habits they're developing. This is how we determine if you're going to live to be a hundred or if I should call 911 right now. Some of the questions are interesting, some are a bit embarrassing, and some may seem dumb, but they are all important. And remember, unless I think you're in grave danger, all your answers are confidential. Should we get started?"

"Okay, but let me tell you, I have had some bad habits and some good ones," Blake answered. "I'm trying to get rid of the bad ones, so don't be too hard on me!"

"Oh, I'm not here to lecture, judge, or punish your behavior," I assured him. "My job is to help you overcome the bad habits and reinforce the good ones. Since you're my patient, I feel we're in this thing together. Besides, I'm too much of a pushover to be a parole officer."

We laughed together and much too soon we were finished, but not until we talked about how he might turn things around in his life. Then I said, "Let me say, I really enjoyed talking with you. Looks like you have tried to get your life back in order and do the right thing. Everybody has done things they aren't proud of, you know. Don't let it get you down. Move on, as they say."

And then I looked him in the eye and said, "If you were my son, I would be proud of you!"

"Really?" he asked in surprise. "If I had a son like me I wouldn't be proud of him." He didn't smile when he said it.

"Hey, I told you I was an old softie; but look, I'm not proud of everything you ever did, I'm not even proud of everything I ever did," I replied, making my case to a teen who had obviously beaten himself down about his conduct as much as others had.

"People make mistakes. People also *stop* making mistakes. I'm proud that you realized what mistakes you were making and are willing to change your life. That would make any dad proud! Just remember, don't try to change too many things at one time. Adjustment isn't that easy, you know."

"Boy, I know that," Blake said. "First I had to adjust to high school, then we moved and I had to adjust to another school. I got in trouble and had to adjust to life in the lock up. I had to adjust to moving to an apartment in Georgia, then we moved to a house and I had to adjust to a new neighborhood. It seems like life is just one adjustment after another." Then he thought a while, smiled, and said, "Maybe we should all be chiropractors and learn how to adjust!"

> LIFE IS JUST ONE ADJUSTMENT AFTER ANOTHER

We both laughed out loud. His use of wit softened the punch after acknowledging one of the sad facts of life: the only thing we can count on is change! But change was a sore point for Blake, and I realized he needed to talk to someone about it.

We discussed the changes that took place in Blake's past and the changes he needed to make in his life habits. When his father came in to take him home, I took the opportunity to tell him what a fine boy I thought he had. "The three of us," I told him, "with the help of Blake's new counselor, just need to play Michelangelo and chip away the excess stone. So let the chips fly. Let me add, I really enjoyed meeting your son. He's got a lot going for him, and he'll do fine. You can be proud of him! I sure am."

The Value of Sincere Praise

I wondered how long it had been since someone had told Blake he was proud of him, despite his troubles. Or when was the last time someone gave him a compliment. Honest compliments and other affirmations are so important in how we see ourselves, how we see others and how we react to and with others, and how successful we are in life. A world-wide study[235] of over four million employees at more than 10,000 businesses found that individuals who receive consistent recognition and praise:

- increase productivity,
- improve relationships with co-workers,
- change jobs less often,
- are better liked by customers,
- have fewer injuries on the job.

To emphasize the strength and value of affirmation, I have two bags of beans in my office desk drawer: one of white beans and one of red beans. I give five of each to any patient who seems too negative and wants to improve his or her attitude and ask them to place the beans in the right front pocket of their pants. I instruct them to take out one bean each time they put a hand into that pocket. If the bean is white, they are to find something they like about the person they are with: their looks, their hair, their jewelry, something they're wearing, something they just said, or anything else they like, and give that person a sincere compliment. If they are by themselves, they are to find someone to compliment. If the bean is red, they are to think of something they like about themselves; and if they are alone, they should voice the self-compliment out loud. If others are present, it is enough to just think about the compliment and smile. In any case, after they give a sincere compliment, they place the bean in their left pocket. The goal is to move all the beans from the right to the left pocket each day. When they accomplish that, I give them more beans. Kids who follow this program change their observation of others; their impression of themselves and others; and in a few short weeks, their attitudes as well.

This program works for several reasons: when we give someone a sincere, heartfelt compliment, the recipient will usually smile and often return the compliment. After receiving two or three compliments, most people will start to notice the admirer, look forward to seeing him or her again, and soon endear themselves to the individual. When we compliment ourselves, we start to realize that we, too, have value. It is important to remember, however, that we must avoid insincerity at all costs. People, especially teenagers, see through false compliments immediately.

Blake displayed an almost despairing attitude; he was not proud of what he had done and not proud of himself. No one, it seems, not even himself, had ever given nod to anything positive about Blake. It's no wonder he needed to use drugs and delinquent behavior to boost his status. He was just the kind of "good kid" who would join a gang and we would all wonder why.

What Blake needed more than anything else was someone to believe in him; someone who believed, like John Locke, that "the sooner you treat [your son] as a man, the sooner he will begin to be one."[236] Someone needed to find the good inside of Blake and nourish it with sincere compliments and affirmations until he knew he was a valuable human being. Like all of us social beings, he needed someone to help him change.

Choosing Happiness

When we are faced with change there are several tacks we can take. We can deny it, we can fight it, we can accept it, or we can embrace it. If the change is unexpected and unwanted, we may progress through all of these stages—from denial to embracing—with difficulty. Our actions will parallel Dr. Elizabeth Kubler-Ross's stages of grief.[237] Her description (as it relates to change) can be paraphrased as follows: denial of the impending event, bargaining with

God or whoever is responsible for the event, becoming angry over the event, becoming depressed, and finally, arriving at resolution and acceptance.

To facilitate change in our lifestyle, it helps to focus first on the good things that may come with change, and try to keep our minds off the negatives. Then by visualizing our new life as better, we will have the energy needed to overcome the anger resulting from a change in our status quo. Most changes in our life turn out to be improvements if we look at them objectively. As we change, we discover that adjusting can be fun. Ben Hogan said, "One of the reasons golf is so fascinating is that the adjustments are endless."[238] So it is with life.

I saw Blake several more times during his last two years of high school. He had some problems with curfew and he met some friends who once helped him get marijuana—but only once. He didn't let a failure get him off track because he really wanted to change his life, and he had enough character to bounce back. By the time he graduated, he was drug free and ready to adjust to college.

I think of Blake often as I deal with life's changes: retirement, new friends, new town, new store, new church, new home, painful shoulder, painful back, sick grandchild, war, 9/11, taxes—the list is endless. But I try to remember what he said: "Life is just one adjustment after another." If we can enjoy the adjustments, our lives will be enriched and we'll be happier. After all, being happy is a habit. As Abraham Lincoln said, "People are just as happy as they make up their minds to be."[239] Take an hour or two and watch *Breaking Away* and do as Dave did: decide to be happy.

As to bouncing back, I'll never forget the lesson my 11-year-old son Brian taught me many years ago when we were skiing. We had taken a hot chocolate break when a fellow skier asked Brian if he was having fun. Brian assured him he was having a great time, so the stranger asked, "Did you have any falls?"

"Yep," Brian replied, "and I had fourteen get-ups today."

"Get-ups?" the man questioned. "What is a get-up?"

Brian looked at him incredulously. "A get-up is what you do when you fall down. Falls don't count, get-ups do!"

We all fall, but it's what we do after we fall that's important. Remember to get up!

CHAPTER 20

CONTROLLING AND USING ANGER

Anger is likely to be both a useful tool to survive and a disease in which the heart turns to stone.

Journal of Child and
Adolescent Psychiatric Nursing

*W*HEN IT COMES to legitimizing anger, actor Peter Finch in the movie *Network* uttered one of the most memorable lines I've heard: "I'm mad as hell and I'm not going to take it anymore!" It thrilled the television studio audience in the movie, and real-life audiences in the movie theaters.

Anger is often considered a righteous and courageous response from the downtrodden and those wronged, and a lot of us feel downtrodden or wronged at some time in our lives. On television and in the comic books, Dr. Bruce Banner could not turn into the crime-fighting Incredible

Hulk unless someone really ticked him off. Then his clothes ripped, his skin turned green, and his body rippled with muscle upon muscle—like a baseball player on steroids—and we cheered as he stomped the bad guys into submission.

Real life, however, is a better venue to witness anger and society's struggle with it. We got angry as a nation after 9/11 and were prepared to go anywhere to vanquish the terrorists who attacked us without provocation. One place we went was Iraq. That war unleashed a new wave of anger across America that we hadn't seen since Vietnam.

This time, as in the Vietnam era, it was Americans against Americans. People disagreed strongly and sometimes violently about the war. The presidential election of 2004 heightened the intensity of feelings between Blue State and Red State Americans, fueling an angry debate about the integrity of the two front-runners. The 2008 presidential election was even more discordant as anger over the war continued to escalate. Anger in our society has clearly become an acceptable tool for human behavior, and in some instances, the preferred one. Arnold Schwarzenegger made his name with shoot-'em-up, fight-back movies filled with anger and revenge, and what did that image get him? The governor's seat in California! Voters saw his "Hasta La Vista, Baby" persona as representative of a nononsense man strong enough to straighten out the state's many problems and knucklehead the lawmakers in Sacramento. In our modern-day culture, anger denotes strength; anger represents bravery. But as Eric Hoffer cautions: "Rudeness is the weak man's imitation of strength." [240]

Anger Isn't Smart

Most anger isn't smart. Smart trumps anger almost every time because smart can deliver better results without all the risk. A recent Duke study found that "the covariation of hostility, anger, depression, and anxiety accounts for the increased risk of coronary heart disease (CHD) associated with each individual factor."[241] In short, that means that each of these negative personality factors increases the risk of CHD, and a combination of them *seriously* increases the risk of CHD.

Being smart instead of angry is not always easy, but I learned two ways of handling anger from Jacob, a high school boy who moved into our neighborhood just in time for me to hire him and his new friend Ryan to help me with some early spring planting. They were hard workers and I continued to use them off and on that spring and summer. Jacob brought his folks over to see the shrubbery screen we had planted and the waterfall we made, complete with pond and circulating pump. He was especially excited to show them the toilet valve we hooked up to the water line to keep the pond full. Through him, Mary and I became friends of his parents. We were all proud of Jacob.

Sometime later that summer, Jacob came to see me for his physical. We proceeded to the habit-review questions and he seemed to enjoy answering them. He was the kind of boy every parent wants, and he and I both knew it.

"How often do you get in a fight?" I asked.

"A fight? You mean like a fistfight or hitting somebody or getting hit? Gosh, never!"

"Good," I said. "I guess that was an unnecessary question, but I ask all the kids all the questions so I don't miss anything. Let me continue. How often do you get angry or mad?"

"Never," Jacob answered.

"Never?"

"Well, almost never. I try never to get mad because I found out that every time I get mad, things get worse."

EVERY TIME I GET MAD, THINGS GET WORSE

I wanted to shout, "Hey, what a great lesson that is!" but I knew that would turn him off and I really wanted to hear more about how he came to this conclusion. So I repeated what he had said. "Every time you get mad things get worse? How so?"

"Well," he said. "You know my little sister. Everybody thinks she's so great because of the way she plays the piano. She can be nice, but sometimes she really bugs me. Like she used to go into my room when I was gone and mess up my things. Then when I got home and found everything a mess, I'd get mad and yell at her and try to get her to undo the mess she'd made. But as soon as I started yelling, Mom or Dad would hear me and I'd get in trouble. Then, to make matters worse, when I did get grounded she would taunt me and make me even madder.

"Then I thought, I got in trouble for what she did! So I came up with a plan. The next time she messed up my desk, instead of getting mad I called Mom up to my room and said, 'Look Mom, someone must have been in my room when I was gone. They threw all the things off my desk and the model I was working on is broken. Do you think we had a burglar?'

"I knew who had done it and Mom knew, too. Her face got bright red and she shouted, 'Donna, get in here! Now!' And she got grounded. I'll never forget that day. So I decided not to get mad at Donna anymore. It worked, too, because now if she does get into my stuff, Mom and Dad get mad at her instead of me. I think she finally learned a lesson, too, because she hardly ever messes with my stuff anymore.

"Then I learned the same thing playing golf. If I missed a shot and got mad, my next shot would be worse. But if I just laughed and said, 'I guess the golf gods are mad at me,' my next shot would be a lot better. So, that's how I figured it out. Don't you think that makes sense?"

"Jacob, I think that makes a lot of sense," I replied, almost dumbfounded by how he'd figured out how to handle such adult emotions so young. "I think most people, including me, could learn a lot from you. That's a lesson many people never seem to learn. You should be proud of yourself for learning it so young."

"Thanks," he said. "But it doesn't always work. I still get mad once in a while."

"I'm sure you do," I replied, not at all surprised. "Developing anger control is a big part of maturing. Many kids, especially boys, and a lot of adults, too, have trouble managing their anger. When you start to feel angry, have you found anything that helps keep you from getting really upset or staying mad?"

"Sure," he answered. "That's why you see me shooting

baskets on the driveway so much. It doesn't take long and I'm over whatever I was angry about in the first place."

Jacob had a degree of sophistication that impressed me. How was it that a kid of barely 17 years knew so much about anger and how to control it? He reminded me of Earl Woods, Tiger's dad. Earl said, "When you get angry, you give up power. You allow outside influences to harm your greatest asset—yourself."[242] Elizabeth Kenny of the famous Kenny Foundation put it even more succinctly: "He who angers you conquers you."[243]

Childhood Lost

Anger is one of the biggest issues involved in delinquent behavior. Many delinquents are chronically angry. Just why this is no one really knows, but researchers are looking for possible causes and ways to prevent anger and help angry kids get in charge of their emotions.

Studies are evaluating the relationship between environment and delinquent behavior. A tough, crime-ridden neighborhood, for instance, can demand a survival-of-the-fittest attitude. Kids learn at a young age from their parents, siblings, and friends that if someone hits you, you hit back. You don't want to be seen as weak because the weak are prime targets of bullies and gangs. Anger is a defense mechanism, a way to survive.

The problem with anger as a defense is that it can be hard to turn off (or on) from one situation to another. And it grows. Picture a kid who gets in trouble for some minor mischievous behavior in school. When a teacher gets after him (or her) for his misconduct, the child will sense that he is being attacked and respond with anger. A student with a poor self-image may even see a teacher's correction as confrontational and again respond with anger. Because of his anger he is sent to the principal's office, to detention, or is suspended. The cycle just spirals out of control—yet this child is only doing what he was taught to do to survive. The child begins to hate school, which is really the only way out of the survival-of-the-fittest environment.

But anger and delinquency are not relegated to the poor parts of town. Every neighborhood will have angry, delinquent kids. Just think of the Steward County, Tennessee, freshman who got angry and shot and killed his school bus driver in front of a bus filled with children.[244] He will never in his lifetime recover from the results of that anger. His victim's husband, to his credit, did not give in to the anger. At a memorial service for his wife, he told the audience that he had already forgiven the teen. In doing so, he helped defuse the anger in the community over the shooting and took control of his life.

I believe that teen anger is often a grief response to losing one's childhood. Kids in a high-risk neighborhood often have *no* childhood as they are forced to pass from toddler to adolescent, maybe even adulthood, in order to survive. They have plenty to grieve. In a more affluent atmosphere, very young kids are often given everything any adolescent or adult could want and are left without any goal to pull them into adulthood. They, too, have missed childhood. Neither group of teens has had the time nor the opportunity to just be kids. They are either ducking bullets or drug dealers in the ghetto or they're busy playing adults in supervised team sports, music lessons, dance lessons, and every other kind of distraction helpful adults can plan for them. Not that all structured play is bad. It isn't. But in excess, it can squeeze out childhood and cause its participants to miss being kids. In short, kids need to do kid things! Although neither group consciously recognizes the loss, it is present subconsciously and causes grief to set in. Grief, as Dr Kubler-Ross taught us, leads to anger. Yet I believe this: anger, if properly directed, helps to overcome grief. It's nature's way of dealing with loss.

Like Mother, Like Daughter

Unbelievable as it may seem, some forms of anger may be genetic. A University of Pittsburgh study of 550 women found that those who had a 2C gene were more likely to be hostile, aggressive, and angry.[245] This gene is responsible for the control of serotonin levels in the brain. Serotonin makes us feel up, happy, even euphoric depending on how much is present in our brains. Low levels have just the opposite effect, making us feel down, sad, and even depressed. Dr. Redford Williams from Duke University also thinks low levels of serotonin make us prone to anger.[246] His opinion is based on work done in his laboratory four years earlier. Some popular scientists refer to this gene as the "Anger gene." But that is an oversimplification; there are many other factors, and perhaps many other genes, which help control our emotions. We know that depression, bipolar disease, and other mood disorders tend to aggregate in families; but we do not know which genes are involved. There are most likely a number of genes that interact with environmental factors to produce the disease. Genetic causes of anger are interesting to study, but most anger is learned directly from one's parents or peers.

The onset of hostility in an otherwise happy child or adult can be the sign of a mood disorder, some other psychiatric disease, drug use, or even organic disease. A previous head injury, brain tumor, diabetes, or Alzheimer's disease are just a few of the physical problems that can lead to hostility. Any major change in personality should be evaluated by a physician and never dismissed without looking for these treatable causes.

When Anger Is Used For Good

Regardless of its cause, anger has some other uses also related to defense. Kids and adults alike often use anger to project superior knowledge. They forget (or don't know) what Bertrand Russell said about anger: "The degree of one's emotion varies inversely with one's knowledge of the facts: the less you know the hotter you become."[247] They strike out when they feel cornered by lack of knowledge or lack of protection and like a trapped squirrel or other wild animal, they attack when threatened. Just knowing that they will get in more trouble if they get angry is not enough. Sometimes teens just can't seem to get a grip on cause and effect, or they would come to Jacob's conclusion.

Anger does not need to be eliminated. As a matter of

fact, it cannot be eliminated. To quote the National Youth Violence Prevention Resource Center:

> Anger is a completely normal, healthy emotion. It is a common reaction when people have been insulted, wronged, hurt, or treated unfairly. When people know how to control and manage their anger, it can actually play a positive role in their lives, helping them to stand up for themselves, to fight against injustices, and to recognize when there is a need to make changes in their lives.[248]

Think of the young people who followed Dr. Martin Luther King—both black and white—and revolutionized civil rights in our country and in the world. Getting angry at social injustice or in defense of liberty is what made our country free and has propelled justice throughout all of history. There are many places in every community where righteous anger is needed and should, perhaps, be used more often. Substandard schools in the inner cities, starving children, hazardous work places, and outrageous salaries for company CEOs readily come to mind; but there are many other causes where anger, rightly used, can be beneficial to individuals and to society. Many of these causes are championed by teens and young adults but are not the challenges most of us face when we become angry.

Learning to Control Anger

Unfortunately, many teens, like the adults who mentor them, do not know how to control their anger. Instead, they let their anger control them, and violence often is the result. In one national survey of junior high and high school students, a third of the students agreed with the following statement: "When I am really angry, there is no way I can control myself."[249] Of the students who agreed with that statement, more than three in four reported getting into physical fights. Students who disagreed were much less likely to report fighting.

Anger is an emotion, a feeling. We cannot control our feelings and should not even try, but we can control our actions. Napoleon Hill said, "No one can make you jealous, angry, vengeful, or greedy unless you let him." In other words, be in charge of your own actions. Don't let someone else control how you behave and live!

All anger, even genetically determined anger, can be controlled. Genetics cannot be used as an excuse to do what is not socially justifiable. It may be more difficult to get a good handle on genetic-coded anger, but with determination it is possible. Many bright psychologists and psychiatrists have studied anger for years and have written much about its control and management. As a teenager, Jacob learned two ways of controlling his anger. Let me mention a few others:

Find Your Trigger: Knowing what triggers your anger is a good place to start. Jacob knew his sister caused his anger and he also knew he could not control her, but his mother could. He enlisted mom's help to improve his life. Keep a log and record the events leading to each episode of anger you experience. Then in a moment of peace, study your log and figure out how to avoid these stimuli or how to face them with dignity. By identifying these clues to getting angry, you can act before anger consumes your life.

Be Honest: Anger is often a response to getting caught in a lie or finding out we were wrong. If being untruthful is causing anger, there will soon be more problems unless the habit of lying is curtailed completely. Lying causes us to believe that others do not tell the truth. This lack of trust for others can only be overcome by learning to trust ourselves. There is no substitute for telling the truth.

Take a Time Out: The time-tested advice to "count to ten" actually works, though for more serious anger it may be necessary to count to one hundred. This distraction will allow time to consider other more noble means of problem solving. Try to relax while counting, and if another person precipitated your anger, try listening to him while you count. It may be that he is right, and your getting angry would be a double embarrassment to you.

Get a Pet: Dr. Redford Williams in his book *Anger Kills* advises getting and caring for a pet.[250] We discussed the advantages of having a pet in Chapter 5, but it is well to note Williams's advice: "Pet ownership can provide you with a safe and non-threatening opportunity to learn how to be an active participant in a trusting, caring relationship that will make few demands of you."[251] It's hard to get mad while your dog is at your side.

Forgive: Williams also suggests we forgive those who make us angry. Remember the boy from Steward County and the husband of his victim? The noble gesture of forgiving helped him to work through the tragedy and resume living. We should all try to be big enough to emulate him. It is not easy letting go of past hurts and resentments, but the only way to move past your anger is to let go of these feelings and start fresh. Don't be afraid to ask for help. Most city and county health departments offer courses in anger management

Laugh: Everybody feels better after a good laugh, that's probably why comedy is such a popular form of entertainment. Laughter really is the best medicine, so laugh, laugh, laugh. Even forced, fake laughter has been shown to increase serotonin and decrease anger.[252] I used to play golf with a man who always seemed terribly angry. If he hit a bad shot, he threw his clubs, swore, and acted like a spoiled toddler. Others playing with us asked me to talk to him about his behavior. I suggested he get some *Three Stooges* films and watch a clip each morning before we played. He agreed. His game didn't improve, but he calmed down and was actually fun to play with. But soon he stopped watching the films and his old behavior returned. At that point nobody would play with him, so he quit the club. The lesson? Learn to laugh at yourself and stop taking things so seriously.

Get Physical: When someone says something you don't like or you don't get what you want, don't let that angry feeling overwhelm you and control your actions. Do like my patient Jacob did and shoot baskets in your backyard: go for a run, work out in a gym, or do anything else physically strenuous enough to erase that anger. Be in charge!

Take It Easy: Finally, learn to relax, not just when you feel anger coming on but in your day-to-day living. Read a book; listen to calming music; visit a museum, a park, or a garden. I find great relaxation in my garden. The shade cools the summer sun and the scent of roses fills the air. I recall my day, reflect on my life, and plan for the future. Often I think about all the kids I have known over the years. Relaxing lets the stress and anger of the day dissolve away.

The tragedy of anger needs to be addressed with greater understanding by our society of educators, doctors, social workers, police, clergy, and most of all, parents. More of us should be using our anger and our energy to defuse the anger in our teenagers and in our communities. We need to understand that anger is an emotion that can be used for good or evil. It can be controlled, and it is our duty as adults to get our anger under control and teach our children to do likewise.

Jacob knew that the best way to control his anger and

its consequences was to avoid it. When that wasn't possible, he learned to force it out of his mind by physical exertion. He has a bright future ahead of him because he won't let anger spoil it. He also knows that on a personal level, anger really can't resolve a thing—unless your skin is green and you're tough on clothes.

CHAPTER 21

WORK FOR WHAT YOU WANT

> *The things, Good Lord, that we pray for, give us the grace to work for.*
>
> Thomas More, c. 1510

O NE OF THE great privileges I had in my career was being the physician for various sport teams. I spent nine years with a public high school in the little town of Hartford, Wisconsin, and followed that with four years at a private religious high school in Milwaukee. During those years, I met hundreds of outstanding high school athletes: outstanding not so much as athletes, but as people. You can watch college football or NFL ball, but unless you have been involved with the enthusiasm, the dedication, the drama, and the emotion of high school competition, you have not really seen or enjoyed sports. The enthusiasm and dedication I speak of is not limited to the players: the coaches share, and perhaps generate, this emotion. It all reaches a peak on Friday nights on the football field, and that's where I started every autumn weekend for thirteen years.

During the course of those years, I learned that sports really do make life more exciting, more interesting, and a whole lot better. Athletes learn discipline, perseverance, and honesty. They learn how to live with disappointment and how to handle success; they learn the value of preparation, goal setting, and the importance of exercise and a good diet. In short, sports teach character. In spite of evidence to the contrary from some professional athletes, high school athletes really care about their health, their school, and their sport. I love what sports do for high school kids.

Dennis' Story

Dennis was a wide receiver I met during his sophomore year. He was attending a religions high school in Milwaukee on scholarship. I saw him for the first time when I gave a talk to the team on nutrition and hygiene. As one of only two black kids on the team, he stuck out from most of the other players. He also stuck out on the field when he snatched a ball out of the hands of a defender and sprinted thirty-five yards for the team's first touchdown of the year.

The following week, his coach brought him into my office with an authorization note from his mother to treat an infection on his leg.

"I told his mom you would call her after you saw him," Coach began. "I hope that's okay. Dennis doesn't have a regular doctor, but he needs to get that leg taken care of before it falls off. I told him you would probably need to amputate it," he finished with a laugh.

I shook Dennis' hand and noted that his smile was only half the intensity of what he had worn during my brief encounters with him and the team.

"Don't worry, Dennis," I said to reassure them both. "We should be able to get you fixed up in time for Friday's game, and we definitely won't need to amputate. Heck, I want to see another catch like you made in the last game. You make the game look easy. But first, why don't you tell me how you hurt your leg."

The forced smile on Dennis's face disappeared as he glanced at the coach.

"It's okay," Coach said. "Tell him how it happened."

Dennis took a deep breath, exhaled briskly, and began. "Well, Coach knows that my mom, my sister, and I live alone and that she's a single mother. But nobody knows that I've never seen my dad." Then he turned to the coach and added, "Please don't tell the team, Coach, because they would all laugh and make me feel like I don't fit in, and I feel that way enough of the time already."

"Anyhow," Dennis continued. "We live in a not very nice part of town; it's all we can afford. I have a job in the summer, but Mom won't let me work very much during the school year. I agree with her; I need the time to study. My high school is hard, you know?" He rubbed his hand over his forehead and through his curly, black hair and sighed.

Why is he telling me this stuff? I wondered. But I'd learned over the years that when my office door closes, any subject is game—relevant or not. In any case, it sounded like he really needed someone to listen to him.

"You're right about that," I agreed. "But what happened to your leg?" I felt I had to get going, even though I really wanted to hear the rest of his story. Perhaps, I could have him come back some time and tell me all the other stuff.

"I'm getting to that," he said, not noticing I was running short on patience. "You see, Saturday afternoon I was shooting hoops with some of my neighbor friends and I fell and scraped my leg in the dirt. When I got home I knew I should have showered and washed it like you said in your talk at school, but it was really cold and ..." He was quiet again, and then continued, mumbling. "We don't have hot water in our apartment, and the landlord hasn't turned the heat on yet." Then he exhaled and in a more moderate voice added, "He says heat costs a lot, and I guess it does."

I nodded in agreement, too numb to talk.

"So by the time I got to shower after practice last night, I guess it was too late and my leg really swelled up. Now it looks like this."

I was pretty sure I could take care of his leg infection—unless it was the virulent staph I had talked about at that high school lecture. Many who play sports contact and spread what we call MRSA (methicillin resistant staph aureus) which can cause minor skin infections or boils and occasionally more serious, even fatal, infections. That's why I am so insistent that all players shower at school right after practice or games and any other time they break open their skin. If an athlete waits until he gets home to shower, other activities like phone calls, computer games, or dinner may delay the removal of staph germs from the skin, allowing them time to reproduce and invade a scratch or an open wound. The Centers for Disease Control (CDC) recommends frequent hand washing, showering after sports participation, and not sharing towels or other personal equipment as the first line of protection against MRSA.[253]

Even if it were staph, I could most likely help him as most strains of staph that athletes carry are not MRSA and are sensitive to most antibiotics. The real question, however, was where and when could I start on his social problem? I examined his leg and found a large red wound with red streaks running up to his groin, which was filled with firm, tender lymph nodes.

"Let's start with an antibiotic shot, and then I'll give you some pills," I explained. "Don't worry about the cost; I'll take care of that."

When I returned with the pills, Nurse Debbie had just finished his injection. He was rubbing his injured muscles while he told her, "That didn't hurt as much as getting hit by a 250-pound linebacker."

Nurse Debbie left and he turned to me and asked, "Is it okay if I work tonight?"

"I thought you said you didn't work during the school year?" I asked, puzzled.

"Oh, I'm sorry," he said, "I meant that I didn't work *much* during school. I only work Monday nights. I help clean Joey's restaurant after they close. I really need to save some money for college."

"Dennis," I said. "I'm sorry, but you can't be on that leg tonight. I'm hoping we'll be able to get you on the field Friday night. Let me see you tomorrow after school and we'll talk more about it then. There are some other things I want to talk about, too."

I saw Dennis the next day and much to my relief, he was markedly improved.

"Hey," I almost shouted. "Looks like we got things under control and you'll be catching passes Friday night. I'll see you before the game to make a final decision."

Then I added, "How do you find the time to play football, work, and study?"

"It's not a matter of finding time," Dennis insisted. "I need to do all those things. If I don't study, I'll lose my scholarship and never get one for college. I have to work during the school year to keep my summer job. And I definitely need the money for college."

He didn't say why he needed to play football and I was afraid to ask him as I thought he might say it was the only place he could get a warm shower. He played basketball in the winter months and baseball in the spring, so I might have been right. While I was lost in thought, he continued.

"My school counselor said not to worry about getting a scholarship to college because I was black and that would give me an advantage. When he said that, I really did a dumb thing. I got mad and just walked out of his office because I think if you want something, you need to want it bad enough to work for it. Otherwise, it will never mean anything to you."

My eyes filled up and my throat tightened. I couldn't respond. I stood and walked over to the sink and washed my hands. I've found that's

> IF YOU WANT SOMETHING, YOU NEED TO WANT IT BAD ENOUGH TO WORK FOR IT

a good place to clear my mind and take a few minutes to think. As I dried my hands, I looked at Dennis and said, "Dennis, you can't imagine how proud I am to know you. Your mother must just be bursting with pride. I think you are 100 percent right. The world needs more men like you!"

"Thanks," he beamed, smiling and showing all his beautiful teeth. He interrupted that smile with a frown and said softly, "It's not easy, you know."

"I'm sure it isn't," I replied. "But like you said … if it were easy, it probably wouldn't mean much." Then I added, "I don't think you did wrong at all by leaving the counselor's office. I think you did exactly the right thing. If you had stayed there, you may have started to argue with him, and then things could have gone really bad for you. But don't you think you're maybe being a bit too hard on yourself?"

"What do you mean?" he asked, unsure if I was criticizing him.

"Well, I think the world of you and so does Coach; he and I both respect you for who you are. But you think of your situation as a weakness while Coach and I think it has strengthened you. I wonder if you think asking for help is also a sign of weakness. You don't need to do everything yourself. Just take your leg infection as an example. If you hadn't asked for help, you would still be sick and you might have ended up losing that leg or even your life."

We talked more about his situation before Dennis left with a bit of the burden off his shoulders. He promised to talk to Coach about some of the things going on in his life. I learned that day that true character can be developed at a young age.

No Shame in Working Hard

There's a lot to be learned from Dennis. Too often we parents try to make everything easy for our kids; we don't want them to have to work too hard. It's a lesson we learned from our parents. Actually, it's a lesson we've learned from antiquity. Working hard—in the absence of compulsion—was not the norm for Hebrew, classical, or medieval cultures.[254] It was not until the Protestant Reformation that physical labor became culturally acceptable for all persons, including the wealthy. Even today we refer to the habit of work as the "Protestant Work Ethic."

We read in the Old Testament that after the fall of Adam, God said, "By the *sweat* of your brow you will eat your food...[emphasis added]." Work was seen as a curse imposed by God upon Adam and Eve and their descendants, a punishment for disobedience and ingratitude. Work was not seen as a source of joy for accomplishment or for its own intrinsic worth, only as a means to prevent poverty and destitution.

The Greeks also thought of work as a curse reserved

for slaves, allowing free men to pursue warfare, large-scale commerce, and the arts—especially architecture or sculpture. Roger B. Hill from the University of Georgia notes:

> [P]hilosophers such as Plato and Aristotle made it clear that the purpose for which the majority of men labored was 'in order that the minority, the elite, might engage in pure exercises of the mind—art, philosophy, and politics (Tilgher, 1930, p. 5).[255]

I learned from Dr. Lannigan, my professor in Philosophy 101, that Aristotle thought work was a waste of time; that it interfered with man's pursuit of virtue; that knowledge for the sake of knowledge was the highest form of knowledge and that learning for the sake of earning was the lowest. (I yearned for knowledge for the sake of earning, and somehow I did not feel I stood out from the rest of the class.)

During the reformation, Martin Luther taught that work was a form of prayer; that God determines a man's profession at birth and it was sinful to try to change your birth occupation.[256] According to John Calvin's theology of predestination, not working and being idle was a sign of being damned and working hard in any occupation was a sign of being one of the Elect—those predestined for heaven.[257] These two theologians were responsible for the change in attitude toward work: we owe the term "Protestant Work Ethic" to them.

Roger Hill says of the early American settlers:

The early adventurers who first found America were searching, not for a place to work and build a new land, but for a new Eden where abundance and riches would allow them to follow Aristotle's instruction that leisure was the only life fitting for a free man.[258]

However, they and other settlers soon learned that America was anything but Eden. Eventually, because of hard work, the industrial revolution came to America and the United States became the nation it is today.

Currently, some argue that we have turned once again to a two-tiered system of workers, with the working-class laborers replacing the "slaves" and white-collar executives functioning as the "masters." (My working-class cousins refer to a *job* as "work" and a *position* as "doing nothing.") The separation of Americans into classes has led, in part, to the conflict between labor and management. (Much more is involved in this issue, however.)

Developing a Positive Work Ethic

There is a story about an average high school boy who told his guidance counselor that he wanted to be a doctor.

"How do you ever expect to get through medical school with *your* brain?" the unprofessional counselor asked him.

"I plan to work like everything depends on me and pray like everything depends on God," was his reply.

Today, they call that former "C" student "Doctor."

Dr. L. Braude in her book *Work and Workers* states that children are often influenced by others' attitudes toward work.[259]

> If a parent demonstrates a dislike for a job or a fear of unemployment, children will tend to assimilate these attitudes. Parents who demonstrate a strong work ethic tend to impart a strong work ethic to their children.[260]

Baude's philosophy was promulgated more than thirty years ago, and it is still true today. If you want your children to have a work ethic like Dennis' or the young boy who became a doctor, you must have one yourself.

Unfortunately, Dale Dauten, writing in the March 25, 2007, *Boston Globe,* says the work ethic is dead. "Younger generations in the workforce have killed it off. If you're under thirty, 'work' has a different meaning than it did." What's needed, he says, is a "way of working beyond mere work, something higher, something finer. What's needed is a Contribution Ethic." He suggests ten ways to develop a Contribution Ethic:

- Make yourself useful.
- Be a team player.
- Know your half of the workload is 60 percent.
- Expect new ideas to be met with resistance.
- Don't expect reward for everything you give.

- Assume the best in others.

- Know that being right is overrated.

- Being wrong is underrated, but leads to wisdom.

- Read.

- Think like a hero; work like an artist.

Dauten's contribution ethic will not guarantee success in the workplace, but it does mean you'll be pleased with your contribution.

Whatever your ethic—Protestant Work Ethic or Contribution Ethic—your attitude will be reflected in your kids' approach to work. As in everything else, they will emulate you. As parents, we all need to encourage our kids to work, not just so they can have a nice car or new clothing or another electronic toy, but because having things too easy can lead kids to an entitlement mentality which destroys creativity, incentive, and ambition.

When we really look at ourselves, how many of us take the easy way out instead of doing the hard, more courageous thing? When I graduated from college in 1960, the commencement speaker gave each of the graduates a small pocket dictionary and a tiny penknife. Then he asked us to look up the word "expedient."

"Look at the second definition," he said. "Now take your knife and cut it out of the book, and out of your lives."

The second definition reads "based on or guided by self-interest." We did as he requested then and there.

Dennis was a senior when I left Wisconsin, so I don't know where he went to college or if he got a scholarship. I do know he made the National Honor Society and continued to do well in sports. I wouldn't be surprised to see his name in the paper someday. And when that happens, I'll know he earned his success because he wanted it bad enough to work for it.

CHAPTER 22

MONEY AND FINANCE

I don't like money, actually,
but it quiets my nerves.

Joe Lewis

F ASHION, SEX, DRUGS, and money dominate the minds
of many teens. The image perpetuated by movies
like *Mean Girls* (2004) and TV programs like "Beverly
Hills 90210" or "The OC" is that teens are materialistic
maniacs who must always look good and have everything,
NOW! It also suggests that to live that lifestyle means
demanding money, money, and more money from mom or
dad or other sources.

Because of this popular image, many teens and their
parents have heated arguments over high credit card
charges and cell phone bills. The result is a growing dissat-
isfaction between parents and their children. Ultimately,
capitalism seems to be the worst economic system in which
to raise a child; at least, that's what I was beginning to

think until Pat came into my office providing me with a more realistic image of teens (even teens with money) than the one Hollywood promulgates as a means to sell movie tickets and boost ratings.

"Sorry about the way I smell," Pat began as I entered the exam room. "I just came from work and I didn't have time to go home and change," he explained. "I have a rash I want you to look at."

Pat was a plain-looking blonde kid of barely 15. His appearance that day was startling. His shorts were dirty, crumpled, and partly hidden by a tattered Braves T-shirt. And he didn't smell much better. I had seen him many times before, but only in prep shirts and pressed pants or his private school uniform—tie and all. He was from a very wealthy family, so I was a bit surprised by the way he looked and even more amazed that he had a job.

"Where do you work?" I asked.

"Peachtree Animal Hospital," he announced with pride. "You know where that is?"

"Sure, I take my dog there. What do you do?"

"I clean dog cages," he answered, betraying no emotion that showed he considered his job below his social or personal standing.

"Oh," I said surprised again. "Are you planning to be a veterinarian?"

"Not a chance."

Now I was confused. "Then why are you working in such a place?"

"Well, I need to fund my IRA, and it's the only job I could get that was close enough to walk or bike to."

That made sense. Too bad more people don't think like Pat. To encourage him I quickly added, "I'm proud of you, Pat. I guess you're never too young to get a job or start making money."

"It's not just making money that's important, you know," he pronounced with that know-it-all-teenage-look in his eye. "Lots of people *make* money but still never *have* money."

"I'm sure that's true," I answered, not revealing whether I was one of those people he singled out. I was still a bit confused but interested enough to take the bait. "So what's important then?"

"Saving money! You see, the best way to make money is to save money. If you make a dollar, you really only have about 75 cents. They take the rest out for taxes and stuff. But if you save a dollar, you

> THE BEST WAY TO MAKE MONEY IS TO SAVE MONEY

have a dollar. And if you invest it right, by the end of the year you should have more than a dollar; maybe a dollar five or ten or even more. It's even better if you put it into a Roth IRA, because then you get it back tax-free. You don't even have to pay taxes on the earnings!"

Pat's grin told me this was a lecture he had heard many times from adults, and he now delighted in giving it back to a grown-up. His parents would be proud.

Learning to Save

Pat is *so* right to urge high school kids to open Roth IRA

or other suitable savings accounts. If they save $2,000 a year during their four high school years and never save another penny, and it grows tax deferred at 10 percent annually, it will be worth just under a million dollars by the time they reach age 65. The chart below shows this remarkable growth.

Of course, the future is hard to predict and annual percentage yields will vary from year to year. At this time, 10 percent interest earnings on an investment is a highly optimistic assumption. Still, regardless of the interest rate obtained, your best choice is to invest early and consistently with your focus on long-term goals.

Investing in an index mutual fund could yield that coveted 10 percent, as the Standard & Poor's (S&P) index has averaged 10.88 percent annually since 1988 and that

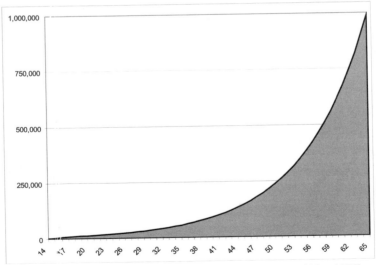

Growth of $2,000 investements made annually between the ages of 14 and 17, Tax Deferred at 10% Annual Return Until Age 65.

includes a 38 percent loss in 2008. Remember that earnings over time are directly related to the interest paid by the borrower and the underlying risk of the investment; remember too that stock prices fluctuate depending on the earnings and public favor of the company; so always seek out a qualified professional for investment advice.

In contrast to investing early, a 45-year-old would have to invest just over $1,000 dollars every month, that's over $12,000 a year, until he reached 67—a total investment of $280,000—to have just over a million dollars (using a 10 percent annual rate of return). I sure wish Pat had talked to me when I was 14.

It is possible for a teen to start a Roth IRA, but it has to be with money they have actually earned.[261] According to a study by Yankelovich, a market research firm in North Carolina,[262] more than six million teens are employed. An additional million are looking for work. Teens in 2006 earned more than $480 monthly; surely they can find a way to save part or all of the $2,000 they are allowed to put into a Roth IRA.

Critics might say that 50 years from now, a million dollars will not be worth the same as it is today. And they would be right. But it will be worth a lot more than the car a high school kid bought 50 years earlier with his $8,000. Yet high school and college kids persist in buying cars, video games, and clothes, knowing that in a few short years the car will be worth little or nothing, the game outdated, and the clothing out of style. Getting an employed adult to save for retirement is hard enough, but talking to a teen about retirement is like trying to convince a rock to roll uphill. So if Pat is going to convince other kids to start a Roth IRA, he has his work cut out for him. Perhaps a nudge from parents will get a high schooler on his way to saving.

The Value of Work

Most neighborhoods have work available for teenagers who want to do it. When my oldest grandson was in fourth grade, his neighbor (who had three large dogs) paid him to clean the dog droppings out of his yard. Each Saturday, Marc made five dollars for what many would consider unpleasant work. When he was older, he began shoveling walks and mowing lawns for other neighbors. Last summer he worked at a Dairy Queen; and right now he's a host at Applebee's, serves ice cream at a local ice cream shop, and continues his mowing jobs. He has a good grade point, has a letter in cross-country track, and is field marshal in Ohio's Oakwood High School marching band. But the best financial news is that he has received an ROTC scholarship which covers tuition and expenses, plus provides a stipend. Hard work pays off!

When I was practicing medicine in Wisconsin many years ago, a "welfare mother" brought her 12-year-old son to see me. He had hurt his leg the night before and X-rays showed a fractured tibia (the large bone in the lower leg). I asked her why she hadn't brought him in when it happened. He answered for her and said he had to deliver his papers.

"How did you manage that with a broken leg?" I asked.

"It wasn't easy," he answered. "I put my papers and my hurt leg in a coaster wagon I found in the garage and pedaled along with my good leg. It worked okay as long as I hit the front porch, but if I missed I had to hop on one leg up to the step and replace the paper. When I got done it was dark, and Mom didn't want to bother you at night."

That was more than 30 years ago, but I can still see the tears in his blue eyes.

"I wish you had called me when it happened. I would have been glad to see you, and I'm sure one of my sons would have delivered the papers for you," I assured him.

Much to his dismay, I put his leg in a cast and told him he would have to get a substitute for his route.

"How long before I can walk?" he asked.

"Let me see you in a week and if you're doing well, we can make a walker out of your cast and you'll be free. Is that soon enough?" I asked.

"I guess," he mumbled, "but I really need to do my route!"

"What are you saving for?"

"I'm not saving any of it," he answered, not trying to cover the fact. "Mom and I need it for food and stuff."

If this 12-year-old could work a paper route with a broken leg, I would think most high school kids could work and save some of their money!

Fortunately, many teens *are* saving money. Teenage Research Unlimited reported that in 2006, 56 percent of teens had savings accounts: 5 percent had Certificates of Deposit (real CDs) and 13 percent owned stocks or bonds. Only 10 percent had checking accounts. The bad news is, none reported that they had a Roth IRA.[263]

Studies show that teens are a lot more like Pat than the media likes to portray. A survey of 4,400 young people (ages 12 to 19) reported in *The Cleveland Plain Dealer* showed that half "try hard" to save money. While a third usually spends most of their money, 60 percent said not being able to buy everything they wanted made them appreciate the things they were able to buy.

The average American teenager spent $107 a week in 2006. And according to a survey by Teenage Research Unlimited, teens spent more than $179 billion that year! Moreover, 63 percent of the teens surveyed thought credit cards were dangerous, that they allowed people to spend more money than they actually had.

Fortunately, only 7 percent of teens in the 12 to 17 age group have credit cards.[264] But once they got those cards, they got into debt fast; they had an average of $1,533 in credit card debt by the time they started college and $3,262 by the time they graduated. In fact, "7% to 10% of students will drop out of college due to credit problems," says Robert Manning, author of *Credit Card Nation*.[265]

The Dangers of Debt

Once again, children are following their parents' examples. Credit card debt in this country is sinking a lot of households under trillions of dollars of red ink. And the stress this creates is affecting family relationships. According to the Federal Reserve Board (which conducts surveys every three years), 76 percent of American households had credit cards in 2004. Of those cardholders, 55 percent paid the debt off every month and had no balance. Those who did not pay the balance in full had an average balance of $5,100, with a median balance of $2,200. But 10 percent of the cardholders had cumulative balances in excess of $10,000.[266]

If you have $1,000 in debt on your card and only pay the minimum, it will take you almost 15 years to pay it off at a cost of over $2,500 in interest. If you ever listen to Dave Ramsey on radio, you will know how threatening debt and its consequent interest are to a family's happiness. That interest can eat you alive! Dave Ramsey suggests you eat beans and rice until you have paid off all your credit cards,[267] but according to an article on the *MSN Money* Web site, there are many other ways to find the money to pay off those cards:

Pay less to Uncle Sam. In 2004, 80% of taxpayers got a refund—on average, $2,400 a pop. By adjusting your withholdings, you can keep that money in your own pocket and put an extra $200 a month toward your debt. (Why give the government an interest free loan?)

Curb your spending. Even small changes, like brown-bagging lunch or renting one DVD a week instead of three, can free up to 10% or 15% of your income. To find expenses you can shave, track your spending for seven days. You may be surprised at how relatively small expenses—like 75 cents for a Diet Coke from the vending machine or $3.25 for a Latté—add up over time.

Control your cards. Paying down a big debt is hard enough without adding more fuel to the fire. To avoid the temptation to spend, lock your credit cards away. People have frozen them in bowls of ice or given them to a trusted friend (to use only if there is a real cash emergency). But we all agree what an emergency is, and a shoe sale at Nordstrom isn't it.[268]

It would be a good idea to include your children in the journey as you get out of debt. Experts say that parents—as with so many things in life—are the most important role models for how their teens will handle money and value it. Rob Brough, senior vice president for marketing at Zion's Bank, was quoted in *The Deseret Morning News* as saying, "If Mom and Dad don't save money and plan their spending, their kids won't be good at it either."[269] That bodes ill for today's teens. Statistics from the U.S. Bureau of Economic Analysis show Mom and Dad often are not providing a good example. Americans saved a negative 0.4 percent of their disposable personal income in the fourth quarter of 2005 and a negative 1 percent in all of 2006.[270] This means they are saving nothing and are, in fact, losing money each quarter by spending more than they earned. That is the worst rate of saving in 73 years; the only years that Americans saved less were 1932 and 1933 during the Great Depression. In the 1940s, Americans saved almost one-fourth of their disposable personal income and as recently as August 2004, saved 4 percent. These reported "savings" do not include what they have put away in a retirement account or have earned as a pension. But money in retirement and pension plans is not available in an emergency. Economists recommend that people have three to six months of living expenses in an emergency saving's account as we never know what the future may bring.

Even though our schools are currently facing an over-load with the classes they are required to provide, it would be great if high schools, like parents, could consider adding money-management classes to their curriculum. (Fortunately, some schools currently offer a little of this information through their Economics classes.) Bob Brough recommended that parents have young children sit down with them "to pay the bills for gas and electricity and the telephone. That will help them realize that all this stuff costs money."[271] He also recommended saving for things like a baseball glove or a CD. If grade-schoolers develop the habit of saving, they will be more open in high school to start saving for retirement by opening a Roth IRA.

The Joy of Giving

Starting young is important. A British survey showed that English teens had about twice as much saved before they entered their later teen years than when they entered their twenties. During these years, savings were cut in half. Cars, auto insurance, gasoline, and dating all started to absorb cash.

Helping older teens navigate the increasingly difficult adult world of finance is critical. We don't want them giving up and cashing in on the most readily available credit card like so many adults. This pattern will lead them to a lifetime of financial woes.

Money management is more that just earning, spending, and saving; it also includes giving back to the community. Every wage earner can learn the joy of giving; it is learned from parents by example and direction. Teens love to work and save and when they start donating to a favorite charity, they love that, too. It helps them feel good about themselves; they know they are contributors and no longer living off the "fat of the land."

Once kids have established the habit of giving and realize that it truly is better to give than receive, they will usually continue it for life. A study in the March 2008 issue of *Science* magazine found that people who give to charity really are happier than those who do not. They sampled 632 adults and had them estimate their level of happiness. Then they had them estimate what percent of their income they gave to charity or gifted to friends or relatives. They found a link between giving and happiness. In order to find out which came first, they gave a small amount of money, $5 to $20, to each of 46 students. Some had to spend the money on themselves while the others had to buy a gift for someone else. Those who spent the money on others were happier than those who kept it, independent of how much money they received.[272]

I have not seen Oprah's show "The Big Give," but reports of it show that even watching someone else enjoy giving money away makes the viewer happy. It was reported in an article in the March 27, 2008, issue of *The Tennessean* that a Nashville woman who was on the show was not able to give away $100,000 during the week she was in Florida. She tried as hard as she could, but she ran out of time. She said, "This experience has changed my life. ... It's like being baptized, because it has changed my sense of purpose. ... It's like seeing life though a set of fresh eyes."

Money may not buy happiness, but giving it away apparently can!

Back to Pat. As we talked, I reemphasized that he was right about the Roth IRA and taxes: when he takes that million dollars out of his Roth IRA, it *will* be tax-free. He made a tough investment choice by finding a place he could walk to work (no car expense), taking a job a lot of folks wouldn't want (cleaning dog cages), and saving his earnings for the future.

I told Pat his CEO dad must be very proud of him. Then, while continuing to talk "high finance," I had a look at his leg. He had a patch of poison ivy dermatitis from a hike in the woods the previous weekend. As he left, he thanked me for the prescription and I thanked him for the lesson on finance.

While I didn't hand over my stock and banking portfolio for Pat to manage, he left me feeling good about the future and the ability of teens to cope with the materialistic world we adults have left them. We don't want our children to think that the acquisition of money is the purpose of life, but we also understand that their ability to manage money will reduce stress in their lives and in their relationships with their spouses and children. Understanding the role of finances will also permit them to donate to charity, become philanthropists, and help the less fortunate. Money does not buy happiness. But teaching our children to manage it well can reduce the kind of stress that keeps adults from taking time to smell life's roses—and being able to buy a few as well.

JUST BE NICE

*If you can't say something
nice, don't say nothing at all.*

Thumper in *Bambi*, Disney–1942

W HEN I WAS in high school, Mrs. Shaw, my English
teacher, said "nice" was an overworked word. "It
is so over-used," she said, "that it no longer has meaning. Don't use it." But dictionaries define "nice" as fastidi-
ous, refined, delicate, precise, subtle, calling for care, tact-
ful, pleasant, attractive, kind, good, or as a general term
of approval. What could be wrong with using a word like
that? Aren't those characteristics we all would like to possess? And if someone does possess them, shouldn't they
be recognized? Yet for the past half-century, every time I
say "nice" or write "nice," I hear Mrs. Shaw admonishing,
"Don't use it!"

Bennett had a different idea. One beautiful Sunday afternoon he, his dad, and I had agreed to play nine holes of golf. But as luck would have it, Dad couldn't make it; so 17-year-old Bennett and I went on without him.

Try to Be Nice

I didn't know Bennett very well. I sang in the church choir with his dad and frequently met Bennett and his mother after Sunday service. He was short; had a round face with small round, brown eyes; and looked more like 13 than 17. His short hair reminded me of the military recruits I had cared for in the past. He was always pleasant. He shook my hand and greeted my wife and me every time we met; but he remained quiet, talking only if we spoke first.

I enjoyed playing golf with this young man, even though he was beating me. Well, let me be honest—he was annihilating me! We had some great conversations. I learned he had two older brothers, was born in Germany, and had spent a couple of years at a boarding school—his dad's alma mater. He was not exactly crazy about school; he wanted to be a chef. He said he had had a few arguments, but had never been in a fight.

As we approached the ninth tee box, I was sorry we were about to finish. (Sorry, too, that he was beating me.) After I hit my tee shot into the lake, Bennett said in sympathy, "Why don't you just take a Mulligan?" To a non-golfer, that means just take another try; we won't count the first one.

"Thanks, Bennett," I responded. "But I think I'll take

my penalty and drop down by the lake. I can probably get on the green from there. Besides, you've beaten me badly today, and I should let the score show that."

"Thanks," he answered as he blushed. "I guess I just feel bad beating you when you invited me to play. Next time you'll probably kick my behind."

"Bennett," I said, "you're just too much. Are you always this kind?"

"Not really," he answered.

"Well, you seem like a pretty great guy to me."

"I'm no Mother Theresa," he responded enjoying the compliment, "but I try to be nice."

"You do a great job of it."

We finished the hole, said good-bye, and I thought no more about it until a few days later when I read an article in the local paper about Dolly Parton. One of her past agents was quoted as saying "Dolly is always so nice. She is just wonderful to everybody." Then I started to think. Bill Clinton, regardless of what you thought of him as a politician, was said to be "nice" to everybody. He was the "man" at every party. He made sure everybody around him had a good time. The late Tim Russert was reported as being nice. If you had watched his shows, you would never have seen him insult a guest or confront them in a mean way.

I always start my day with the comics, and my favorite is "Red and Rover." Cartoonist Brian Basset has captured the innocence and imagination of childhood and managed to avoid any meanness. Red is always nice, as is his dog Rover. They're a great pair and they warm my heart at every breakfast. I like Snoopy too, but Lucy can be mean!

Bill Murray in *Groundhog Day* (1993) plays the role of a very wacky, self-centered, miserable weatherman who by some unexplained quirk of nature is forced to live the same Groundhog Day over and over again. After the first few reruns of the same day in Punxsutawney, Pennsylvania, Murray becomes frightened, even suicidal. Even after killing himself, the alarm clock rings, he's back in his hotel bed, and Groundhog Day starts again. Then, as he realizes only he knows the days are reruns, and because he knows what will happen next, he tries to take advantage of people. That doesn't work either; he's still unhappy. Gradually, his attitude changes. He saves a boy's life, takes piano lessons, and gives to his colleagues and the community. He becomes more concerned about other people than about himself, and all these changes make him happy. When he becomes totally unselfish, loving, and "nice," his alarm rings and it is February 3; Groundhog Day is finally over and Bill Murray awakes a new man. What a story! What a lesson!

But *Groundhog Day* was fiction. Does being nice really make a difference? Can real people be nice, and successful, too?

Being Remembered for Being Nice

Bart Starr was perhaps the greatest quarterback of all time. I know many give this honor to Peyton Manning or Tom Brady, but to us *old* Packer fans, even Brett Favre is in second place. Starr was the Packers seventeenth-round draft pick in 1956 and played fifteen seasons, leaving the team in 1971. He won six Western Division Titles, five NFL Championships, Super Bowls I and II, and was named MVP for both those bowl games. He went on to coach the Packers from 1975–83, and he earned induction into the Pro Football Hall of Fame in 1977. And he was known as a nice guy.

My son Rafe tells a couple of stories that show just how nice a guy Starr really was. Rafe lived in Kansas City and Bart Starr was there at the opening of a sporting goods store to sign autographs. The lines were long and when Rafe finally got to the counter with Starr, he was surprised to see Bart standing, not sitting, while signing various items the patrons had brought for his signature.

"To whom shall I address this?" Starr asked Rafe.

"My son Harrison," Rafe replied. Then, while Bart was writing, Rafe asked, "Do you have to just stand here? Can't they find a chair for you to sit down?"

"They could," Bart replied, "but I told them if people have to stand and wait to see me, the least I can do is stand to greet them. Seems fair, doesn't it?"

"I guess it does at that," Rafe answered. "And thanks for signing this picture. It will have a place of honor in my son's room."

And it does.

Rafe's other story concerning Bart Starr involves Rafe's boss, Kerry Hafner, who played tight end for The University of Wisconsin-Stout in the 1980s. After leaving Stout, he attended training camp with the Green Bay Packers. When he was released, Coach Starr apologized to Hafner. "I'm sorry we didn't get enough time to work you like we should have. We just have too many tight ends in camp right now. Another time, things might have been different."

Hafner was awed that the Packers head coach would talk to him, let alone apologize for releasing him. Hafner went on to earn a Ph.D. in biostatistics, was inducted into 1998 UW-Stout Athletic Hall of Fame and, according to Rafe, continues to be as nice a guy as Bart Starr.

Another luminary noted for being nice was former President Jimmy Carter. In fact, he was affectionately known as "Mr. Nice Guy." Mike Nizza in an October 3, 2007, article for *The New York Times* wrote, "Jimmy Carter's nice-guy image has always been a reason to like him, loathe him or laugh at him. ..." Then he went on to tell how the President stood up to a local security chief during his visit to the Darfur region of Sudan when he was told he could not visit a tribal leader in Kabkabiya. He ended the article stating, "In the end, the dispute was resolved in Mr. Carter's usual Nobel-peace-prize style: First a cessation of yelling, and then a compromise. The tribal leader he planned to meet came to him, and they drove off together...."

A final example of being "nice" involves my college roommate's mother, Grace. Grace was refined, delicate, pleasant, attractive, kind, and good. In short, she was all the things dictionaries say "nice" should be. When she talked with you she looked at you, and only at you; you knew she was sincerely interested in what you were saying. When you were with Grace you always felt special. Grace sent many care packages to Rod while he was in school, always with a note to be sure to share with his friends. And Rod had a lot of friends because he was so much like his mother. Rod's intelligence, his determination, and his perseverance made him an oral surgeon; and his kindness (niceness) helped him to become successful as a surgeon and as a colonel in the U.S. Air Force. I was blessed to have such a nice roommate.

When I married, Mary met Grace; she loved her immediately, probably because they are very much alike. Mary has done a wonderful job of being nice. I appreciate it every day.

Nice and Successful

Patrick Steffen, assistant professor of clinical psychology at Brigham Young University, reported in the December 2005 issue of *Annals of Behavioral Medicine* that students with compassion enjoyed better health than those without such an attribute. He defined compassion as "being moved by the suffering of others and having the desire to alleviate that suffering."[273] Since compassion is a part of being nice, Steffen has provided a scientific reason for listening to Bennett.

There's even a book about being nice: *The Power of Being Nice*: *How to Conquer the Business World With Kindness,* by Linda Kaplan Thaler and Robin Koval. In it they say, "It is often the small kindnesses—the smiles, gestures, compliments, favors—that make our day and can even change our lives."[274]

Do-gooders (nice people) "are the glue that holds offices together."[275] We have all experienced that type of person in our workplaces, but there is a difference between being nice and being a wimpy, passive Milquetoast. Thaler and Koval state, "Nice is not naïve. Nice does not mean smiling blandly while others walk all over you. It is valuing niceness—in yourself and in others—the same way you respect intelligence, beauty, or talent."[276] Like nice co-workers at the office, nice parents are the glue that holds families together. Shouldn't we all have a mission, like Bennett, to try to be nice?

I began to wonder how much being nice has to do with success, so I talked with my neighbor Don who is considered one of the nicest guys on the golf course. Yet I know that he can be firm, too. Don retired as CFO from one of the Fortune 500 companies, so I know he was successful.

"Tell me, Don," I began, "What is the relationship between being nice and being successful in corporate America? Is it true that nice guys finish last?"

"Par, that's a complicated question," Don answered. "Fortunately, I had a lot of good people working for me and with me." (Why is it that successful people always mention first the good people who worked for them? I think it says something about the "good people's" boss.)

Don continued. "Sure, people who are too nice can get run over, but I don't think that's so much about being nice as it is about being weak. Nice, Par, is a difficult word to define. I think," he added, "it has to do with knowing the company's goals and staying focused on those goals and being nice to those who are committed to those goals. You can be nice to those who are not committed by helping them understand the goals or letting them find other work. The mean, egotistical boss seldom succeeds."

I thought nice guys finished last! I was wrong. So why not try to be nice? What can it hurt? Why not listen to Bennett? He showed me how to play golf, he showed me how to be nice, and then he let me in on his personal philosophy. And what a great philosophy it is: Try to be nice!

Parenting Tips

- *Decide to be happy! Be positive; throw out the negative.*

- *Laugh! Share humor with your kids.*

- *Learn to adjust to the difficulties that may come into your life. Be open to change, welcome it, and do not fear the unknown.*

- *Be lavish with sincere praise.*

- *Control your anger. Use it wisely to change those things you can change. Attend an anger management course, if needed.*

- *Review your health and your living habits. Change those that are harmful to you and your family.*

- *Forgive your child often, but be sure you work out a plan to prevent the offense from happening again.*

- *Work hard, but don't be afraid to ask for help.*

- *Insist your teen finds a summer or weekend job. All work and no play may make Johnny a dull boy, but all play and no work gives him an entitlement mentality that may well doom him, as well as society.*

- *Be nice, especially to the people who mean the most to you—your family.*

- *Be nice to everyone, whether they can do you good or not. It is a sign of real character.*

WHAT DOES IT ALL MEAN?

> *If you really live your beliefs*
> *and make them attractive,*
> *you won't have to ram them*
> *down other people's throats—*
> *they will steal them.*
>
> Dick Gregory

A NUMBER OF YEARS ago, my family and I attended a pro-life rally in Milwaukee commemorating the tragic January 22, 1973, *Roe v. Wade* decision on abortion. As Milwaukee is in January, it was cold. I mean really cold! At mid-day, we still had our coats on in Turner Hall, but our spirits were warmed by the keynote speaker, Brother Booker Ashe. Brother Booker was often portrayed as a "Portly, jovial Capuchin monk," a moniker he relished. Years earlier, he had founded a nonprofit institution—House of Peace—to provide food, counseling, and education to Milwaukee's poorest of the poor. This champion of the poor had earned the title of "Milwaukee's Social Conscience." He had a smile that could melt butter and a laugh that could crack plaster; he accepted people as they were and offered food, clothing, and sometimes cash—but seldom a sermon.

And this day was to be no different.

The Source of Wisdom

Brother Booker enlightened, inspired, and motivated, but he did not preach. He stood over six feet tall and must have weighed more than 400 pounds. Standing in his brown monk's robe, he looked ever the picture of Robin Hood's Friar Tuck. Story after story took us from tears to laughter and then back again; then to cheers, and finally to the applause of a standing ovation. It was apparent that he had studied drama and used it to make his point.

After he was finished, I dried the tears from my eyes and approached him with my wife and kids to thank him and ask permission to use some of his stories and quote his wisdom in my own presentations.

He thanked me for being gracious and said, "Use anything I said if it can help someone. And you don't need to quote me. These are not my stories; they are stories of God's people. They are God's stories, or maybe I should say they are everybody's stories. You know, Brother," he went on, "there are no new stories, just old recycled stories, just like there are no new ideas and no new wisdom. Everything I said has been said before and will be said again, either by you or by somebody else ... most likely both. So, don't worry about who said it first. Learn from it if you can; and remember, everybody learns from everybody else."

Then he smiled his great big butter-melting smile (which on that day was ice melting) and threw his big arms around my four kids and my wife and me and pulled us all into his big, teddy bear self. "Thanks for coming," he said. "And God bless you and all you do."

"Thank you," I muttered as I pulled myself and my family from his grip. "I won't forget this day. God has blessed us by bringing us here. May he continue to bless you and the House of Peace."

My frozen car didn't want to start when I cranked the engine, and when it did, white steam rose from the exhaust pipe and covered the red setting sun. *I'll never get this thing warm enough to put the kids in,* I thought as I pulled up to the front door of Turner Hall. They ran across the ice strip that covered the curb and jumped into the self-propelled icebox seemingly unaware of the temperature. Their by now frozen mother joined us and we were on our way. The kids were especially quiet on the hour-long ride home, which gave me some time to think. Finally, my daughter Maura broke the silence.

"Dad, Brother Booker is a really holy man, isn't he?"

I was thinking of something to say when a cacophony of conversation began in the back seat.

"Of course he is."

"He takes care of hundreds of poor people!"

"Do you think he's a saint?"

"How can he be so happy when he's so poor?"

"Why aren't there more people like him?"

"Just think of all the people he's helped!"

"I bet Jesus was a lot like him."

And their comments continued all the way home. I didn't get a chance to answer any of their questions during the trip; I just enjoyed hearing them answer each other. But during dinner that night and for many nights thereafter, Brother Booker and the House of Peace were the topics of conversation.

Brother Booker has a message for us, too. There really aren't any new stories—either good or bad—just like there is no new wisdom. Consequently, the wisdom of these teenagers is not new and as Brother said, it isn't even theirs. The wisdom they have shared in this book was given to them by someone they admired: parents, teachers, coaches, aunts, and uncles. They all had a hand in developing the philosophies these teens were willing to share with me. But as parents, we need to know that we are the *most* influential voices in our kids' lives, and live accordingly.

Wisdom Of All Ages

One summer noon when I was a pediatric resident, I was walking down a street in Milwaukee on my way to lunch when the light turned red. Directly in front of me was a young man with a small toddler. As we waited for the light to change, the father squatted to talk to his son. As he did so, the son also squatted. What a picture! Kids do what they see their parents do, and at every age. Country music artist Rodney Atkins in his 2007 hit song "Watching You" hits it on the head. In the lyrics, a young boy curses and when the dad asks where he learned the offensive word the boy explains that he's been watching his dad. He thinks what his dad does is "cool," and he wants to emulate everything he sees his dad do.[277]

So to paraphrase Eric from Chapter 19, "Be the adult you want your child to become."

When my son Rafe was in seventh grade, he was asked to write a paper about what he would consider to be the perfect age. Since he did his homework without interference from me, I didn't know about this paper until Parent-Teacher conference some weeks later. At the conference, Mrs. Carey asked if Mary and I had seen his paper. Mary had; I had not.

"Shame on you!" she chastised. "It was one of the best I have ever received, and I've been assigning this topic for over 23 years. The papers never change much: 16 so I can drive, 18 so I can drink, 21 so I can vote, or some variation on that theme. But you must read Rafe's! He said the perfect age would be 84 because by then he would have experienced many things and acquired so much knowledge that people would come to him and say: 'Rafe, old timer, what should we do about this problem, or what should we do with this thing?' Or would ask a million other questions; and he would know, because he would have wisdom."

Now, as I sneak closer to 84, I'm not so sure that it is the perfect age. Too much pain for one thing. But I have learned that you don't have to be 84, or even 64 or 24, to have wisdom; Rafe had it at age 13. The kids you have read about all had it as teenagers. I have seen wisdom in people of all ages, and so have you. It is wherever we seek it. It comes, as Brother Booker suggested, from those who go before us. You have some wisdom, your parents have some wisdom, and your teenager has some wisdom. Look for it in each other and in all of your acquaintances.

One last story before I close.

Telling It like It Is

When I got the contract to write this book, I called my 94-year-old mother in Minnesota.

"Good news!" I announced. "I got a contract to write another book!"

"Congratulations," Mom answered. "What is this one about?"

"Teenagers," I replied.

"Oh, I guess you told me that before," she remembered. "Just be sure you say something good about them. There are so many good ones, and they do so much good stuff, but all you ever hear about is the bad ones. It's about time someone tells it like it is!"

And my mom knows how it is. She and Dad raised nine kids (7 girls and 2 boys) and through years of hard work, brought us from the Great Depression into the space age and beyond. Now, after 72 years of marriage, they enjoy 32 grandchildren, 59 great-grandchildren, and 6 great-great-grandchildren (and still counting).

Twenty-two years ago when my folks celebrated their Golden Wedding Anniversary, I thought I would try to get some words of wisdom from my dad. Awed that he had raised seven daughters and stayed married for 50 years, I asked: "Dad, however did you manage to live with eight women and not go crazy?"

He looked at me and without smiling said, "All together, they didn't give me as much trouble as you did." (He was, of course, lying through his teeth.)

That ended the discussion, but I had a different recollection of those years at home than he did. I don't remember giving him any trouble at all, and I can name many, many things my sisters did to annoy and worry him. The point is, our memories have a way of revising history to serve our needs; the things we remember about our childhood, especially adolescence, may not really be the way they were. When I first heard that in a medical school psych lecture, I thought, *That's not true. I remember things just as they were.* Of course, I was only 22 at the time so my mind had not had enough time to suppress the memories of my past that made me look bad. Healthy brains actually revise our personal history by deleting uncomfortable memories and embellishing pleasant memories. This mental gymnastics helps us use the past to adjust to the present and create a better future.

The point is, don't be so sure of how it was when you tell your kids about your saintly teenage years, and try not to compare their reality with your perception of history. Try instead to concentrate on finding the things about them you like, admire, and respect. Tell them frequently and sincerely, because they have spent their lives, brief as they may be, liking, admiring, and respecting you—even if you don't deserve it. This mutual admiration society will be the basis on which they will build their moral value system, imitating you in almost every way.

Your teenager is still the angel you held in your arms a decade ago, only now your angel is wearing denim and bears a message from God. If you listen with patience, respect, and love you will decipher that message and help your teen become an adult you can respect, love, and cherish. You already know why teens should listen to their parents—now you know why parents should listen to the wisdom of their teens.

Fathering four children has been the highlight of my life. When I look back at all the things I have done, every accomplishment pales compared to the pride I have in these four young adults. I never imagined parenting could be so much fun and so rewarding. My prayer is that reading this book has helped you so that you, too, can have an equally wonderful experience as a parent. God bless you all!

Appendicies

GUIDELINES FOR ADOLESCENT PREVENTIVE SERVICES†

*I*N AN ATTEMPT to improve medical care for adolescents, the American Medical Association released Guidelines for Adolescent Preventive Services (GAPS) in 1992. A synopsis of GAPS is contained in this appendix. These guidelines should be reviewed with every teen as part of their annual physical. Appendix B lists the questions I ask each teen to assure I am heeding the AMA's guidelines.

I. Recommendations for delivery of health services

   1. All adolescents ages 11–21 should have an annual health visit.

   2. Preventive services should be age and developmentally appropriate.

---

† This appendix is summarized from a document by the American Medical Association and is used with permission.

3. Policies regarding confidential adolescent care should be clear to adolescents and their parents.

II. Recommendations for health guidance

1. Parents should receive health guidance at least once during early adolescence, once during middle adolescence and, once during late adolescence.

2. All adolescents should receive health guidance annually to promote:

- an understanding of growth and development and become actively involved in decisions regarding their health care.

- reduction of injuries.

- good dietary habits to achieve a healthy diet and safe weight management.

- regular exercise.

- responsible sexual behavior, including abstinence.

- avoidance of tobacco, alcohol, and substance abuse.

III. Recommendations for screening

1. All adolescents should be screened for:

- hypertension.

- use of tobacco, including cigarettes and smokeless tobacco.

- eating disorders and obesity as determined by weight and stature.

- use of alcohol and other substances of abuse.

- depression and risk of suicide.

- history of emotional, physical, or sexual abuse.

- learning disorders or other school problems.

- sexual behaviors, including sexual orientation, use of condoms and contraception, number of partners, history of STDs or pregnancy.

2. Selected adolescents should be asked about and screened as follows:

- Those with family history of hyperlipidemia should be screened for cholesterol.

- Sexually active adolescents for sexually transmitted diseases: especially those at risk for HIV including teens with more than one sexual partner in the past six months, who trade sex for drugs, who use intravenous drugs, who have had other STDs, who have a sexual partner at risk for HIV, and males who have had sex with other males.

- females should be screened for pregnancy and cervical cancer.

IV. Recommendations for immunizations

1. All adolescents should receive prophylactic immunizations as recommended by the federally convened Advisory Committee on Immunization Practices. (See Appendix C.)

2. Selected adolescents should receive a tuberculin skin test if they have been exposed, are homeless or living in a shelter, have been incarcerated, or are currently working in a health care facility.

REWIEW OF HEALTH HABITS

*T*HESE QUESTIONS, IN addition to the usual health history, should be discussed with each adolescent at every annual health evaluation. These revealing questions only take a few minutes, provide valuable information about the teenager, and fulfill the Guidelines for Adolescent Preventive services.

1. Do you play any sports or get any daily exercise?

2. How many hours of homework do you do each day?

3. What is your GPA?

4. Do you have a job?

5. How many hours do you work each week during the school year?

6. How many hours of TV or video games do you watch/play each day?

7. Do you have a TV or computer in your room?

8. How many brothers and sisters do you have?

9. Are your parents married, divorced, single, or widowed?

10. How happy do you think your parents are in their marriage?

11. How strict are your parents?

12. How many servings of fruit and/or vegetables do you eat in the average day?

13. How many nights each week do you have dinner with your family?

14. How important is religion in your life?

15. How often do you go to church, temple, or synagogue?

16. Think about your best friend. How often does he or she:

   wear a seat belt?
   smoke cigarettes?
   chew tobacco?
   drink alcohol?
   drive after drinking?
   use drugs?
   carry a gun?

17. Do you think he/she has ever had sex?

18. How often do you:

    wear a seat belt?
    smoke cigarettes?
    chew tobacco?
    drink alcohol?
    use drugs?
    carry a gun?
    ride in a car when the driver has been drinking?
    drive after drinking?

19. How old were you when you first saw porn?

20. How often do you watch porn?

21. How much do you worry about being gay?

22. How concerned are you about the size of your penis/breasts?

23. How old were you the first time you had sex?

24. How old was your first partner?

25. Did you/he use a condom the first time?

26. When was the last time you had sex?

27. How old was your partner?

28. Did you/he use a condom the last time?

29. How many sex partners have you had?

30. What percent of the time did you/he use a condom?

31. Have you ever been pregnant or gotten a girl pregnant?

32. Have you ever had an STD?

33. What problems do you think masturbation causes?

34. Have you ever been:

    emotionally or psychologically abused?
    physically abused?
    sexually abused?

35. How often do you get sad enough to be depressed for a day or more?

36. How often do you get depressed enough to think about suicide?

37. Have you ever attempted suicide?

38. How often do you get angry?

39. How often do you get in a fight?

40. Have you ever been in trouble with the law?

A P P E N D I X   C

IMMUNIZATION SCHEDULE

*T*HE CHART ON the following page outlines standard immunization schedules from birth to age 18. If your child has not received all of the listed immunizations, contact your physician to get a "catch-up" schedule.

Information for these schedules was drawn from the American Academy of Pediatrics.

http://www.aap.org/immunization

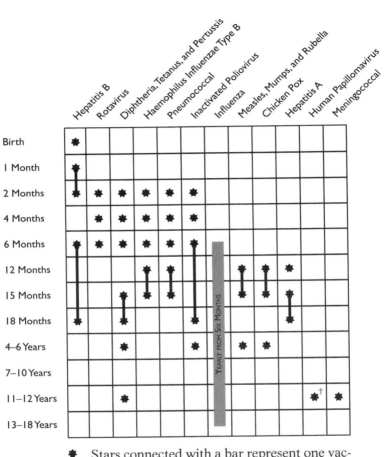

	Hepatitis B	Rotavirus	Diphtheria, Tetanus, and Pertussis	Haemophilus Influenzae Type B	Pneumococcal	Inactivated Poliovirus	Influenza	Measles, Mumps, and Rubella	Chicken Pox	Hepatitis A	Human Papillomavirus	Meningococcal
Birth	★											
1 Month	★											
2 Months	★	★	★	★	★	★						
4 Months		★	★	★	★	★						
6 Months	★	★	★	★	★	★						
12 Months				★	★			★	★	★		
15 Months			★	★	★			★	★	★		
18 Months	★		★			★				★		
4–6 Years			★			★		★	★			
7–10 Years							Yearly from Six Months					
11–12 Years		★									★†	★
13–18 Years												

★ Stars connected with a bar represent one vaccination within the indicated time period.

† Three doses are recommended between ages
11 and 12 for both boys and girls.

ENDNOTES

1   Perioperative genomics is a branch of science and medicine that studies genetic factors that can make an operation either go well or lead to complications; e.g., Brian characterized (discovered) a gene variant which, if present, decreases the need for blood transfusion in cardiac surgery.

2   "The State of our Nation's Youth 2005–2006," *Horatio Alger Association*, http://www.horatioalger.com/pdfs/state05.pdf.

3   Michael Resnick, "National Longitudinal Study of Adolescent Health," *JAMA* 278(10) (September 10, 1997):823–32.

4   James Dobson, "What is the answer to curbing teenage sexual activity?"*Focus on the Family*, April 2001. Can be accessed at http://family.custhelp.com/cgi-bin/family.cfg/php/enduser/std_adp.php?p_faqid=828.

5   Lynn Minton, "Fresh Voices," *Parade Magazine*, August 22, 1999.

6   Tom Boyle, "St. Pius Men Hear Talk on Fatherhood," *The Georgia Bulletin*, February 22, 2001.

7   Kate Howard, "Parents can keep GPS eye on teen driver's every turn," *The Tennessean,* June 20, 2007, Main News Section, A1.

8   John O'Sullivan, *The President, the Pope, and the Prime*

Minister, Three Who Changed the World (Washington, DC: Regnery Publishing, Inc., 2006), 164.

9 Martha Marino and Sue Butkus, "Eat Better; Eat Together: Research on Family Meals," *Washington State University,* http://nutrition.wsu.edu/ebet/background.html; "For happy teens, pass the peas," *The Atlanta Journal-Constitution,* August 16, 1997, A7.

10 The National Center on Addiction and Substance Abuse at Columbia University Annual Report, September 2007, Accompanying Statement by Joseph A. Califano, Jr., Chairman and President of the Board of Directors, "The Importance of Family Dinners IV," Sponsored by The Safeway Foundation, accessed at http://www.casacolumbia.org/absolutenm/ articlefiles/380-Importance%20of%20Family%20Dinners%20IV.pdf.

11 Op. cit., Marino and Butkus.

12 Ibid

13 Katharine Coon, et al., "Relationships Between Use of Television During Meals and Children's Food Consumption Patterns," *Pediatrics* 107(1) (January 2001):e7.

14 Renee Boynton-Jarrett, et al., "Impact of Television Viewing Patterns on Fruit and Vegetable Consumption Among Adolescents," *Pediatrics* 112(6) (2003): 1321–26.

15 Karen Olson, "Eating Out Poses Health Risks for Kids," (paper presented at the American Heart Association 2005 Scientific Sessions, Dallas, Texas, November 13–16, 2005).

16 Mark A. Pereira, et al., "Fast-food habits, weight gain, and insulin resistance (the CARDIA study): 15-year prospective analysis," *The Lancet* 365 (2005): 36–42.

17 Gerald Berenson of the Tulane Center for Cardiovascular Health, "The Bogalusa heart study" (paper presented at the annual meeting of the American Society of Hypertension, New Orleans, Louisiana, May 20, 2008).

18 Ibid.

19 FTC Releases Research on Children's Exposure to Television

Advertising (June 1, 2007), "Children Not Seeing More Food Ads on Television," *FTC.gov,* http://www.ftc.gov/opa/2007/06/childrenadsstudy.shtm; Kaiser Family Foundation Report (March 2007), "Food for Thought: Television Food Advertising to Children in the United States," *The Henry J. Kaiser Family Foundation,* http://www.kff.org/entmedia/upload/7618.pdf.

20   Restaurant news (July 8, 2007: news release August 7, 2007), "Study Finds Children Swayed by Brand Preferences," *QSR Magazine.com,* http://www.qsrmagazine.com/articles/news/story.phtml?id=5665.

21   Dwight Lewis, "Know right where your teen is; it is life and death," *The Tennessean,* December 15, 2005.

22   Ibid.

23   BrainyQuote, "Ronald Reagan Quotes," *BrainyMedia.com,* http://www.brainyquote.com/quotes/authors/r/ronald_reagan_5.html.

24   Traffic Safety Facts (July 2007), "2006 Traffic Safety Annual Assessment–A Preview," *NHTSA,* http://www-nrd.nhtsa.dot.gov/Pubs/810791.PDF; Traffic Safety Facts (updated March 2008), "Alcohol Impaired Driving," *NHTSA,* http://www-nrd.nhtsa.dot.gov/Pubs/810801.PDF.

25   One-Minute World News (March 23, 2004), "Mother calls for tougher gun law," *BBC News,* http://news.bbc.co.uk/2/hi/uk_news/3561071.stm.

26   Album & Victim's stories, "Anton Hyman," MAMAA, http://www.mamaa.org/infalah.html.

27   Sylvia Slaughter, "Family sees dream home come to life," *The Tennessean,* August 5, 2006, Main News section.

28   Lisa Fernandez and Ben Aguirre, Jr., "Mother's sacrifice saves son from pit bull," *Oakland Tribune,* September 6, 2007, Media News story.

29   Myrna Weissman, et al., "Remissions in Maternal Depression and Child Psychopathology," *JAMA* 295(12) (March 22/29, 2006):1389–98.

30   I. Akman, et al., "Mothers' postpartum psychological adjustment and infantile colic," *Archives of Disease of Children* 91(5) (May 2006): 417–19.

31   Lindsey O'Connor, *If Mama Ain't Happy, Ain't Nobody Happy!: Making the Choice to Rejoice,* (Eugene, Oregon: Harvest House Publishers, 2006).

32   Kris and Brian Gillespie, *When Mama Ain't Happy, Ain't Nobody Happy: 52 Secrets Uncovered! Rules That Women Want Men to Know* (Tulsa, OK: Insight International, 2000).

33   Michael J. Formica, "Gender Differences, Sexuality and Emotional Infidelity," *Psychology Today,* January 8, 2009, http://www.psychologytoday.com/blog/enlightened-living/200901/gender-differences-sexuality-and-emotional-infidelity.

34   Kyle Pruett and Marsha Kline Pruett, *Partnership Parenting, How Men and Women Parent Differently and How it Helps Your Kids,* (Cambridge:Da Capo Lifelong Books, 2009).

35   Cal Thomas, "Hope for conservative woman president," *Dispatch Politics,* a division of *The Columbus Dispatch,* June 7, 2008.

36   Ibid.

37   J. Serpell, "Beneficial effects of pet ownership on some aspects of human health and behavior," *Journal of the Royal Society of Medicine* 84 (1991): 717–20.

38   "14 Ways to Show Love for Your Child This Valentine's Day," *American Academy of Pediatrics,* February 2009, http://www.aap.org/advocacy/releases/febvaltips.cfm.

39   Dennis Ownby, et al., "Exposure to dogs and cats in the first year of life and risk of allergic sensitization at 6 to 7 years of age," *JAMA* 288(8) (2002): 963–72.

40   P. Cullinan, et al., " Early allergen exposure, skin prick responses, and atopic wheeze at age 5 in English children: a cohort study." Thorax 59 (October 2004): 855–61; Eva Rönmark, et al., "Four-year incidence of allergic sensitization

among schoolchildren in a community where allergy to cat and dog dominates sensitization: Report from the obstructive lung disease in northern sweden study group," *The Journal of Allergy and Clinical Immunology* 112(4) (October 2004): 747–54; Sid Kirchheimer, "Pets May Prevent Allergies in Kids," *WebMD Health News,*{END ITALICS http://www.webmd.com/allergies/news/20031014/pets-may-prevent-allergies-in-kids.

41   C. M. Chen, et al., "Dog ownership and contact during childhood and later allergy development," *European Respiratory Journal* 31(5) (May 2008 [Epub Febuary 6, 2008]): 963–73.

42   Karen Allen, Jim Blascovich, and Wendy B. Mendes, "Cardiovascular Reactivity and the Presence of Pets, Friends, and Spouses: The Truth About Cats and Dogs," *Psychosomatic Medicine* 64 (2002):727–39.

43   Julie V. Iovine, "The healing ways of Dr. Dog," *The New York Times*, October 28, 2001.

44   Ibid.

45   Jeff Fisher, "Exercise has proven mental benefits, so come run to beat the blues," *The Tennessean*, March 28, 2008.

46   University of Tennessee College of Veterinary Medicine: a nonprofit program benefiting adolescents and dogs, "Humans & Animals Learning together," *HALT,* http://www.vet.utk.edu/halt/about.shtml.

47   Kris Bulcroft, "Pets in the American Family," *People, Animals, Environment* 8(4) (1990): 13–14.

48   Bill Strickland, "The Benefits of Pets," *Parents.com,* http://www.parents.com/family-life/pets/kids/pets-good-for-kids/.

49   James Serpell, "Guest Editor's Introduction: Animals in Children's Lives," *Society and Animals, Journal of Human-Animal Studies* 7, no. 2 (1999): 87–93.

50   Abby Deliz, "Newborns Need Touch," *Suite 101.com,* September 29, 2008, http://massagetherapy.suite101.com/

article.cfm/newborns_need_touch.

51 A. Dougall and J. Fiske, "Surving child sexual abuse: the relevance to dental practice," *Dental Update* 36(5) (June 2009): 294–96, 298–300, 303–04.

52 Industry Statistics and Trends (2007–2008), "Pet Ownership," *APPA*, http://americanpetproducts.org/press_industrytrends.asp.

53 Christian Smith and Melinda Lundquist Demon, "Soul Searching: The Religious and Spiritual Lives of American Teenagers" (New York: Oxford University Press, 2005), 129–130.

54 B. M. Yarnold, "Cocaine use among Miami's public school students, 1992: religion versus peers and availability," *Journal of Health and Social Policy* 11(2) (1999): 69–84.

55 R. L. Poulson, et al., "Alcohol consumption, strength of religious beliefs, and risky sexual behavior in college students," *Journal of American College Health* 46(5) (March 1998): 277–32.

56 J. M. Wallace, et al., "Religion's role in promoting health and reducing risk among American youth," *Health Education and Behavior* 25(6) (December 1, 1998): 721–41.

57 Eric Goldscheider, "Seeking a Role for Religion on Campus," *The New York Times*, February 2, 2002.

58 Institute for American Values, "Hardwired to Connect: The New Scientific Case for Authoritative Communities," report by the Commission on Children at Risk, September 9, 2003, http://www.americanvalues.org/html/hardwired_press_release.html.

59 Ibid.

60 Robert Shaw, *The Epidemic*, (New York: Regan Books, 2003), xii, 4.

61 Ibid., p. 21.

62 Op. cit., Institute for American Values.

63 Amanda Aikman, "Do Children Need Religion?" *Reach*, September 1995.

64   Janet Daling, et al., "Risk of Breast Cancer Among Young Women: Relationship to Induced Abortion,"*Journal of the National Cancer Institute* 86(21) (1994): 1584–92.

65   Karin Michels, et al., "Abortion and breast cancer risk in seven countries," *Cancer Causes and Control* 6:(1) (January 1995): 75–82.

66   Mads Melbye, et al., "Induced Abortion and the Risk of Breast Cancer," *The New England Journal of Medicine* 336(2) (January 9, 1997): 81–5.

67   Karin Michels, et al., "Induced and Spontaneous Abortion and Incidence of Breast Cancer Among Young Women: A Prospective Cohort Study," *Archives of Internal Medicine* 167 (April 2007): 814–20.

68   Abortion and breast cancer study seriously flawed, "Commentary on the Study, Michels, et al. 2007," *ABC*, http://www.abortionbreastcancer.com/commentary/070423.

69   Joel Brind, "Induced Abortion and Breast Cancer Risk: A Critical Analysis of the Report of the Harvard Nurses Study II," *Journal of American Physicians and Surgeons* 12 no. 2 (2007).

70   Jesse R. Cougle, et al., "Depression associated with abortion and childbirth: a long-term analysis of the NLSY cohort," *Medical Science Monitor* 9(4) (2003): 105–12.

71   Christian Smith with Melinda Lundquist Denton, *Soul Searching, The Religious and Spiritual Lives of American Teenagers* (New York: Oxford University Press, 2005).

72   Ibid., p. 216–17.

73   Op. Cit., Smith and Demon, 154–156; 218–258.

74   Armand M. Nicholi, *The New Harvard Guide to Psychiatry* (Cambridge: The Belknap Press of Harvard University Press, 1988).

75   Lynn Minton, "Fresh Voices," *Parade Magazine,* February 14, 1999, 18.

76   T. A. Wills and S. D. Cleary, "Peer and adolescent substance use among 6th–9th graders: latent growth analyses of

influence versus selection mechanisms," *Health Psychology* 18(5) (September 1999): 453–63.

77   R. W. Blum, et al., *Protecting Teens, Beyond Race, Income and Family Structure* (Minneapolis, MN: Center for Adolescent Health, University of Minnesota, 2000)24.

78   Stephen Allen Christensen, "Adolescents and Cigarette Smoking: Teens Appear to Be Using Tobacco at an Increasing Rate," *Suite 101.com: The genuine article. Literally,* December 8, 2008, http://substanceabuse.suite101.com/article.cfm/adolescents_and_cigarette_smoking.

79   Luther Terry, *Smoking and Health, Report of the Advisory Committee to the Surgeon General of the Public Health Service* (Washington, DC: U.S. Department of Health Education, and Welfare, 1964).

80   Duane Stanford, "TEEN DRIVING: Young drinkers sentenced, Gwinnett girl leaving party died in wreck," *The Atlanta Journal and Constitution,* November 28, 2000.

81   Fred M. Hechinger, *Fateful Choices* (New York, NY: Carnegie Corporation of America, 1992), 110.

82   Media Center, "Ensuring Solutions to Alcohol Problems," *The George Washington University Medical Center,* http://www.ensuringsolutions.org/media/.

83   Op. cit., Hechinger.

84   Office of National Drug Control Policy (2004), "The economic costs of drug abuse in the United States, 1992–2002," Washington, DC: Executive Office of the President (Publication No. 207303).

85   Monica H. Swahn, et al., "Age of Initiating Alcohol Use, Suicidal Behavior and Dating Violence Among High Risk Seventh-Grade Adolencnts," *Pediatrics* 121 (February 2008): 297–305.

86   N. Peleg-Oren, et al., "Drinking Alcohol before Age 13 and Negative Outcomes in Late Adolescence," *Alcoholism: Clinical Experimental Research,* 31 August 2009.

87   Sandy Fertman Ryan, "Wasted lives: the truth about teen

girls and drinking," *Girls' Life*, Oct/Nov 2004.

88 Office of Applied Studies, "SAMHSA's Latest National Survey on Drug Use & Health," U.S. Department of Health and Human Services, Last updateds September 10, 2009, http://www.oas.samhsa.gov/NSDUHlatest.htm.

89 Girl Talk: Choices and Consequences of Underaged Drinking, "A Guide For Mothers and Daughters to Prevent Underage Drinking," *The Century Council*, www.girlsanddrinking.org.

90 Ibid.

91 Distillers Fighting Drunk Driving and Underaged Drinking, "Fight Drunk Driving," *The Century Council*, www.century-council.org.

92 Robert Davis, "'Hands-on' parent can keep kids off drugs," *USA TODAY*, February 22, 2001.

93 Op. cit., Hechinger, p. 111.

94 "How Parents Can Prevent Drug Abuse," *National Crime Prevention Council*, 2009, http://www.ncpc.org/topics/drug-abuse/drug-abuse/alcohol-tobacco-and-other-drugs.

95 Lisa Miller, et al., "Religiosity and Substance Use and Abuse Among Adolescents in the National Survey," *Journal of the American Academy of Child and Adolescent Psychiatry* 39(9) (September 2000): 1190–97.

96 Tony Hendra, *Father Joe* (New York: Random House, 2004).

97 Karen Shideler, "Youthful health mistakes that will come back to haunt you," *Dayton Daily News*, August 31, 2000.

98 National Center for Health Statistics (July 24, 2002), "New Report Sheds Light on Trends and Patterns in Marriage, Divorce, and Cohabitation," *CDC.gov*, http://www.cdc.gov/nchs/pressroom/02news/div_mar_cohab.htm.

99 Baby, Pregnancy, and Parenting Information, "Causes for Infertility," *Babies Online*, http://www.babiesonline.com/articles/ttc/causes-for-infertility.asp.

100 Department of Health and Human Services Centers for

Disease Control and Prevention, "Sexually Transmitted Diseases: Chlamydia - CDC Fact Sheet," *USA.gov,* December 20, 2007, http://www.cdc.gov/std/Chlamydia/STDFact-Chlamydia.htm; Steve Sternberg, "Chlamydia tops 1 million cases with STDs rising slightly overall," *USA Today,* November 14, 2007.

101 Basic Statistics (Volume 19, 2007), "Cases of HIV Infection and AIDS in the United States and Dependent Areas: HIV/AIDS Survelliance Report," *CDC.gov,* http://www.cdc.gov/hiv/topics/surveillance/basic.htm#aidscases.

102 Gypsyamber D'Souza, et al., "Case-Control Study of Human Papillomavirus and Oropharyngeal Cancer," *New England Journal of Medicine* 356(19) (May 10, 2007): 1944–56.

103 Sexually Transmitted Diseases (1999 data), "Tracking the Hidden Epidemics: Trends in STDs in the United States," *CDC.gov,* http://www.cdc.gov/std/Trends2000/herpes-close.htm.

104 Global HIV/AIDS (last modified January 7, 2009), "CDC Global HIV/AIDS Activities–Botswana," *CDC.gov,* http://www.cdc.gov/globalaids/countries/Botswana; Global HIV/AIDS (last modified October 23, 2008), "HIV/AIDS Surveillance Reports–Swaziland," *CDC.gov,* http://www.cdc.gov/search.do?action=search&queryText=hiv+Swaziland.

105 Ibid.

106 Elizabeth Donegan (October 2003), "Transmission of HIV by Blood, Blood Products, Tissue Transplantation, and Artifical Insemination," *HIV InSite,* http://hivinsite.ucsf.edu/InSite?page=kb-07-02-09#S2.1X.

107 "Reported Cases of Selected Notifiable Diseases in Georgia, (Profile for December 2006), *The Georgia Epidemiology Report* 23(3) (March 4, 2007): 4.

108 Joseph Nolen, "Is premarital sex a sin?" *Liguori,* January 15, 2006.

109 Kevin McDonald, "The cost of a divorce," *Bankrate.com,* http://www.bankrate.com/brm/news/advice/19990903a.

asp.

110 Ellen Rock, et al., "A rose by any other name? Objective Knowledge, Perceived Knowledge, and Adolescent Male Condom Use," *Pediatrics* 115(3) (March 2005): 667–72.

111 Linda Johnson, "Groups push for condom labeling to be more precise," *The Tennessean*, May 30, 2005.

112 Ibid.

113 Lisa Manhart, et al., "Mycoplasma genitalium Among Young Adults in the United States: an Emerging Sexually Transmitted Infection," *American Journal of Public Health* 97, no. 6 (June 2007):1118–25.

114 Leandro Mena, et al., "Mycoplasma genitalium infections in asymptomatic men and men with urethritis attending a sexually transmitted diseases clinic in New Orleans," *Clinical Infectious Diseases* 35 (2002): 1167–73.

115 Peter J. Smith quoting Matt Barber, "New STD Infection Rates '4 times higher among those who used condoms during their last vaginal intercourse': Study–M. Genitalium Surpasses Gonorrhea among Young Adults Reports Health Journal," *LifeSiteNews.com*, http://www.lifesitenews.com/ldn/2007/jun/070612.html#5.

116 "Sex: The White House ban on condoms," *The Week*, January 24, 2003.

117 2008 National STD Prevention Conference, "3.2 Million Female Adolescents Estimated to Have at Least One of the Most Common STDs: Other Studies Featured at 2008 National STD Prevention Conference Show Missed Opportunities for STD Screening and Innovative Solutions for STD Prevention and Treatment," *CDC.gov*, http://www.cdc.gov/STDConference/2008/media/release-11march2008.htm.

118 Cal Thomas, "Steamy Teen 'love' in Tampa," *JWR Review*, December 15, 2005.

119 Christopher Trenholm, et al., "Impacts of Four Title V, Section 510 Abstinence Education Programs Final Report," *Mathematica Policy Research, Inc.*, April 2007,

http://www.mathematica-mpr.com/publications/PDFs/impactabstinence.pdf.

120   Steven C. Marino, et al., "Beyound the 'Big Talk': The Importance of Breadth and Repetition in Parent-Adolescent Communication About Sexual Issues," *Pediatrics* 121 (March 2008): e612–e618; Dr. Michael A. Carrera of The Children's Aid Society agrees when he says: "Repetitions of these messages throughout their development and daily adult role modeling will provide the needed emphasis on the specific view a parent wants to convey to their child." Cited October 12, 2009, from: http://www.advocatesforyouth. org/index.php?option=com_content&task=view&id=165 &Itemid=206.

121   Michael A. Carrera of The Children's Aid Society, "Parents and Their Children's Learning about Sexuality," *Advocates for Youth*, http://www.advocatesforyouth.org/index. php?option=com_content&task=view&id=165&Itemid=2 06.

122   Victor Strasburger, "'Clueless': Why Do Pediatricians Underestimate the Media's Influence on Children and Adolescents?" *Pediatrics* 117(4) (2006): 1427–31.

123   Peter Millet, "Does abstinence education work? Teen sexuality more complicated than that," *The Tennessean*, May 27, 2007, 23A.

124   Sara Forhan, "Nationally Representative CDC Study Finds 1 in 4 Teenage Girls Has a Sexually Transmitted Disease," *CDC.gov*, March 11, 2008, http://www.cdc.gov/stdconference/2008/media/release-11march2008.htm.

125   R. Lowry, et al., "Substance use and HIV-related sexual behaviors among U.S. high school students: Are they related?" *American Journal of Public Health* 84 (1994):1116–20.

126   Bruce Noland quoting Rev. Jerrode Keys, "Teens getting message on sex,"*The Atlanta Journal and Constitution,*June 26, 1999.

127   American Academy of Pediatrics, Committee on Public

Education, "Children, Adolescents, and Television," *Pediatrics* 107(2) (February 2001):423–26.

128 "Pull the Plug," *The Tennessean*, February 7, 2004.

129 Ibid.

130 Carla Kemp, "Health Briefs, Parents not following AAP TV Guidelines," *AAP News*, January 2004, 24:2.

131 Op. cit., American Academy of Pediatrics, Committee on Public Education, p. 423–26.

132 "Family News," *Focus on the Family*, April 2001.

133 Stephanie Strauss, "Is Media Violence Affecting Your Kids?" *Nashville Parent*, February 2005, 49–50. Can be viewed online at http://www.parentworld.com/news.php?viewStory=1428.

134 Daheia J. Barr-Anderson, et al., "Characteristics Associated With Older Adolescents Who Have a Television in Their Bedrooms," *Pediatrics* 121(4) (April 2008):718–24.

135 Ibid.

136 Op. cit., Kemp, p. 24, 1:2.

137 Op. cit., American Academy of Pediatrics, Committee on Public Education, p. 423–26.

138 Dimitri A. Christakis, "Can We Turn a Toxin Into a Tonic? Toward 21st-Century Television Alchemy," *Pediatrics* 120(3) (September 2007): 647–48.

139 Kevin Downey, "Bring the Family," *Wall Street Journal*, March 10, 2008.

140 Ibid.

141 "In the Matter of Violent Television Programming And Its Impact On Children," a report before the Federal Communications Commission, Washington, D.C., adopted April 6, 2007, released April 25, 2007, http://www.c-span.org/pdf/fcc_tvviolence.pdf page 14. This is an excellent article filled with lots of well-documented facts, easy to read, but a bit long. I would recommend it for anyone interested in learning more about Television's effect on children.

142 Kelli Turner, "V-chip doesn't protect kids, so TV industry

now must clean up its act," *The Tennessean,* June 2, 2007.

143 Frederick J. Zimmerman, et al., "Associations between Media Viewing and Language Development in Children Under Age 2 Years, *The Journal of Pediatrics* 151(4) (October 2007): 364–68.

144 Ibid.

145 C. E. Landhuis, et al., "Does Childhood Television Viewing Lead to Attention Problems in Adolescence? Results From a Prospective Longitudinal Study," *Pediatrics* 120(3) (September 2007): 532–37.

146 Dimitri A. Christakis, et al., "Early Television Exposure and Subsequent Attentional Problems in Children," *Pediatrics* 113(4) (April 2004): 708–13.

147 Judith Owens, et al., "Television viewing Habits and Sleep Disturbance in School Children," *Pediatrics* 104(3) (September 1999): e27.

148 Op. cit., Coon, p. e7.

149 Ibid.

150 Ibid.

151 Robert DuRant, et al., "The Relationship Among Television Watching, Physical Activity, and Body Composition of Young Children," *Pediatrics* 94(4) (October 1994): 449–55.

152 M. S. Tremblay and J. D. Willms, "Is the Canadian child obesity epidemic related to physical inactivity?" *International Journal of Obesity* 27 (2003): 1100–05.

153 Barbara Dennison, et al., "Television Viewing and Television in Bedroom Associated With Overweight Risk Among Low-Income Preschool Children," *Pediatrics* 109(6) (June 2002): 1028–35.

154 Pradeep P.Gidwani, et al., "Television Viewing and Initiation of Smoking Among Youth," *Pediatrics* 110(3) (September 2002): 505–08.

155 Op. cit., American Academy of Pediatrics, Committee on Public Education, p. 423–26.

156 Erica Weintraub Austin, et al., "The Role of Interpretation Processes and Parental Discussion in the Media's Effects on Adolescents' Use of Alcohol" *Pediatrics* 105(2) (February 2000): 343–49.

157 Rebecca Collins, et al., "Watching sex on television predicts adolescent initiation of sexual behavior," *Pediatrics* 114(3) (September 2004): e280–289.

158 Diana M. Zuckerman and Barry S. Zuckerman, "Television's Impact on Children," *Pediatrics* 75(2) (February 1985): 233–40.

159 Kenneth Gadow and Joyce Sprafkin, "Field Experiments of Television Violence with Children: Evidence for an Environmental Hazard?" *Pediatrics* 83(3) (March 1989): 399–405.

160 Dimitri A. Christakis, "The Effects of Infant Media Usage: What Do We Know and What Should We Learn?" *Acta Paediatrica* 98(1) (Jan 2009): 8–16.

161 David Kleeman, "The Good Things About Television," *Media Awareness Network,* http://www.media-awareness.ca/english/parents/television/good_things_tv.cfm cited October 15, 2009.

162 Op. cit., American Academy of Pediatrics, Committee on Public Education, p. 423–26.

163 Kimberly Daly, "Reap the riches of family game night," *The Tennessean,* January 9, 2006.

164 Horatio Alger Study of Our Nations Youth (2005), "Teens Willing to Work Harder and Expect More From Education," *Horatio Alger Association,* http://www.horatioalger.com/news/05sony.cfm.

165 Op. cit., Christakis, "Early Television Exposure and Subsequent Attentional Problems in Children."

166 Ibid.

167 Heidi Aase and Terje Savolden, "Infrequent, but not frequent, reinforcers produce more variable responding and deficient sustained attention in young children with

attention-deficit/hyperactivity disorder (ADHD)," *The Journal of Child Psychology and Psychiatry* 47(5) (May 2006): 457–71.

168   Carla Kemp, "Survey ranks top 5 drugs for children based on spending," *AAP News,* December 2007, 28:12:2.

169   Richard M. Scheffler, et al., "Positive Association Between Attention-Deficit/Hyperactivity Disorder Medication Use and Academic Achievement During Elementary School," *Pediatrics* 123(5) (May 2009): 1273–79.

170   Shari Roan, "Flu shot gave you the flu? It's a myth," *Los Angeles Times,* November 03, 2003.

171   Lauran Neergaard, ""New nasal-spray flu vaccine is costly, not for everyone," *The Tennessean,* September 23, 2003.

172   Karen Hunter (podcast February 27, 2008), "Influenza Vaccination Now Recommended for Children 6 months to 18 years of Age," *CDC.gov,* http://www2a.cdc.gov/podcasts/player.asp?f=8383; Maggie Fox, Health and Science Editor (February 27, 2008), "All U.S. kids should get flu vaccine, panel says," *Reuters.com,* http://www.reuters.com/article/healthNews/idUSWAT00897520080227.

173   Joint News Release (March 10, 2006), "Global measles deaths plunge by 48% over past six years," *World Health Organization,* www.who.int/mediacentre/news/releases/2006/pr11/en/print.html.

174   Gina Kolata, *Flu. The Story Of The Great Influenza Pandemic,* (New York: Touchstone, 2001).

175   John M. Barry, *The Great Influenza: The Epic Story of the 1918 Pandemic,* (New York: Viking, 2004) 359.

176   Report prepared by the Majority Staff: U.S. House of Representatives (January 2009), "Getting Beyond Getting Ready for Pandemic Influenza," *Committee on Homeland Security,* http://homeland.house.gov/SiteDocuments/20090114124322-85263.pdf.

177   Bill Snyder, "How did we get here and how bad will H1N1 be?" *Vanderbilt University MedicalCenter Reporter* Vol

XIX, #38. Oct 2, 2009.

178   Ibid.

179   American Academy of Pediatrics Task Force on Circumcision, "Circumcision policy statement," *Pediatrics* 103(3) (March 1999): 686–93.

180   I. O. W. Leitch, "Circumcision: a Continuing Enigma," *Australian Paediatric Journal* 6 (June 1970): 59–65.

181   "Neonatal circumcision revisited. Fetus and Newborn Committee, Canadian Paediatric Society," *Canadian Medical Association Journal* 154(6) (15 March 1996): 769–80.

182   "The decline of circumcision," *The Week,* March 14, 2003.

183   David M. Fergusson, et al., "Circumcision Status and Risk of Sexually Transmitted Infection in Young Adult Males: An analysis of a Longitudinal Birth Cohort," *Pediatrics* 118(5) (November 2006): 1971–76.

184   E.O. Laumann, et al., "Circumcision in the United States: prevalence, prophylactic effects, and sexual practice," *JAMA* 277(13) (April 2, 1997): 1052–57.

185   S. S. Dave, et al., "Male Circumcision in Britain: findings from a national probability sample survey," *Sexually Transmitted Infections* 79 (2003): 499–500.

186   J. Richters, et al., "Circumcision in Australia: prevalence and effect on sexual health," *International Journal of STD & AIDS* 17 (2006): 547–54.

187   Nigel P. Dickson, et al., "Male Circumcision and Risk of Sexually Transmitted Infections in a Birth Cohort," *Journal of Pediatrics* 152(3) (March 2008): 383–87.

188   R. C. Bailey, et al., "Male circumcision for HIV prevention in young men in Kisumu, Kenya: a randomized controlled trial," *The Lancet* 369(9562) (24 February 2007): 643–56.

189   Ronald H. Gray, et al., "Male circumcision for HIV prevention in men in Rakai, Uganda: a randomized trial," *The Lancet* 368(9562) (24 February 2007): 657–66.

190   Seth Kalichman, et al., "Male Circumcision in HIV

prevention," *The Lancet* 369(9573) (12 May 2007): 1597.

191 Nigel O'Farrell, et al., "Male Circumcision in HIV prevention," *The Lancet* 369(9573) (12 May 2007): 1598.

192 George Dennison and George Hill, "Male Circumcision in HIV prevention," *The Lancet* 369(9573) (12 May 2007): 1598.

193 Devon D. Brewer, et al., "Male and Female Circumcision Associated With Prevalent HIV Infection in Virgins and Adolescents in Kenya, Lesotho, and Tanzania," *Annals of Epidemiology* 17(3) (March 2007): 217–26.

194 Global Campaign for Microbicides, "Male Circumcision: What Does It Mean For Women?" Global-Campaign.org, http://www.global-campaign.org/clientfiles/FS-MaleCircumcision%5BE%5D.pdf.

195 Country Profiles, "2006 Report on the Global Aids Epidemic," *UNAids.org,* http://data.unaids.org/pub/GlobalReport/2006/2006_GR_ANN1M-Z_en.pdf.

196 A. Zoosmann-Diskin, "No protective effect of circumcision on human immunodeficiency virus incidence," *Journal of Infectious Disease* 181(5) (May 2000): 1865–68.

197 Anna Taddio, et al., "Effect of neonatal circumcision on pain response during subsequent routine immunizations," *The Lancet* 349(9052) (March 1997): 599–603.

198 Circumcision of male infants research paper (Brisbane 1993: Section 2), "The History of Male Circumcision," *Cirp. org,* http://www.cirp.org/library/legal/QLRC/02.html.

199 John Harvey Kellogg, *Plain Facts for Old and Young* (written in 1877, republished in Charleston, SC: BiblioLife, 2008) 295.

200 Lewis Sayre, "Lecture III: Deformities: Etiology (continued)–Congenital Phimosis and Adherent Prepuce–Prognosis–Diagnosis," *History of Circumcision,* http://www.historyofcircumcision.net/index.php?option=content&task=view&id=58.

201 K. R. Shankar and A. M. Rickwood, "The Incidence of

Phimosis in Boys," *British Journal of Urology* 84(1) (July 1999): 101–2.

202 M. A. Monsour, et al., "Medical management of phimosis in children: our experience with topical steroids," *Journal of Urology* 162(3 pt. 2) (September 1999): 1162–64.

203 Op. cit., "The decline of circumcision," p. 13.

204 Jack Paradise, et al., "Tympanostomy Tubes and Developmental Outcomes at 9 to 11 Years of Age," *New England Journal of Medicine* 356(3) (18 January 2007): 248–61.

205 James M. Steckelberg, "Honey: An effective cough remedy?" *MayoClinic.com,* March 18, 2008, http://www.mayoclinic.com/health/honey/AN01799.

206 Frank Pittman, *Man Enough* (New York: Putnam's and Sons, 1993) 212.

207 Lawrence S. Neinstein, *Adolescent Health Care* (Baltimore: Urban & Schwarzenberg, 1984) 28. Neinstein gives the measurement of the average size adult penis as 13.2 centimeters, which converts to 5.5 inches.

208 Generation Rx.com survey (released December 11, 2001), "Survey: more young people going online for health information than to shop, check sports scores or chat," *The Kaiser Family Foundation,* http://www.kff.org/entmedia/Press%20Release..pdf.

209 Janis Wolak, et al., "Unwanted and Wanted Exposure to Online Pornography in a National Sample of Youth Internet Users," *Pediatrics* 119(2) (February 2007): 247–57.

210 Stuart Sheperd, "Teens Ambivalent About Internet Porn," *family.org,* 17 December 2001; Editorial, "Fence Off Internet Porn," *USA Today,* 16 September 2005. http://www.urbanministry.org/wiki/teens-ambivalent-about-internet-porn.

211 W. Marshall, "Report on the Use of Pornography by Sexual Offenders," Report to the Federal Department of Justice, Ottawa, Canada, 1983.

212 Gary R. Brooks, *The Centerfold Syndrome: How Men*

Can Overcome Objectification and Achieve Intimacy with Women (San Francisco: Jossey-Bass, 1996), 2.

213 Samuel Roberts, "Fantasy-Reality Alignment: a Cognitive-Behavorial Technique to Help Men Overcome Pornography Addiction or Compulsion," *PornographyAddictionHelp. Info,* 2008, http://www.PornographyAddictionHelp.Info.

214 Dolf Zillmann and Jennings Bryant, editors, *Pornography: Research Advances & Policy Considerations* (Mahway, NJ: Lawrence Erlbaum, 1989), 143.

215 The National Coalition for the Protection of Children and Families, quoting Dr. Reo M. Christensen, "The Subtle Dangers of Pornography," *Troubledwith.com,* http://www.troubledwith.com/AbuseandAddiction/A000000775. cfm?topic=abuse%20and%20addiction%3A%20 pornography%20and%20cybersex.

216 Cal Thomas (March 13, 2008), "Sex and the Married Governor," *CalThomas.com,* http://www.calthomas.com/index. php?news=2209.

217 Morris Green, "Myth of the Month: The 10-minute visit: Anything but routine," *Contemporary Pediatrics* (August 1992): 53–61.

218 Gerald Caplan and Serge Lebovici, editors, *Adolescence: psychosocial perspectives* (New York: New York Basic Books, 1969), 244–51.

219 Leonard Pitts, "This Just In: Parents Matter as Role Models," *The Tennessean,* September 13, 1997.

220 Ibid.

221 "Study: Links between symptoms of depression among young people and relationships with others," *The Daily,* February 16, 2005. This release is based on a research paper entitled, "Youth depressive symptoms and changes in relationships with parents and peers." Data used in this study were taken from the National Longitudinal Survey of Children and Youth (NLSCY), a long-term study of children in Canada that collects information on a wide range of

factors influencing the social, emotional, and behavioural development of children from birth to early adulthood. The NLSCY began in 1994 and is jointly conducted by Statistics Canada and Social Development Canada.

222 Gunilla Ringbäck Weitoft, et al., "Mortality, severe morbidity, and injury in children living with single parents in Sweden: a population-based study," *The Lancet* 361(9354) (25 January 2003): 289–95.

223 National Center for Health Statistics. Multiple cause-of-death public-use data files, 1990 through 2004. Hyattsville, MD: U.S. Department of Health and Human Services, CDC, National Center for Health Statistics; 2007.

224 Douglas F. Levinson, "The genetics of Depression: A review," *Biological Psychiatry* 60(2) (15 July 2006): 84–92. Cited at http://depressiongenetics.med.upenn.edu/DLResearch/Levinson_GeneticsDepression.pdf.

225 Meg Meeker, *Strong Fathers, Strong Daughters* (Washington, DC: Regnery Publishing, Inc., 2006): 104.

226 Denise Hallfors, et al., "Which Comes First in Adolescence: Sex and Drugs or Depression?" *American Journal of Preventive Medicine* 29(3) (October 2005): 163–70.

227 Facts for Families (No. 10: updated May 2008), "Teen Suicide," *American Academy of Child & Adolescent Psychiatry*, http://www.aacap.org/cs/root/facts_for_families/teen_suicide.

228 C. S. Lewis, *The Screwtape Letters* (New York: Harper Collins, 1942, renewed 1996): 50.

229 Jack Nicklaus, *Golf My Way* (New York: Simon & Shuster, 1972).

230 Tom Rath and Donald Clifton, *How Full Is Your Bucket?* (New York: Gallop Press, 2004), 28.

231 Jim Myers, "Look on the sunny side, and children will follow," *The Tennessean*, September 9, 2005, p. D-1.

232 Deborah D. Danner, et al., "Positive Emotions in Early Life and Longevity: Findings from the Nun Study," *Journal of*

Personality and Social Psychology 80(5) (2001): 804–13.

233 Detailed Guide: Cervical Cancer, "What Are the Risk Factors for Cervical Cancer?" *American Cancer Society,* last revised May 13, 2009, http://www.cancer.org/docroot/CRI/content/CRI_2_4_2X_What_are_the_risk_factors_for_cervical_cancer_8.asp; Cervical Cancer & STDs, "Sexually Transmitted Diseases (STDs) and Cervical Cancer," *Information-on-Cervical-Cancer.com,* http://www.information-on-cervical-cancer.com/articles/sexually-transmitted-diseases.

234 Ian Newby-Clark, "Five Things You Need to Know About Effective Habit Change," *Zenhabits,* http://zenhabits.net/2007/11/five-things-you-need-to-know-about-effective-habit-change/.

235 Op. cit., Rath, p. 24.

236 John Locke, *Some Thoughts Concerning Education,* Vol. XXXVII, Part 1, The Harvard Classics (New York: P.F. Collier & Son, 1909–14; Bartleby.com, 2001), 160.

237 Elisabeth Kübler-Ross, *On Death and Dying* (New York: Scribner Classics, 1997).

238 "How to play target golf," *Golf Digest Woman,* April 2001, 99–100.

239 "Abraham Lincoln Quotes," *BrainyQuote,* http://www.brainyquote.com/quotes/keywords/happy.html.

240 Eric Hoffer (1902–1983) was a self-educated American long-shoreman who became famous for his social commentary. He received the Presidential Medal of Freedom in February 1983 by then President of the United States, Ronald Reagan.

241 Stephen H. Boyle, et al., "Covariation of Psychological Attributes and Incident Coronary Heart Disease in U.S. Air Force Veterans of the Vietnam War," *Psychosomatic Medicine* 68(6) (November/December 2006): 844–50.

242 Guy Yocom, "My Shot: Earl Woods," *Golf Digest,* February 2004, 115.

243 Elizabeth Kenny Quote, "He who angers you conquers

you," *FamousQuotes.com*, http://www.famousquotes.com/show/1001603/.

244 Ryan Gray, "Tennessee School Bus Driver Slain by High School Student," *School Transportation News*, April 2005, http://www.stnonline.com/stn/stnarticles/tenn_driver_slain_0405.htm.

245 Indrani Halder, "Gene Variations Contribute to Aggression and Anger in Women" (paper presented at the American Psychosomatic Society's Annual Meeting held in Budapest, Hungary, March 6–11, 2007).

246 Dr. Redford Williams on *Good Morning America*, ABC News, New York City, NY, 28 April 2002; Rozanne M. Puleo, excerpt by, "Could Anger Be a Hereditary Trait?" ABCNews.com, http://preventdisease.com/news/articles/anger_hereditary.shtml.

247 Quote attributed to Bertrand Russell (source unknown), "Positive Atheism's Big List of Bertrand Russell Quotations," *Positive Atheism's Big List of Bertrand Russell Quotations*, http://www.positiveatheism.org/hist/quotes/russell.htm. Bertrand Russell (May 18,1872–February 2, 1970) was a British philosopher, historian, logician, mathematician, advocate for social reform, and pacifist. He was awarded the Nobel Prize for Literature in 1950.

248 Human Betterment Programs, "Anger Management and Stabilization Program," *Applied Behavioral Sciences*, http://www.absrehabilitation.com/anger.html.

249 School of Public Health researchers in collaboration with Louis Harris Associates, "Anger and Violence in Public Schools Documented in New SPH Survey," *The Harvard University Gazette*, October 22, 1998.

250 Redford Williams and Virginia Williams, *Anger Kills: Seventeen Strategies for Controlling the Hostility That Can Harm Your Health* (New York: HarperCollins, 1993), 111–17.

251 Ibid., p. 112.

252 Bonna Johnson, "That's funny, even fake laughter is good for

you," *The Tennessean*, May 16, 2008, Features section.

253 Department of Health and Human Services, "About Methicillin-Resistant Staphylococcus aureus (MRSA) among Athletes," *CDC.gov*, http://www.cdc.gov/ncidod/dhqp/ar_MRSA_AthletesFAQ.html#5.

254 M. Rose, *Reworking the work ethic: Economic values and socio-cultural politics* (London: Schocken, 1985).

255 Roger B. Hill, "Attitudes Toward Work During the Classical Period," *History of Work Ethic*, http://www.coe.uga.edu/workethic/hatcp.html.

256 Roger B. Hill, "Protestantism and the Protestant Ethic," *History of Work Ethic*, http://www.coe.uga.edu/workethic/hpro.html.

257 Ibid.

258 Roger B. Hill, "The Work Ethic in America," *History of Work Ethic*, http://www.coe.uga.edu/workethic/hweam.html.

259 L. Braude, *Work and Workers* (New York: Praeger, 1975).

260 Roger B. Hill, "Influences Shaping the Contemporary Work Ethic," *History of Work Ethic*, http://www.coe.uga.edu/~rhill/workethic/hist.htm.

261 "Roth IRA For Teenagers," *Frugaldad.com*, http://frugaldad.com/2009/01/27/roth-ira-for-teenagers/.

262 Alison Wellner, "Teens view jobs as first step to wealth," *USA Weekend*, June 10, 2007.

263 NAA Business Analysis & Research Department: Newspaper Association of America (August 2007 p. 9), "Targeting Teens," *Consumer Insight*, http://www.naa.org/docs/Research/TargetingTeensBrief.pdf.

264 Ibid., p. 10.

265 Robert D. Manning, *Credit Card Nation: The Consequences of America's Addiction to Credit* (New York: Basic Books, 1st Ed., 2001).

266 Brian K. Bucks, et al., "Recent changes in U.S. family finances: evidence from the 2001–2004 survey of consumer

finances," *Federal Reserve Bulletin,* 2006, A30–31.

267   The Early Show, "Dave Ramsey, Money Answer Man," *CBS News.com,* http://www.cbsnews.com/stories/2007/01/30/earlyshow/living/money/main2413314.shtml.

268   Melody Warnick, "The Basics: Your credit card payment just doubled," MSN's *Money Central,* http://moneycentral.msn.com/content/Banking/creditcardsmarts/P117014.asp.

269   Carma Wadley quoting Rob Brough, "Bank on it: It pays to teach kids about money management," *Deseret News,* February 6, 2005, Life section.

270   Associated Press (February 1, 2007), "Personal savings drop to a 73-year low: Development comes as 78 million boomers nearing retirement," *MSNBC,* http://www.msnbc.msn.com/id/16922582.

271   Op. cit., Wadley.

272   Elizabeth W. Dunn, et al., "Spending money on others promotes happiness," *Science* 319(5870) (21 March 2008): 1687–88.

273   Patrick R. Steffen and Kevin S. Masters, "Does compassion mediate the intrinsic religion-health relationship?" *Annals of Behavioral Medicine* 30(3) (2005): 217–24.

274   Linda Kaplan Thaler and Robin Koval, *The Power of Nice, How to Conquer the Business World with Kindness* (New York: Currency/Doubleday, 2006).

275   Patricia Kitchen quoting Maggie Mistal, "Niceness works: A little kindness can make workplace better," *Los Angeles Times-Washington Post,* January 21, 2007.

276   Op. cit., Thaler and Koval, p. 3.

277   Rodney Atkins, "Watching You," www.azlyrics.com, http://www.azlyrics.com/lyrics/rodneyatkins/watchingyou.html.

Sources Cited

Aase, Heidi, and Terje Savolden. "Infrequent, but not frequent, reinforcers produce more variable responding and deficient sustained attention in young children with attention-deficit/hyperactivity disorder (ADHD)." *The Journal of Child Psychology and Psychiatry* 47(5) (May 2006): 457–71.

Abortion and breast cancer study seriously flawed. "Commentary on the Study, Michels, et al., 2007." *Abortion Breast Cancer.* http://www.abortionbreastcancer.com/commentary/070423/index.htm.

"Abraham Lincoln Quotes." *BrainyQuote.* http://www.brainyquote.com/quotes/keywords/happy.html.

Aikman, Amanda. "Do Children Need Religion?" *Reach,* September 1995.

Akman, I., K, Kuçu, N. Özdemir, Z. Yurdakul, M. Solakoglu, L. Orhan, A. Karabekiroglu, and E. Özek. "Mothers' postpartum psychological adjustment and infantile colic." *Archives of Disease of Children* 91(5) (May 2006): 417–19.

Album & Victim's stories. "Anton Hyman." MAMAA. http://www.mamaa.org/infalah.html.

Allen, Karen, Jim Blascovich, and Wendy B. Mendes. "Cardiovascular Reactivity and the Presence of Pets, Friends, and Spouses: The Truth About Cats and Dogs." *Psychosomatic Medicine* 64

(2002):727–39.

American Academy of Pediatrics Committee on Public Education. "Children, Adolescents, and Television." *Pediatrics* 107(2) (February 2001):423–26.

American Academy of Pediatrics Task Force on Circumcision. "Circumcision policy statement." *Pediatrics* 103(3) (March 1999): 686–93.

Associated Press (February 1, 2009). "Personal savings drop to a 73-year low: Development comes as 78 million boomers nearing retirement." *MSNBC*. http://www.msnbc.msn.com/id/16922582/.

Atkins, Rodney, "Watching You." www.azlyrics.com. http://www.azlyrics.com/lyrics/rodneyatkins/watchingyou.html.

Austin, Erica Weintraub, Bruce E. Pinkleton, and Yuki Fujioka. "The Role of Interpretation Processes and Parental Discussion in the Media's Effects on Adolescents' Use of Alcohol." *Pediatrics* 105(2) (February 2000): 343–49.

Auvert B., D. Taljaard, E. Lagard, J. Sobingwi-Tambekou, R. Sitta, A. Puren. "Randomized, controlled intervention trial of male circumcision for reduction of HIV infection risk: the ANRS 1265 Trial." *PLoS Medicine* (2005): e298, Epub 2005.

Baby, Pregnancy, and Parenting Information. "Causes for Infertility." *Babies Online*. http://www.babiesonline.com/articles/ttc/causes-for-infertility.asp.

Bailey, Robert C., Stephen Moses, Corette B. Parker, Kawango Agot, Ian Maclean, John N. Krieger, Carolyn F. M. Williams, Richard T. Campbell, and Jeckoniah O. Ndinya-Achola. "Male circumcision for HIV prevention in young men in Kisumu, Kenya: a randomized controlled trial." *The Lancet* 369(9562) (24 February 2007): 643–56.

Barna, George. *Transforming Children into Spiritual Champions*. Ventura, California: Regal, 2003.

Barr-Anderson, Daheia J., Patricia van den Berg, Dianne Neumark-Sztainer, and Mary Story. "Characteristics Associated With Older Adolescents Who Have a Television in Their

Bedrooms." *Pediatrics* 121 (April 2008): 718–24.

Barry, John M. *The Great Influenza: The Epic Story of the 1918 Pandemic.* New York, NY: Viking, 2004.

Basic Statistics (Volume 19, 2007). "Cases of HIV Infection and AIDS in the United States and Dependent Areas: HIV/AIDS Survelliance Report." *CDC.gov.* http://www.cdc.gov/hiv/topics/surveillance/basic.htm#aidscases.

Berenson, Gerald. "The Bogalusa heart study." Paper presented at the annual meeting of the American Society of Hypertension, New Orleans, Louisiana, May 20, 2008.

Blum, Robert W., Trisha Beuhring, and Peggy Mann Rinehart. *Protecting Teens, Beyond Race, Income and Family Structure.* Minneapolis, MN: Center for Adolescent Health, University of Minnesota, 2000.

Boyle, Stephen H., Joel E. Michalek, and Edward C. Suarez. "Covariation of Psychological Attributes and Incident Coronary Heart Disease in U.S. Air Force Veterans of the Vietnam War." *Psychosomatic Medicine* 68(6) (November/December 2006): 844–50.

Boyle, Tim. "St. Pius Men Hear Talk on Fatherhood." *The Georgia Bulletin,* February 22, 2001.

Boynton-Jarrett, Reneé, Tracy N. Thomas, Karen E. Peterson, Jean Wiecha, Arthur M. Sobol, and Steven L. Gortmaker. "Impact of Television Viewing Patterns on Fruit and Vegetable Consumption Among Adolescents." *Pediatrics* 112(6) (2003): 1321–26.

BrainyQuote. "Ronald Reagan Quotes." *BrainyMedia. com,*Copyright 2009. http://www.brainyquote.com/quotes/authors/r/ronald_reagan_5.html.

Braude, L. *Work and Workers.* New York: Praeger, 1975.

Brewer, Devon D., John J. Potterat, John M. Roberts, and Stuart Brody. "Male and Female Circumcision Associated With Prevalent HIV Infection in Virgins and Adolescents in Kenya, Lesotho, and Tanzania." *Annals of Epidemiology* 17(3) (March 2007): 217–26.

Brind, Joel. "Induced Abortion and Breast Cancer Risk: A Critical Analysis of the Report of the Harvard Nurses Study II." *Journal of American Physicians and Surgeons* 12 no. 2 (2007).

Brooks, Gary R. *The Centerfold Syndrome: How Men Can Overcome Objectification and Achieve Intimacy with Women.* San Francisco, CA: Jossey-Bass, 1996.

Bucks, Brian K., Arthur B. Kennickell, and Kevin B. Moore prepared this article with assistance from Gerhard Fries and A. Michael Neal. "Recent changes in U.S. family finances: evidence from the 2001–2004 survey of consumer finances." *Federal Reserve Bulletin,* 2006, A30–31.

Bulcroft, Kris. "Pets in the American Family." *People, Animals, Environment* 8(4) (1990): 13–14.

Caplan, Gerald, and Serge Lebovici, editors. *Adolescence: psychosocial perspectives.* New York: New York Basic Books, 1969.

Carrera, Dr. Michael A. of The Children's Aid Society. "Parents and Their Children's Learning about Sexuality." *Advocates for Youth.* http://www.advocatesforyouth.org/index.php?option=com_content&task=view&id=165&Itemid=206.

Cervical Cancer & STDs. "Sexually Transmitted Diseases (STDs) and Cervical Cancer." *Information-on-Cervical-Cancer.com,* http://www.information-on-cervical-cancer.com/articles/sexually-transmitted-diseases/index.php.

Chen, C. M., V. Morgenstern, W. Bischof, O. Herbarth, M. Borte, H. Behrendt, U. Krämer, A. von Berg, D. Berdel, C. P. Bauer, S. Koletzko, H. E. Wichmann, and J. Heinrich. "Dog ownership and contact during childhood and later allergy development." *European Respiratory Journal* 31(5) (May 2008 [Epub Febuary 6, 2008]): 963–73.

Christakis, Dimitri A. "Can We Turn a Toxin Into a Tonic? Toward 21st-Century Television Alchemy." *Pediatrics* 120(3) (September 2007): 647–48.

Christakis, Dimitri A., "The Effects of Infant Media Usage: What Do We Know and What Should We Learn?" *Acta Paediatrica*

98(1) (January 2009): 8–16.

Christakis, Dimitri A., Frederick J. Zimmerman, David L. Di-Giuseppe, and Carolyn A. McCarty. "Early Television Exposure and Subsequent Attentional Problems in Children." *Pediatrics* 113(4) (April 2004): 708–13.

Christensen, Stephen Allen. "Adolescents and Cigarette Smoking: Teens Appear to Be Using Tobacco at an Increasing Rate." *Suite 101.com.* December 8, 2008, http://substanceabuse.suite101. com/article.cfm/adolescents_and_cigarette_smoking.

Circumcision of male infants research paper (Brisbane 1993: Section 2). "The History of Male Circumcision." *Cirp.org.*(END ITALICS) http://www.cirp.org/library/legal/QLRC/02.html.

Collins, Rebecca, Marc N. Elliott, Sandra H. Berry, David E. Kanouse, Dale Kunkel, Sarah B. Hunter, and Angela Miu. "Watching sex on television predicts adolescent initiation of sexual behavior." *Pediatrics* 114(3) (September 2004): e280–289.

Coon, Katharine A., Jeanne Goldberg, Beatrice L. Rogers, and Katherine L. Tucker. "Relationships Between Use of Television During Meals and Children's Food Consumption Patterns." *Pediatrics* 107(1) (January 2001):e7.

Cougle, Jesse R., David C. Reardon, and Priscilla K. Coleman. "Depression associated with abortion and childbirth: a long-term analysis of the NLSY cohort." *Medical Science Monitor* 9(4) (2003): 105–12.

Country Profiles. "2006 Report on the Global Aids Epidemic." *UNAids.org.* http://data.unaids.org/pub/GlobalReport/2006/2006_GR_ANN1M-Z_en.pdf.

Cullinan, P., S. J. MacNeill, J. M. Harris, S. Moffat, C. White, P. Mills, and A. J. Newman Taylor. " Early allergen exposure, skin prick responses, and atopic wheeze at age 5 in English children: a cohort study." *Thorax* 59 (October 2004): 855–61.

Daling, Janet R., Kathleen E. Malone, Lynda F. Voigt, Emily White, and Noel S. Weiss. "Risk of Breast Cancer Among Young Women: Relationship to Induced Abortion." *Journal of* the National Cancer Institute 86(21) (1994): 1584–92.

Daly, Kimberly. "Reap the riches of family game night." *The Tennessean,* January 9, 2006.

Danner, Deborah D., David A. Snowdon, and Wallace V. Friesen. "Positive Emotions in Early Life and Longevity: Findings from the Nun Study." *Journal of Personality and Social Psychology* 80(5) (2001): 804–13.

Dave, S. S., A. M. Johnson, K. A. Fenton, C. H. Mercer, B. Erens, and K. Wellings. "Male Circumcision in Britain: findings from a national probability sample survey." *Sexually Transmitted Infections* 79 (2003): 499–500.

Deliz, Abby. "Newborns Need Touch." *Suite 101.com.* September 29, 2008. http://massagetherapy.suite101.com/article.cfm/newborns_need_touch.

Dennison, Barbara A., Tara A. Erb, and Paul L. Jenkins. "Television Viewing and Television in Bedroom Associated With Overweight Risk Among Low-Income Preschool Children." *Pediatrics* 109(6) (June 2002): 1028–35.

Dennison, George, and George Hill. "Male Circumcision in HIV prevention." *The Lancet* 369(9573) (12 May 2007): 1598.

Department of Health and Human Services. "About Methicillin-Resistant Staphylococcus aureus (MRSA) among Athletes." *CDC.gov.* http://www.cdc.gov/ncidod/dhqp/ar_MRSA_AthletesFAQ.html#5.

Department of Health and Human Services Centers for Disease Control and Prevention. "Sexually Transmitted Diseases: Chlamydia - CDC Fact Sheet." *USA.gov,* December 20, 2007. http://www.cdc.gov/std/Chlamydia/STDFact-Chlamydia.htm#Common.

Detailed Guide: Cervical Cancer. "What Are the Risk Factors for Cervical Cancer?" *American Cancer Society,* last revised May 13, 2009. http://www.cancer.org/docroot/CRI/content/CRI_2_4_2X_What_are_the_risk_factors_for_cervical_cancer_8.asp.

Dickson, Nigel P., Thea van Roode, Peter Herbison, and Charlotte

Paul. "Circumcision and Risk of Sexually Transmitted Infections in a Birth Cohort." *The Journal of Pediatrics* 152(3) (March 2008): 383–87.

Distillers Fighting Drunk Driving and Underaged Drinking. "Fight Drunk Driving." *The Century Council.* http://www.century-council.org/fight-drunk-driving.

Dobson, James. "What is the answer to curbing teenage sexual activity?"*Focus on the Family,* April 2001.

Donegan, Elizabeth (October 2003). "Transmission of HIV by Blood, Blood Products, Tissue Transplantation, and Artifical Insemination." *HIV InSite.* http://hivinsite.ucsf.edu/InSite?page=kb-07-02-09#S2.1X.

Dougall, A., and J. Fiske. "Surving child sexual abuse: the relevance to dental practice." *Dental Update* 36(5) (June 2009) 294–96, 298–300, 303–04.

Downey, Kevin. "Bring the Family." *Wall Street Journal,* March 10, 2008.

D'Souza, Gypsyamber, Aimee R. Kreimer, Raphael Viscidi, Michael Pawlita, Carole Fakhry, Wayne M. Koch, William H. Westra, and Maura L. Gillison. "Case-Control Study of Human Papillomavirus and Oropharyngeal Cancer." *New England Journal of Medicine* 356(19) (May 10, 2007): 1944–56.

Dunn, Elizabeth W., Lara B. Aknin, and Michael I. Norton. "Spending money on others promotes happiness." *Science* 319(5870) (21 March 2008): 1687–88.

DuRant, Robert H., Tom Baranowski, Maribeth Johnson, and William O. Thompson. "The Relationship Among Television Watching, Physical Activity, and Body Composition of Young Children." *Pediatrics* 94(4) (October 1994): 449–55.

Dyer, Wayne. *The Power of Intention: Learning to Co-create Your World Your Way.* Carlsbad, CA: Hay House, 2005.

Editorial. "Fence Off Internet Porn." *USA Today,* 16 September 2005. http://www.urbanministry.org/wiki/teens-ambivalent-about-internet-porn.

Elster, Authur B., and Naomi J. Kuznets. *AMA Guidelines for*

Adolescent Preventive Services (GAPS). Baltimore, MD: Williams & Wilkins, 1994.

Facts for Families (No. 10: updated May 2008). "Teen Suicide." *American Academy of Child & Adolescent Psychiatry.* http://www.aacap.org/cs/root/facts_for_families/teen_suicide.

"Family News." *Focus on the Family,* April 2001.

Feiler, Bruce. *Abraham, A Journey to the Heart of Three Faiths.* New York: Perennial, 2004.

Fergusson, David M., Joseph M. Boden, and L. John Horwood. "Circumcision Status and Risk of Sexually Transmitted Infection in Young Adult Males: An analysis of a Longitudinal Birth Cohort." *Pediatrics* 118(5) (November 2006): 1971–76.

Fernandez, Lisa and Ben Aguirre, Jr. "Mother's sacrifice saves son from pit bull." *Oakland Tribune,* September 6, 2007, Media News story.

Fisher, Jeff. "Exercise has proven mental benefits, so come run to beat the blues." *The Tennessean,* March 28, 2008.

"For happy teens, pass the peas." *The Atlanta Journal-Constitution,* August 16, 1997, A7.

Forhan, Sara (Press release March 11, 2008). "Nationally Representative CDC Study Finds 1 in 4 Teenage Girls Has a Sexually Transmitted Disease." *CDC.gov.* http://www.cdc.gov/stdconference/2008/media/release-11march2008.htm.

Formica, Michael J. "Gender Differences, Sexuality and Emotional Infidelity." *Psychology Today,* January 8, 2009. http://www.psychologytoday.com/blog/enlightened-living/200901/gender-differences-sexuality-and-emotional-infidelity.

"Fourteen Ways to Show Love for Your Child This Valentine's Day." *American Academy of Pediatrics* February 2009. View at http://www.aap.org/advocacy/releases/febvaltips.cfm.

Fox, Maggie, Health and Science Editor (February 27, 2008). "All U.S. kids should get flu vaccine, panel says." *Reuters.com.* http://www.reuters.com/article/healthNews/idUSWAT00897520080227.

FTC Releases Research on Children's Exposure to Television Advertising (June 1, 2007). "Children Not Seeing More Food Ads on Television." *FTC.gov.* http://www.ftc.gov/opa/2007/06/childrenadsstudy.shtm.

Furnham, Adrian. "The saving and spending habits of young people." *Journal of Economic Psychology* 20(6) (December 1999): 677–97.

Gadow, Kenneth, and Joyce Sprafkin. "Field Experiments of Television Violence with Children: Evidence for an Environmental Hazard?" *Pediatrics* 83(3) (March 1989): 399–405.

Generation Rx.com survey (released December 11, 2001). "Survey: more young people going online for health information than to shop, check sports scores or chat." *The Kaiser Family Foundation.* http://www.kff.org/entmedia/Press%20Release..pdf.

Gidwani, Pradeep P., Arthur Sobol, William DeJong, James M. Perrin, and Steven L. Gortmaker. "Television Viewing and Initiation of Smoking Among Youth." *Pediatrics* 110(3) (September 2002): 505–08.

Gillespie, Kris and Brian. *When Mama Ain't Happy, Ain't Nobody Happy: 52 Secrets Uncovered! Rules That Women Want Men to Know.* Tulsa, OK: Insight International, 2000.

Girl Talk: Choices and Consequences of Underaged Drinking. "A Guide For Mothers and Daughters to Prevent Underage Drinking." *The Century Council.* http://www.girlsanddrinking.org.

Global Campaign for Microbicides. "Male Circumcision: What Does It Mean For Women?" *Global-Campaign.org.* http://www.global-campaign.org/clientfiles/FS-MaleCircumcision%5BE%5D.pdf.

Global HIV/AIDS (last modified January 7, 2009). "CDC Global HIV/AIDS Activities–Botswana." *CDC.gov.* http://www.cdc.gov/globalaids/countries/Botswana/default.html.

Global HIV/AIDS (last modified October 23, 2008). "HIV/AIDS Surveillance Reports–Swaziland." *CDC.gov.* http://www.cdc.gov/hiv/topics/surveillance/resources/reports/index.htm.

Goldscheider, Eric. "Seeking a Role for Religion on Campus." *The New York Times,* February 2, 2002.

Gray, Ronald H., Godfrey Kigozi, David Serwadda, Frederick Makumbi, Stephen Watya, Fred Nalugoda, Noah Kiwanuka, Lawrence H. Moulton, Mohammad A. Chaudhary, Michael Z. Chen, Nelson K. Sewankambo, Fred Wabwire-Mangen, Melanie C. Bacon, Carolyn F. M. Williams, Pius Opendi, Steven J Reynolds, Oliver Laeyendecker, Thomas C. Quinn, and Maria J. Wawer. "Male circumcision for HIV prevention in men in Rakai, Uganda: a randomized trial." *The Lancet* 368(9562) (24 February 2007): 657–66.

Gray, Ryan. "Tennessee School Bus Driver Slain by High School Student." *School Transportation News,* April 2005. http://www.stnonline.com/stn/stnarticles/tenn_driver_slain_0405.htm.

Green, Morris. "Myth of the Month: The 10-minute visit: Anything but routine." *Contemporary Pediatrics* (August 1992): 53–61.

Halder, Indrani. "Gene Variations Contribute to Aggression and Anger in Women." Paper presented at the American Psychosomatic Society's Annual Meeting held in Budapest, Hungary, March 6–11, 2007.

Hallfors, Denise D., Martha W. Waller, Daniel Bauer, Carol A. Ford, and Carolyn T. Halpern. "Which Comes First in Adolescence: Sex and Drugs or Depression?" *American Journal of Preventive Medicine* 29(3) (October 2005): 163–70.

Hechinger, Fred M. *Fateful Choices.* New York: Carnegie Corporation of America, 1992.

Hendra, Tony. *Father Joe.* New York: Random House, 2004.

Hill, Roger B. "Attitudes Toward Work During the Classical Period." *History of Work Ethic.* http://www.coe.uga.edu/workethic/hatcp.html.

Hill, Roger B. "Influences Shaping the Contemporary Work Ethic." *History of Work Ethic.* http://www.coe.uga.edu/~rhill/workethic/hist.htm.

Hill, Roger B. "Protestantism and the Protestant Ethic." *History of Work Ethic.* http://www.coe.uga.edu/workethic/hpro.html.

Hill, Roger B. "The Work Ethic in America." *History of Work Ethic.* http://www.coe.uga.edu/workethic/hweam.html.

Horatio Alger Study of Our Nations Youth (2005). "Teens Willing to Work Harder and Expect More From Education." *Horatio Alger Association.* http://www.horatioalger.com/news/05sony.cfm.

Horrell, Ed. *The Kindness Revolution, The Company-wide Culture Shift that Inspires Phenomenal Customer Service.* New York: AMACOM, 2006.

"How Parents Can Prevent Drug Abuse." *National Crime Prevention Council,* 2009. http://www.ncpc.org/topics/drug-abuse/drug-abuse/alcohol-tobacco-and-other-drugs.

"How to play target golf." *Golf Digest Woman,* April 2001.

Howard, Kate. "Parents can keep GPS eye on teen driver's every turn." *The Tennessean,* June 20, 2007, Main News Section, A1.

Howard, Marion. *How To Help Your Teenager Postpone Sexual Involvement.* New York: Continuum, 1988.

Human Betterment Programs. "Anger Management and Stabilization Program." *Applied Behavioral Sciences.* http://www.absrehabilitation.com/anger.html.

Hunter, Karen (podcast February 27, 2008). "Influenza Vaccination Now Recommended for Children 6 months to 18 years of Age." *CDC.gov.* http://www2a.cdc.gov/podcasts/player.asp?f=8383.

"In the Matter of Violent Television Programming And Its Impact On Children." A report before the Federal Communications Commission, Washington, D.C. Adopted April 6, 2007. Released April 25, 2007. http://www.c-span.org/pdf/fcc_tvviolence.pdf.

Industry Statistics and Trends (2007—2008). "Pet Ownership." *APPA.* http://americanpetproducts.org/press_industrytrends.asp.

Institute for American Values. "Hardwired to Connect: The New Scientific Case for Authoritative Communities." Report by the Commission on Children at Risk. September 9, 2003. http://www.americanvalues.org/html/hardwired_press_release.html.

Iovine, Julie V. "The healing ways of Dr. Dog." *The New York Times*, October 28, 2001.

Johnson, Bonna. "That's funny, even fake laughter is good for you." *The Tennessean*, May 16, 2008.

Johnson, Linda. "Groups push for condom labeling to be more precise." *The Tennessean*, May 30, 2005.

Joint News Release (March 10, 2006). "Global measles deaths plunge by 48% over past six years." *World Health Organization.* http://www.who.int/mediacentre/news/releases/2006/pr11/en/print.html.

Kaiser Family Foundation Report (March 2007). "Food for Thought: Television Food Advertising to Children in the United States." *The Henry J. Kaiser Family Foundation.* http://www.kff.org/entmedia/upload/7618.pdf.

Kalichman, Seth C., Lisa Eaton, and Steven D. Pinkerton. "Male Circumcision in HIV prevention." *The Lancet* 369(9573) (12 May 2007): 1597.

Kellogg, John Harvey. *Plain Facts for Old and Young.* Written in 1877, republished in Charleston, SC: BiblioLife, 2008.

Kemp, Carla. "Health Briefs, Parents not following AAP TV Guidelines." *AAP News,* January 2004, 24:2.

Kemp, Carla. "Survey ranks top 5 drugs for children based on spending." *AAP News,* December 2007, 28:12:2.

Kirchheimer, Sid. "Pets May Prevent Allergies in Kids." *WebMD Health News.* http://www.webmd.com/allergies/news/20031014/pets-may-prevent-allergies-in-kids.

Kitchen, Patricia, quoting Maggie Mistal. "Niceness works: A little kindness can make workplace better." *Los Angeles Times-Washington Post,* January 21, 2007.

Kolata, Gina. *Flu. The Story Of The Great Influenza*

Pandemic. New York: Touchstone, 2001.

Kübler-Ross, Elisabeth. *On Death and Dying.* New York: Scribner Classics, 1997.

Landhuis, Carl Erik, Richie Poulton, David Welch, and Robert John Hancox. "Does Childhood Television Viewing Lead to Attention Problems in Adolescence? Results From a Prospective Longitudinal Study. *Pediatrics* 120(3) (September 2007): 532–37.

Laumann, Edward O., Christopher M. Masi, and Ezra W. Zuckerman. "Circumcision in the United States: prevalence, prophylactic effects, and sexual practice." *JAMA* 277(13) (April 2, 1997): 1052–57.

Leitch, I. O. W. "Circumcision: a Continuing Enigma." *Australian Paediatric Journal* 6 (June 1970): 59–65.

Levinson, Douglas F. "The genetics of Depression: A review." *Biological Psychiatry* 60(2) (15 July 2006): 84–92.

Lewis, C. S. *The Screwtape Letters.* New York: Collier Books, 1982.

Lewis, Dwight. "Know right where your teen is; it is life and death." *The Tennessean*, December 15, 2005.

Locke, John (1632–1704). *Some Thoughts Concerning Education.* Vol. XXXVII, Part 1. The Harvard Classics. New York: P.F. Collier & Son, 1909–14; Bartleby.com, 2001.

Lowry, R. D. Holtzman, B. I. Truman, L. Kann , J. L. Collins, L. J. Kolbe. "Substance use and HIV-related sexual behaviors among U.S. high school students: Are they related?" *American Journal of Public Health* 84 (1994):1116–20.

Ludingron, Aileen, and Hans Diehl. *Health Power, Health by Choice Not Chance.* Hagerstown, MD: Review and Harold Publishing Association, 2005.

Manhart, Lisa E., King K. Holmes, James P. Hughes, Laura S. Houston, and Patricia A. Totten. "Mycoplasma genitalium Among Young Adults in the United States: an Emerging Sexually Transmitted Infection." *American Journal of Public Health* 97(6) (June 2007):1118–25.

Manning, Robert D. *Credit Card Nation: The Consequences of America's Addiction to Credit*. New York: Basic Books, 1st Ed., 2001.

Marino, Martha, and Sue Butkus. "Eat Better; Eat Together: Research on Family Meals." *Washington State University*. http://nutrition.wsu.edu/ebet/background.html.

Marshall, W. "Report on the Use of Pornography by Sexual Offenders." Report to the Federal Department of Justice. Ottawa, Canada, 1983.

Martino, Steven C., Marc N. Elliott, Rosalie Corona, David E. Kanouse and Mark A. Schuster. "Beyound the 'Big Talk': The Importance of Breadth and Repetition in Parent-Adolescent Communication About Sexual Issues." *Pediatrics* 121 (March 2008): e612–e618.

McDonald, Kevin. "The cost of a divorce." *Bankrate.com*. http://www.bankrate.com/brm/news/advice/19990903a.asp.

Media Center. "Ensuring Solutions to Alcohol Problems." *The George Washington University Medical Center*. http://www.ensuringsolutions.org/media/.

Meeker, Meg. *Strong Fathers, Strong Daughters*. Washington, DC: Regnery Publishing, Inc., 2006.

Melbye, Mads, Jan Wohlfahrt, Jørgen H. Olsen, Morten Frisch, Tine Westergaard, Karin Helweg-Larsen, and Per Kragh Andersen. "Induced Abortion and the Risk of Breast Cancer." *The New England Journal of Medicine* 336(2) (January 9, 1997): 81–5.

Mena, Leandro, Xiaofei Wang, Tomasz F. Mroczkowski, and David H. Martin. "Mycoplasma genitalium infections in asymptomatic men and men with urethritis attending a sexually transmitted diseases clinic in New Orleans." *Clinical Infectious Diseases* 35 (2002): 1167–73.

Michels, Karin B., Chung-cheng Hsieh, Dimitrios Trichopoulos and Walter C. Willett. "Abortion and breast cancer risk in seven countries." *Cancer Causes and Control* 6(1) (January 1995): 75–82.

Michels, Karin, Fei Xue, Graham A. Colditz, Walter C. Willett. "Induced and Spontaneous Abortion and Incidence of Breast Cancer Among Young Women: A Prospective Cohort Study." *Archives of Internal Medicine* 167 (April 2007): 814–20.

Miller, Lisa, Mark Davies, and Steven Greenwald. "Religiosity and Substance Use and Abuse Among Adolescents in the National Survey."*Journal of the American Academy of Child and Adolescent Psychiatry* 39(9) (September 2000): 1190–97.

Millet, Peter. "Does abstinence education work? Teen sexuality more complicated than that." *The Tennessean,* May 27, 2007, 23A.

Minton, Lynn. "Fresh Voices." *Parade Magazine,* February 14, 1999; August 22, 1999.

Monsour, M. A., H. H. Rabinovitch, and G. E. Dean. "Medical management of phimosis in children: our experience with topical steroids." *Journal of Urology* 162(3 pt. 2) (September 1999): 1162–64.

Moritsugu, Kenneth. *The Surgeon General's Call to Action to Prevent and Reduce Underage Drinking 2007.* Washington, DC: U.S. Department of Health Education, and Welfare, 2007.

Myers, Jim. "Look on the sunny side, and children will follow." *The Tennessean,* September 9, 2005.

NAA Business Analysis & Research Department: Newspaper Association of America (August 2007 p. 9). "Targeting Teens." *Consumer Insight.* http://www.naa.org/docs/Research/TargetingTeensBrief.pdf.

National Center for Health Statistics. Multiple cause-of-death public-use data files 1990 through 2004. Hyattsville, MD: U.S. Department of Health and Human Services, CDC, 2007.

National Center for Health Statistics (July 24, 2002). "New Report Sheds Light on Trends and Patterns in Marriage, Divorce, and Cohabitation." *CDC.gov..* http://www.cdc.gov/nchs/pressroom/02news/div_mar_cohab.htm.

National Center on Addiction and Substance Abuse at Columbia

University Annual Report of September 2007, The. Accompanying Statement by Joseph A. Califano, Jr., Chairman and President of the Board of Directors. "The Importance of Family Dinners IV." *The Safeway Foundation.* http://www.casacolumbia.org/absolutenm/articlefiles/380-Importance%20of%20Family%20Dinners%20IV.pdf.

National Coalition for the Protection of Children and Families, The. Quoting Dr. Reo M. Christensen. "The Subtle Dangers of Pornography." *Troubledwith.com.* http://www.troubledwith.com/AbuseandAddiction/A000000775.cfm?topic=abuse%20and%20addiction%3A%20pornography%20and%20cybersex.

National STD Prevention Conference 2008. "3.2 Million Female Adolescents Estimated to Have at Least One of the Most Common STDs: Other Studies Featured at 2008 National STD Prevention Conference Show Missed Opportunities for STD Screening and Innovative Solutions for STD Prevention and Treatment." *CDC.gov.* http://www.cdc.gov/STDConference/2008/media/release-11march2008.htm.

Neergaard, Lauran. ""New nasal-spray flu vaccine is costly, not for everyone." *The Tennessean,* September 23, 2003.

Neinstein, Lawrence S. *Adolescent Health Care.* Baltimore, MD: Urban & Schwarzenberg, 1984.

"Neonatal circumcision revisited. Fetus and Newborn Committee, Canadian Paediatric Society." *Canadian Medical Association Journal* 154(6) (15 March 1996): 769–80.

Newby-Clark, Ian. "Five Things You Need to Know About Effective Habit Change." *Zenhabits.* http://zenhabits.net/2007/11/five-things-you-need-to-know-about-effective-habit-change/.

Nicholi, Armand M. *The New Harvard Guide to Psychiatry.* Cambridge: The Belknap Press of Harvard University Press, 1988.

Nicklaus, Jack. *Golf My Way.* New York: Simon & Shuster, 1972.

Noland, Bruce. Quoting Rev. Jerrode Keys. "Teens getting message on sex." *The Atlanta Journal and Constitution,* June 26,

1999.

Nolen, Joseph. "Is premarital sex a sin?" *Liguori,* January 15, 2006.

O'Connor, Lindsey. *If Mama Ain't Happy, Ain't Nobody Happy!: Making the Choice to Rejoice.* Eugene, OR: Harvest House Publishers, 2006.

O'Farrell, Nigel, Prashini Moodley, and A. Wim Sturm. "Male Circumcision in HIV prevention." *The Lancet* 369(9573) (12 May 2007): 1598.

Office of Applied Studies. "SAMHSA's Latest National Survey on Drug Use & Health." U.S. Department of Health and Human Services, Last updateds September 10, 2009. http://www.oas.samhsa.gov/NSDUHlatest.htm.

Office of National Drug Control Policy (2004). "The economic costs of drug abuse in the United States, 1992–2002." Washington, DC: Executive Office of the President (Publication No. 207303).

Olson, Karen. "Eating Out Poses Health Risks for Kids." Paper presented at the American Heart Association 2005 Scientific Sessions, Dallas, Texas, November 13–16, 2005.

One-Minute World News (March 23, 2004). "Mother calls for tougher gun law." *BBC News.* http://news.bbc.co.uk/2/hi/uk_news/3561071.stm.

O'Sullivan, John. *The President, the Pope, and the Prime Minister, Three Who Changed the World.* Washington, DC: Regnery Publishing, Inc., 2006.

Owens, Judith, Rolanda Maxim, Melissa McGuinn, Chantelle Nobile, Michael Msall, and Anthony Alario. "Television-viewing Habits and Sleep Disturbance in School Children." *Pediatrics* 104(3) (September 1999): e27.

Ownby, Dennis R., Christine Cole Johnson, and Edward L. Peterson. "Exposure to dogs and cats in the first year of life and risk of allergic sensitization at 6 to 7 years of age." *JAMA* 288(8) (2002): 963–72.

Paradise, Jack L., Heidi M. Feldman, Thomas F. Campbell,

Christine A. Dollaghan, Howard E. Rockette, Dayna L. Pitcairn, Clyde G. Smith, Kathleen Colborn, Beverly S. Bernard, Marcia Kurs-Lasky, Janine E. Janosky, Diane L. Sabo, Rollanda E. O'Connor, and William E. Pelham. "Tympanostomy Tubes and Developmental Outcomes at 9 to 11 Years of Age." *New England Journal of Medicine* 356(3) (18 January 2007): 248–61.

Peleg-Oren, N., G. Saint-Jean, G. A. Cardenas, H. Tammara, C. Pierre. "Drinking Alcohol before Age 13 and Negative Outcomes in Late Adolescence." *Alcoholism: Clinical Experimental Research,* 31 August 2009.

Pereira, Mark A., Alex I. Kartashov, Cara B. Ebbeling, Linda Van Horn, Martha L. Slattery, David R. Jacobs, David S. Ludwig. "Fast-food habits, weight gain, and insulin resistance (the CARDIA study): 15-year prospective analysis." *The Lancet* 365 (2005): 36–42.

Pittman, Frank. *Man Enough.* New York: Putnam's and Sons, 1993.

Pitts, Leonard. "This Just In: Parents Matter as Role Models." *The Tennessean,* September 13, 1997.

Pollack, William S. *Real Boy's Voices.* New York: Random House, 2000.

Positive Atheism's Big List of Bertrand Russell Quotations. http://www.positiveatheism.org/hist/quotes/russell.htm.

Poulson, R. L., M. A, Eppler, T.N. and Satterwhite, K.L. "Alcohol consumption, strength of religious beliefs, and risky sexual behavior in college students." *Journal of American College Health* 46(5) (March 1998): 277–32.

Pruett, Kyle and Marsha Kline Pruett. *Partnership Parenting, How Men and Women Parent Differently and How it Helps Your Kids.* Cambridge:Da Capo Lifelong Books, 2009.

"Pull the Plug." *The Tennessean,* February 7, 2004.

Rath, Tom, and Donald Clifton. *How Full is Your Bucket? Positive Strategies for Work and Life.* New York: Gallop Press, 2004.

Report prepared by the Majority Staff, U.S. House of Representatives

(January 2009). "Getting Beyond Getting Ready for Pandemic Influenza." *Committee on Homeland Security.* http://homeland.house.gov/SiteDocuments/20090114124322-85263. pdf.

"Reported Cases of Selected Notifiable Diseases in Georgia (Profile for December 2006)." *The Georgia Epidemiology Report* 23(3) (March 4, 2007): 4.

Resnick, Michael. "National Longitudinal Study of Adolescent Health." *JAMA* 278(10) (September 10, 1997): 823–32.

Restaurant News (July 8, 2007: News Release August 7, 2007). "Study Finds Children Swayed by Brand Preferences." *QSR Magazine.com.* http://www.qsrmagazine.com/articles/news/story.phtml?id=5665.

Richters, J., A. M. Smith, R. O. de Visser, A. E. Grulich, and C. E. Rissel. "Circumcision in Australia: prevalence and effect on sexual health." *International Journal of STD & AIDS* 17 (2006): 547–54.

Roan, Shari. "Flu shot gave you the flu? It's a myth." *Los Angeles Times,* November 03, 2003.

Roberts, Samuel. "Fantasy-Reality Alignment: a Cognitive-Behavorial Technique to Help Men Overcome Pornography Addiction or Compulsion." *PornographyAddictionHelp.Info,* 2008. http://www.PornographyAddictionHelp.Info.

Rock, Ellen M., Marjorie Ireland, Michael D. Resnick, and Clea A. McNeely. "A rose by any other name? Objective Knowledge, Perceived Knowledge, and Adolescent Male Condom Use." *Pediatrics* 115(3) (March 2005): 667–72.

Rönmark, Eva, Matthew Perzanowski, Thomas Platts-Mills, and Bo Lundbäck. "Four-year incidence of allergic sensitization among schoolchildren in a community where allergy to cat and dog dominates sensitization: Report from the obstructive lung disease in northern sweden study group." *The Journal of Allergy and Clinical Immunology* 112(4) (October 2004): 747–54.

Rose, M. *Reworking the work ethic: Economic values and socio-*

cultural politics. London: Schocken, 1985.

Rosemond, John. *Parenting by the Book, Biblical Wisdom for Raising Your Child.* New York: Howard Books, 2007.

"Roth IRA For Teenagers." *Frugaldad.com.* http://frugaldad. com/2009/01/27/roth-ira-for-teenagers/.

Ryan, Sandy Fertman. "Wasted lives: the truth about teen girls and drinking." *Girls' Life,* Oct/Nov 2004.

Sayre, Lewis. "Lecture III: Deformities: Etiology (continued)–Congenital Phimosis and Adherent Prepuce–Prognosis–Diagnosis." *History of Circumcision.* http://www.historyofcircumcision.net/index.php?option=content&task=view&id=58.

Scheffler, Richard M., Timothy T. Brown, Brent D. Fulton, Stephen P. Hinshaw, Peter Levine, and Susan Stone. "Positive Association Between Attention-Deficit/Hyperactivity Disorder Medication Use and Academic Achievement During Elementary School." *Pediatrics* 123(5) (May 2009): 1273–79.

School of Public Health researchers in collaboration with Louis Harris Associates. "Anger and Violence in Public Schools Documented in New SPH Survey." *The Harvard University Gazette,* October 22, 1998.

Schwartz, Kimberly A., Sara A. Pyle, M. Denise Dowd, Karen Sheehan. "Attitudes and Beliefs of Adolescents and Parents Regarding Adolescent Suicide." *Pediatrics* 125 (2) (February 2010): 221–227.

Serpell, James. "Beneficial effects of pet ownership on some aspects of human health and behavior." *Journal of the Royal Society of Medicine* 84 (1991): 717–20.

Serpell, James. "Guest Editor's Introduction: Animals in Children's Lives." *Society & Animals, Journal of Human-Animal Studies* 7, no. 2 (1999):87–93.

"Sex: The White House ban on condoms." *The Week,* January 24, 2003.

Sexually Transmitted Diseases (1999 data). "Tracking the Hidden Epidemics: Trends in STDs in the United States." *CDC. gov.* http://www.cdc.gov/std/Trends2000/herpes-close.htm.

Shankar, K. R., and A. M. Rickwood. "The Incidence of Phimosis in Boys." *British Journal of Urology* 84(1) (July 1999): 101–2.

Shaw, Robert. *The Epidemic.* New York: Regan Books, 2003.

Sheperd, Stuart. "Teens Ambivalent About Internet Porn." *family.org,* 17 December 2001. http://www.urbanministry.org/wiki/teens-ambivalent-about-internet-porn.

Shideler, Karen. "Youthful health mistakes that will come back to haunt you." *Dayton Daily News,* August 31, 2000.

Slaughter, Sylvia. "Family sees dream home come to life." *The Tennessean,* August 5, 2006.

Smith, Christian with Melinda Lundquist Denton. *Soul Searching, The Religious and Spiritual Lives of American Teenagers.* New York: Oxford University Press, 2005.

Smith, Peter J. quoting Matt Barber. "New STD Infection Rates '4 times higher among those who used condoms during their last vaginal intercourse': Study–M. Genitalium Surpasses Gonorrhea among Young Adults Reports Health Journal." *LifeSiteNews.com.* http://www.lifesitenews.com/ldn/2007/jun/070612.html#5.

Stanford, Duane. "TEEN DRIVING: Young drinkers sentenced, Gwinnett girl leaving party died in wreck." *The Atlanta Journal and Constitution,* November 28, 2000.

"State of our Nation's Youth 2005—2006, The." *Horatio Alger Association.* http://www.horatioalger.com/pdfs/state05.pdf.

Steckelberg, James M., M.D. "Honey: An effective cough remedy?" *MayoClinic.com,* March 18, 2008. http://www.mayoclinic.com/health/honey/AN01799.

Steffen, Patrick R., and Kevin S. Masters. "Does compassion mediate the intrinsic religion-health relationship?" *Annals of Behavioral Medicine* 30(3) (2005): 217–24.

Sternberg, Steve. "Chlamydia tops 1 million cases with STDs rising slightly overall." *USA Today,* November 14, 2007.

Strasburger, Victor. "'Clueless': Why Do Pediatricians Underestimate the Media's Influence on Children and Adolescents?"

Pediatrics 117(4) (2006): 1427-31.

Strasburger, Victor. *Getting Your Kids to Say "No" in the '90s When You Said "Yes" in the '60s.* New York: Fireside Books, 1993.

Strauss, Stephanie. "Is Media Violence Affecting Your Kids?" *Nashville Parent,* February 2005, 49–50.

Strickland, Bill. "The Benefits of Pets." *Parents.com.* http://www.parents.com/family-life/pets/kids/pets-good-for-kids/.

"Study: Links between symptoms of depression among young people and relationships with others." *The Daily,* February 16, 2005.

Swahn, Monica H., Robert M. Bossarte, Ernest E. Sullivent, III. "Age of Initiating Alcohol Use, Suicidal Behavior and Dating Violence Among High Risk Seventh-Grade Adolescents." *Pediatrics* 121 (February 2008): 297–305.

Taddio, Anna, Joel Katz, A. Lane Ilersich, and Gideon Koren. "Effect of neonatal circumcision on pain response during subsequent routine immunizations." *The Lancet* 349(9052) (March 1997): 599–603.

Terry, Luther. *Smoking and Health, Report of the Advisory Committee to the Surgeon General of the Public Health Service.* Washington, DC: U.S. Department of Health Education, and Welfare, 1964.

Thaler, Linda Kaplan, and Robin Koval. *The Power of Nice, How to Conquer the Business World with Kindness.* New York: Currency Doubleday, 2006.

"The decline of circumcision." *The Week,* March 14, 2003.

The Early Show. "Dave Ramsey, Money Answer Man." *CBS News.com.* http://www.cbsnews.com/stories/2007/01/30/earlyshow/living/money/main2413314.shtml.

Thomas, Cal. "Hope for conservative woman president." *Dispatch Politics,* a division of *The Columbus Dispatch,* June 7, 2008.

Thomas, Cal (March 13, 2008). "Sex and the Married Governor." *CalThomas.com.* http://www.calthomas.com/index.

php?news=2209.

Thomas, Cal. "Steamy Teen 'love' in Tampa." *JWR Review,* December 15, 2005.

Traffic Safety Facts (July 2007). "2006 Traffic Safety Annual Assessment–A Preview." *NHTSA.* http://www-nrd.nhtsa.dot.gov/Pubs/810791.PDF.

Traffic Safety Facts (updated March 2008). "Alcohol Impaired Driving." NHTSA. http://www-nrd.nhtsa.dot.gov/Pubs/810801.PDF.

Tremblay, M. S., and J. D. Willms. "Is the Canadian child obesity epidemic related to physical inactivity?" *International Journal of Obesity* 27 (2003): 1100–05.

Trenholm, Christopher, Barbara Devaney, Ken Fortson, Lisa Quay, Justin Wheeler, Melissa Clark. "Impacts of Four Title V, Section 510 Abstinence Education Programs Final Report." *Mathematica Policy Research, Inc.* (April 2007). http://www.mathematica-mpr.com/publications/PDFs/impactabstinence.pdf.

Turner, Kelli. "V-chip doesn't protect kids, so TV industry now must clean up its act." *The Tennessean,* June 2, 2007.

University of Tennessee College of Veterinary Medicine. "Humans & Animals Learning together." *HALT.* http://www.vet.utk.edu/halt/about.shtml.

Wadley, Carma, quoting Rob Brough. "Bank on it: It pays to teach kids about money management."*Deseret News,* February 6, 2005.

Wallace, John M., Jr. and Tyrone A. Forman. "Religion's role in promoting health and reducing risk among American youth." *Health Education and Behavior* 25(6) (December 1, 1998): 721–41.

Warnick, Melody. "The Basics: Your credit card payment just doubled." MSN.Money. http://moneycentral.msn.com/content/Banking/creditcardsmarts/P117014.asp.

Weigel, George. *Witness to Hope, The Biography of Pope John Paul II.* New York: Harper Perennial, 2001.

Weissman, Myrna, Daniel J. Pilowsky, Priya J. Wickramaratne, Ardesheer Talati, Stephen R. Wisniewski, Maurizio Fava, Carroll W. Hughes, Judy Garber, Erin Malloy, Cheryl A. King, Gabrielle Cerda, A. Bela Sood, Jonathan E. Alpert, Madhukar H. Trivedi, A. John Rush. "Remissions in Maternal Depression and Child Psychopathology." *JAMA* 295(12) (March 22/29, 2006):1389–98.

Weitoft, Gunilla Ringbäck, Anders Hjern, Bengt Haglund, and Måns Rosén. "Mortality, severe morbidity, and injury in children living with single parents in Sweden: a population-based study." *The Lancet* 361(9354) (25 January 2003): 289–95.

Wellner, Alison. "Teens view jobs as first step to wealth." *USA Weekend,* June 10, 2007.

Williams, Redford and Virginia Williams. *Anger Kills, Seventeen Strategies for Controlling the Hostility That Can Harm Your Health.* New York: Times Books, 1993.

Wills, T. A., and S. D. Cleary. "Peer and adolescent substance use among 6th–9th graders: latent growth analyses of influence versus selection mechanisms" *Health Psychology* 18(5) (September 1999): 453–63.

Wolak, Janis, Kimberly Mitchell, and David Finkelhor. "Unwanted and Wanted Exposure to Online Pornography in a National Sample of Youth Internet Users." *Pediatrics* 119(2) (February 2007): 247–57.

World Health Organization: Top News (June 11, 2009). "World at start of N1H1 pandemic." *UPI.com.* http://www.upi.com/Top_News/2009/06/11/WHO-World-at-start-of-N1H1-pandemic/UPI-34451244732904/.

Yarnold, B. M. "Cocaine use among Miami's public school students, 1992: religion versus peers and availability." *Journal of Health and Social Policy* 11(2) (1999): 69–84.

Yocom, Guy. "My Shot: Earl Woods." *Golf Digest,* February 2004, 115.

Zillmann, Dolf, and Jennings Bryant, editors. *Pornography: Research Advances & Policy Considerations.* Mahway, NJ:

Lawrence Erlbaum, 1989.

Zimmerman, Frederick J., Christakis, Dimitri A. Christakis, Andrew N. Meltzoff. "Associations between Media Viewing and Language Development in Children Under Age 2 Years." *The Journal of Pediatrics* 151(4) (October 2007): 364–68.

Zoosmann-Diskin, A. "No protective effect of circumcision on human immunodeficiency virus incidence." *Journal of Infectious Disease* 181(5) (May 2000): 1865–68.

Zuckerman, Diana M. and Barry S. Zuckerman, "Television's Impact on Children," *Pediatrics* 75(2) (February 1985): 233–40.

ABOUT THE AUTHOR

*D*R. PARNELL DO-
NAHUE was born
in 1938 on a farm near
Westbrook, Minnesota,
the third child in a family
of nine. Believe it or not,
he attended a one-room
school house where one
teacher taught all eight
grades! He earned his
medical degree from
Marquette University
School of Medicine,
now Medical College of
Wisconsin. He was a

General Medical Officer in the USAF before his specialty
training in pediatrics. He practiced pediatrics, adolescent
medicine, and adolescent sports medicine in Hartford and
Milwaukee, Wisconsin, and in Atlanta, Georgia.

Par (as he likes to be called) is a master gardener. He enjoys playing golf, reading, wood-working, cooking for friends and family, and is currently learning to play the bag pipe. Since his retirement he has volunteered at Salvus, a clinic for underinsured children; taught at-risk teens in an after-school program; and served on the board of CASA, a program which advocates for kids who, through no fault of their own, end up in the court system. He is a member of the parish council at his church.

He and his scientist wife Mary live in Brentwood, Tennessee, near their three sons—all of whom are on the faculty at Vanderbilt's School of Medicine. Their daughter Maura teaches international business and is the director of The Program for Christian Leadership at the University of Dayton in Ohio. They have thirteen grandchildren between the ages of ten and nineteen.

Par is a member of the Irish and American Pediatric Society, the American Academy of Pediatrics, and a past member of the AMA, the Society for Adolescent Medicine, the American College of Sports Medicine, the Georgia Chapter of the Academy of Pediatrics, and the Wisconsin Chapter of the Academy of Pediatrics.

http://www.MessengersInDenim.org

INDEX

medical decisions, 209
medical home, adolescents need a, 171
medical practices to avoid, 218–220
medical science, 153
medically accurate, make condom package
label, 163
medically underserved population, 171
Meeker, Meg, 249
meningococcal, immunization schedule
for, 352
meningitis strain of, 200
Mental Health Association of Middle Tennessee, The, 57
mental health officer, Margaret Pepe is,
56
minor skin infections or boils caused by
MRSA, 296
Mexico, swine flu (H1N1) developed in,
204
Michelangelo, 272
Millet, Peter, 167
Milwaukee (Wisconsin), 7, 71, 293–294,
333-334, 336
"Milwaukee's Social Conscience," 334
Minnesota, 11, 58, 158, 180, 217, 338
Minton, Lynn, 14, 102
miscarriages, 85
MMR (measles, mumps and rubella vaccine), 199–200
moderation:
drink in, 90, 91 ftnt
live in, 84
Molinari, Susan, 125
money management, 317–318
monogamous relationship(s), 152, 167
monogamous sex, 213
Monopoly, 186
mood disorders, 284–285
More, Thomas (quote from), 293
moral compass, 94, 101, 131
moral vacuum, 74
Mormon kids, 87–88
Mother Theresa, 323
mothers:
hero, 44–45
herpes and, 151

home and, 45–47
in society, 43–44
inept, 73
influence of, 48–49
pets and, 61
save lives, 39–41
teenage drinking and, 125
Mothers Against Drunk Drivers (MADD),
43
Mothers Against Guns, 43–44
"Mr. Nice Guy," 326
MRSA (methicillin resistant staph aureus),
296–297
MSN Money Web site, 315
Much Ado About Nothing by Shakespeare
(quote from), 51
multigenerational, 75
murders, 44, 179, 228
Murray, Bill, 324
mutant strain, 203
Mycoplasma genitalium, 164

N

Nashville Metro Police, 42
Nashville, Tennessee, 44, 319
National Center for Health statistics,
147, 167
National Institute for Health Care Re-
search, conference in 1997, 71
National Institute of Health, 163
National Institute on Alcohol Abuse and
Alcoholism, 124
National Longitudinal Study of Adolescent
Health, 246
National Longitudinal Survey of Youth, 86
National Strategy for Suicide Prevention
(NSSP), The, 253
National Study of Youth and Religion,
88, 91
National Survey of Drug Use and Health,
124
National Youth Violence Prevention Re-
source Center, 286
negative attitude, worse than smoking,
265

THE AMERICAN ST. NICK

978-1-886249-08-0 • Hardback • 175pg
$14.95 • Peter Lion • WWII History

American soldiers are more than combatants on a battlefield, they are also representatives of America and her people. On an overcast day in 1944, two soldiers from the 28th Infantry Division gave a remarkable Christmas gift to the people of Wiltz, Luxembourg — a gift that changed the people of Wiltz forever.

http://www.SilvertonHousePublishing.com/
Products/9781886249080

GOODBYE, WALTER

978-0-9728071-2-8 • Paperback • 192pg
$13.95 • Hogue • Inspiration & Self-Discovery
First Place, Memoirs, 2006 Communications Award, Arizona Press Women; Second Place, 2006 National Federation of Press Women Communications Contest

In February 1997, RuthAnn Hogue was asked to write an article about hospice care and to interview terminal cancer patient Walter Schifter. Her experiences opened her eyes to compassion and the strength of the human spirit in a way that changed her life forever.

http://www.SilvertonHousePublishing.com/
Products/9780972807128